On the Lord's Appearing

❀ The Lord appears to me in this life in five ways:

He who ascends to the fifth has scaled a great height.

Jacopone da Todi

Jonathan Robinson of the Oratory

On the Lord's Appearing

An Essay on Prayer and Tradition

The Catholic University of America Press
Washington, D.C.

The paper used in this publication meets the minimum
requirements of American National Standards for
Information Science—Permanence of Paper for Printed
Library materials, ANSI Z39.48-1984.
∞

Library of Congress Cataloging-in-Publication Data
Robinson, Jonathan, 1929–
    On the Lord's appearing / by Jonathan Robinson.
       p.   cm.
    Includes bibliographical references and index.
    1. Prayer—Catholic Church.   2. Spiritual life—
Catholic Church.   3. Jacopone da Todi, 1230–1306.
Laude.   4. Tradition (Theology)   I. Title.
    BX2350.65.R63   1997
    248.3'2'08822—dc21
    96-36924
    ISBN 0-8132-0886-6 (cloth : alk. paper)
    ISBN 0-8132-0887-4 (pbk. : alk. paper)

❧ Fratribus meis in domo

Sancti Philippi Nerii

Torontinense

❧ ut deus in terris quos hic coniunxit amicos,

gaudentes pariter iungat in arce poli

Hrabanus Maurus

❧ *The Five Ways in Which God Reveals Himself*

The Lord appears to me in this life in five ways:
He who ascends to the fifth has scaled a great height.

The first is the state of fear, the second healing love;
The third manifestation is of tender sustenance,
Followed in turn by fatherly love
And lastly by conjugal love, the love of the bridegroom.

In the first stage the Lord God in His power
Raises my soul from the dead;
Putting to flight the demons who bound me in error,
He touches the heart with contrition.

The reawakened and still fragile soul
Is then visited by the Healer,
Who nurses and comforts
And strengthens with Sacraments.

My Love then appears as the noble companion
Who succours me and saves me from my wretchedness;
He endows me with virtues that lead to salvation.
Can I leave hidden, unsung, the good He has wrought?

In the fourth mode He appears as a tender father
With gifts of great largesse;
Once the soul tastes of that goodness, that love,
It exults in its inheritance.

In the fifth mode Love leads me to the conjugal bed
And I lie in the embrace of the Son of God. O my soul,
Led by grace, you are the queen of the angels,
In wondrous fusion transformed into Christ.

Jacopone da Todi (123?–1306)

❊ Contents

❧ *Acknowledgments*

My first debt is to the members of the Toronto Oratory on whom I have tested parts of this study over the past few years. Then, I will always treasure what the late Father Stephen Dessain of the Birmingham Oratory taught me by word and example about the spiritual life. I have also learned much from Father Paul Türks of the Aachen Oratory. Father Robert Pelton of the Madonna House Apostolate has had a longtime and valued influence on my thinking. To John and Anne Muggeridge, and Jacques and Michèle Vauthier, I am indebted for friendship, support, and criticism over the years. I have also to thank Matthew Daigler, Derek Cross, and Carl Still for helping me to revise the manuscript. Professor Thomas Langan and Father Ron Tacelli, S.J., have also encouraged me. I am also extremely grateful to my editor, Susan Needham, for her help in preparing my manuscript for publication.

❧ *Abbreviations*

Church Documents

CCC	*Catechism of the Catholic Church*
CM	*Christian Meditation*
DV	*Dei Verbum*
FC	*Familiaris Consortio*
LH	*The Liturgy of the Hours*
RP	*Reconciliation and Penance*
SvD	*Salvifici Doloris*

Classic Works

Ascent	St. John of the Cross. *The Ascent of Mount Carmel*
Cloud	Anonymous. *The Cloud of Unknowing*
Conf	St. Augustine. *Confessions*
DN	St. John of the Cross. *Dark Night of the Soul*
DS	*Dictionnaire de Spiritualité*
IC	St. Teresa of Avila. *Interior Castle*
IDL	St. Francis de Sales. *Introduction to the Devout Life*
LFL	St. John of the Cross. *Living Flame of Love*
NE	Aristotle. *Nicomachean Ethics*
TLG	St. Francis de Sales. *Treatise on the Love of God*

Works by John Henry Newman

Apo	*Apologia Pro Vita Sua*
Dev	*Development of Doctrine*
GA	*Grammar of Assent*
HS	*Historical Sketches*
Idea	*Idea of a University*
Jfc	*Lectures on Justification*
LD	*Letters and Diaries*
MD	*Meditations and Devotions*
OS	*Sermons on Various Occasions*
PS	*Parochial and Plain Sermons*
SD	*Sermons on Subjects of the Day*
US	*Oxford University Sermons*
VM	*Via Media*

※ Introduction

This book is about personal prayer in the tradition of the Catholic Church. It deals both with the nature of tradition itself and with what this tradition teaches about prayer. The prayer of a Christian, for all its personal and intimate character, is made possible by, and takes place within, this tradition. Tradition provides the living context for the prayer of the individual by nourishing him with its teaching and sustaining him through the community of the faithful, both the living and the dead.

What is tradition? Tradition in the Church, including the tradition's teaching on prayer, has two aspects that cannot in practice be isolated. First of all, it is what is handed on from the earliest days of the Church until our own time. We may call this the content, or the material aspect, of tradition.[1] Then, secondly, tradition is also the activity of receiving and handing on this content to subsequent generations.[2] Both aspects are necessary to an ade-

---

1. *CCC* 96: "What Christ entrusted to the Apostles, they in turn handed on by their preaching and writing, under the inspiration of the Holy Spirit, to all generations, until Christ returns in glory."

2. *DV* 8: "The words of the holy Fathers witness to the living presence of this tradition, whose wealth is poured into the practice and life of the believing and praying Church."

quate view of tradition. Unless tradition has some stable content, whether written or unwritten, then it loses any lived connection with the given elements of Christianity. By these given elements, I mean "the things [God] had once revealed for the salvation of all peoples [and which] remain in their entirety, throughout the ages, [to] be transmitted to all generations."[3] These given elements are what theologians call the *depositum fidei,* which the *Catechism of the Catholic Church* translated as the heritage of faith.[4] On the other hand, unless it is realized that the tradition of the apostles is encountered only in the lived and developing experience of the Church, then there is a very real danger of imagining that it is possible to abstract from the tradition its "real" content in isolation from its historical context.[5] Tradition is not a Platonic Idea whose being is unrelated to time and place; rather, it is an historical reality that has been formed by its passage through time.

The first part of this book concerns tradition and how it functions in the Church. My thesis is that tradition should be seen as analogous to *lectio divina,* or meditative reading.[6] Meditative reading requires a book to be read, and it also requires an effort to assimilate the contents of the book under the guidance of the Holy Spirit. In a similar way, the given elements of the tradition (what corresponds to the book in meditative reading) are conveyed to us through our life in the Church. These given elements are the object of personal appropriation by the saints and doctors of the Church, as well as by more ordinary Christians. What is handed

3. CCC 75.

4. CCC 84. The translation of the *CCC* emphasizes the active side of the tradition—a heritage is something received and handed on. The notion of a deposit, which does seem to mean a fixed material object left on deposit for safekeeping, is found in St. Paul, for example in 1 Timothy 6:20, where the Apostle tells Timothy to guard the deposit—ἡ παραθήχη.

5. Ratzinger, "Dogmatic Constitution on Revelation, Origin and Background," 3.188.

6. See below, 2.3.

on is derived from Revelation, but it issues from the work of this *lectio* in a form that is both fresh and new.

St. Philip Neri (1515–95), the founder of the Oratory, illustrates this interpretation of tradition. St. Philip spoke out of the tradition that he himself lived, and his speaking gave fresh impetus to the tradition. His teaching was more than his own, because he was conveying the Church's experience concerning prayer, an experience that goes back to Christ himself; yet, at the same time, it *was* very much his own, as the expression of the way he himself experienced and taught the tradition.

There is an example of St. Philip's method of teaching in a sketch, preserved in the archives of the Roman Oratory, of a talk he gave on one of the *Lauds* of the thirteenth-century Franciscan Jacopone da Todi.[7] The *Laud,* number 45 in the English translation,[8] deals with the five ways in which the Lord reveals himself in this life. The structure of the talk was determined by the text itself, and St. Philip moves through Jacopone's poem with comments designed to incline the hearts of his hearers toward a deeper knowledge and love of Christ.[9]

In outlining the spiritual tradition of the Church I have used the same *Laud* of Jacopone da Todi, and I have allowed the poem to determine the development of my discussion on the practice of prayer and the obstacles that it meets. Jacopone's poem, which highlights some of the themes of the spiritual life, provides us with a freer and a looser structure than is sometimes found in books about spirituality.

7. See 2.3.

8. In Italian it is number 23 in the edition of Franco Mancini: "En cinque modi aparame lo Signor 'nn esta vita." The Lauds have no titles in this edition. The English title, "The Five Ways in Which God Reveals Himself," is a rough translation of the work of an early Italian editor, "Como Dio appare ne l'anima en cinque modi."

9. St. Philip's treatment of the *Laud* is discussed in Ponnelle and Bordet, *St. Philip Neri,* 576.

Let us say that Jacopone is telling us a story. It is a true story
because it deals with the love of God for His creation and describes
the lengths to which He is prepared to go to rescue the work of
His hands. But it is a story, because it has a beginning and an end.
It moves through time and experience, and it is never quite the
same, no matter how many times it is relived and no matter how
many times it is retold. The very best versions of the story have
been left to us by the saints and the doctors of the Church, but
Jacopone's tale bears comparison with the best. With freshness
and vividness he hymns both the tradition which brings us the
Gospel of redemption, as well as the response of the individual
who answers to the appearing of the Lord.

The first part of this book, then, is a brief explanation and defense of some crucial elements in the Catholic view of tradition as
this tradition is related to the spiritual life. The second part is my
meditation on Jacopone's story. I have followed St. Philip's example and used Jacopone's *Laud* as a vehicle for discussing some
of the major themes of the tradition concerning the spiritual life.
Jacopone did not try to talk about everything in one poem, nor
have I tried to provide a map of the entire spiritual life in one book.
Furthermore, just as I have not tried to cover all the themes of the
spiritual life, so I have not tried to deal with all of the authors who
have discussed a particular theme. Many of the subjects I consider
have been illustrated by other authors—for example, Thomas
Merton—but, because I am dealing with the traditional spirituality of the Church, I have for the most part illustrated my account by works from classical writers. I hope my own meditation
will provide us with a heightened sense of some fundamental
Christian truths, and of their relation to our prayer.

Jacopone's tale runs this way:

God first of all seeks the sinful soul and touches the heart with
contrition, and the response to this seeking is the prayer of petition. From the practice of petition we gradually obtain a deeper
sense of the sovereignty of God.

Then God heals and strengthens the "reawakened and still fragile soul" with the sacraments. Here we find that meditation on
God's dealings with us is the appropriate form of prayer, and the
practice of meditation leads us to a deeper awareness of the truths
of faith.

Meditation gives way to a time of light and darkness during
which God endows the soul with virtues, and to this we reply with
a prayer of thanksgiving. This thanksgiving is the cause of a
deeper appreciation of the love of God.

The peace and quietness of the prayer of thanksgiving are then
abruptly taken from us, and we are faced with the reality of a God
whose Fatherhood reveals itself in harsh and unfathomably difficult trials. The only prayer during these times is to will in the
darkness what God has given us to suffer. This prayer, which Father de Caussade called the *sacrament of the present moment,* gives us
an altogether more realistic and tougher appreciation of the providence of God.

Finally, the approach of God as the bridegroom of the soul
brings with it the peace of union, a prayer of the heart. With this
prayer we begin to understand something about God's involve-
ment in His creation through love, and how it is that the saints
love God's creation with God's own love.

PART I. Toward a Theory of Tradition

And he said to me, "Son of man, can these bones live?"

Some persons speak of [Christianity] as if it were a thing of history, with only indirect bearing upon modern times; I cannot allow that it is a mere historical religion. Certainly it has its foundations in past and glorious memories, but its power is in the present. It is no dreary matter of antiquarianism; we do not contemplate it in conclusions drawn from dumb documents and dead events, but by faith exercised in ever-living objects, and by the appropriation and use of ever-recurring gifts.

J. H. Newman, *GA,* Chapter 10, 2

1 ❧ *Tradition*

> It is not true in fact, and never will be, that the mass of serious
> Christians derive their faith for themselves from the Scriptures.
> No; they derive it from Tradition, whether true or corrupt; and
> they are intended by Divine Providence to derive it from the true,
> viz., that which the Church Catholic has ever furnished . . .
>
> J. H. Newman, *VM*, I, lecture 10, section 5

1.1 *The vindication of tradition*

Tradition obviously has some reference to the past, and it is by
means of tradition that the past of a society or group is given to
those living in the present. The past, like the future, seems to lack
the immediate and indubitable character of the present. Neither
the past nor the future is here and now, yet they cannot be dismissed as unreal. A successful theory of tradition would require
an essay in the philosophy of history and on the nature of time,
and that is beyond the scope of this book. It is, however, important
to see from the outset that the question of tradition is central to
our understanding of Catholicism. When people say that Christianity is an historical religion, they must mean at least that the
past as past has to be taken seriously, and that the future as future
has to be reckoned with.

Christianity makes statements about the past which it claims are true, and it asserts propositions about the future which it affirms will be verified. "God created the world" and "Christ became man" are statements about the past; "Christ will come again in glory to judge the living and the dead" is a proposition about the future. St. Augustine, after he had become a Christian, was faced with trying to give due weight to history, in which both the creation and the Incarnation had taken place.[1] His efforts to deal with this question of the historical dimension of Christianity help us to see the intrinsic importance of tradition. Augustine recognized clearly the evanescent character of the past. Yet he also saw that what went on in that evanescent past was crucial for the salvation of mankind. It is tradition that brings those past, crucial events into the present. Both the knowledge and the practice of our faith are given to us by the community of believers we call the Church. And what the Church brings to us has an irreducibly historical dimension.

The historical dimension of Catholicism led Newman to say there was an "utter incongruity" between Protestantism and historical Christianity. "To be deep in history," he said, "is to cease to be a Protestant."[2] Leaving aside the polemical side of the remark, he was drawing attention to the fact that the origin and development of Catholicism are in history, and what God has revealed in history is conveyed to us not only by Scripture but by tradition as well.

Newman's position was vindicated by the Second Vatican Council, which taught that tradition plays an indispensable role in our appropriation of God's Revelation. The Council, in *Dei Verbum,* asserted the existence of a tradition in the Church which

1. Rist, *Augustine,* 58: "In accordance with the world-view of Platonic metaphysics Augustine at first did his best to restrict the impact of some of the historical claims of Christianity . . . nevertheless, from the time of his conversion he held that . . . the historical must become a part of any account of 'reality,' however 'Platonic' it might otherwise be."

2. Newman, *Dev,* introduction, sect. 5.

helps to perpetuate what God has revealed for the salvation of all nations.[3] The Council also said that "both Sacred Tradition and Sacred Scripture are to be accepted and venerated with the same sense of devotion and reverence."[4]

The importance of the idea of tradition is clear enough. Tradition helps to perpetuate what has been revealed for our salvation, and it is to be accepted and reverenced. But any discussion of tradition today has to take account of two different factors. In the first place there exists both in society and within the Church a strong distrust of anything connected with tradition. Secondly, even when the necessity of tradition is recognized, there remain serious disagreements as to how it functions, or ought to function, in the Church.

The contemporary distrust of tradition is a variation on the old theme that the past is more of a hindrance than a help. An authority on the spiritual life has written that "tradition does not prove; it is content with showing up error that is foreign to it— a simple innovation."[5] But "innovation" is precisely what is valued by those who view tradition with suspicion, and it must be said that very few people seem to accept the authority of a tradition that is content merely to assert itself by "showing up error that is foreign to it." It remains true, as T. S. Eliot wrote in "Tradition and the Individual Talent" that the word *tradition* seldom appears in English writing "except as a word of censure."[6] Eliot was commenting on literary criticism, but his judgment appears particularly apt when applied to the way tradition is regarded today. When people say that a belief or a practice is traditional, they often mean that the belief or the practice is either archaic and ir-

3. *DV* 7: "In his gracious goodness, God has seen to it that what He had revealed for the salvation of all nations would abide perpetually in its full integrity and be handed on to all generations."

4. *DV* 9.

5. Bouyer, *The Church of God,* 96.

6. Eliot, *Selected Essays,* 13. The essay in question was written in 1917.

relevant, or even positively harmful. For many, the word conjures up the notion of a force that casts a cold and deadening shadow over everything that is fresh and living. People are said to be shackled by dead tradition, or oppressed with the heavy weight of obsolete beliefs and practices.

Most of this should be dismissed as incompatible with any reasonable understanding of the nature and role of tradition in the Church. This is not to deny the painful fact that tradition and the institutions that embody it have sometimes been used to treat people unfairly. One has to admit the fact, but this is no argument for throwing away an essential element, not only of life in the Church, but of ordinary secular living as well.[7]

There still remains, however, the much more difficult question of stating just what the nature and role of tradition in fact are. The effort to establish the nature and importance of tradition has been called the *rediscovery* (or vindication) of tradition; it is the necessary first step toward a *recovery*[8] of what is in danger of being lost. The vindication of tradition might seem for a Catholic a superfluous enterprise; it is, after all, a bit difficult to talk about rediscovering something whose existence was defined by a council of the Church. But if by vindication we mean a reappraisal of what the Council is supposed to have taught, then a vindication is indeed necessary. Today the existence of tradition is admitted in theory, while at the same time it is understood in a way that has robbed it of any real force. So, while the vindication of tradition in the Church does

---

7. The existence and nature of tradition are living issues in our post-Enlightenment age. It is, therefore, an error to think that tradition is of interest only to those who are writing *ex professo* about religion. For example, Alasdair MacIntyre, in *After Virtue,* Chapter 15, has argued that living as a moral human being requires a community, and there is no community without tradition. "What I am . . . is in key part what I inherit, a specific past that is present in some degree in my present. I find myself part of a history and that is generally to say, whether I like it or not, whether I recognize it or not, one of the bearers of a tradition" (221).

8. The distinction is taken from Pelikan, *The Vindication of Tradition.*

not have to start from the ground up, we do have to reassert three fundamental propositions about it. First, tradition is a lived experience, but it is not only a lived experience; second, it is only the given elements in tradition that enable the Church to distinguish true from false tradition; third, authentic tradition operates within the parameters of the heritage of faith and has both a divine and a human component, and this applies as well to the life of prayer within the tradition.

1.2 Modern discussions of tradition

The theological discussions in the Church about tradition at the time of the Second Vatican Council have tended to obscure the fact that all the parties in the debate acknowledged that tradition had a function in assuring that the Gospel of Christ was preached to succeeding generations. The various controversies had to do with the account to be given of the role of tradition in the Church.[9] What strikes one today is not so much the differences between the contending parties but the extent to which they were operating within a common view of Catholicism and how much the situation has changed since 1965, when the Constitution on Divine Revelation was promulgated.

The problem of tradition first became acute in the Church at the time of the Protestant Reformation. As Cardinal de Lubac has shown, patristic and medieval theology worked with an idea of tradition that was largely unexamined. Theology was the study of Scripture as the Church understood it.

Since the first century of the Church, since the first generation of Christians, [theology] was a question of Scripture read or the word of God understood in the Church and interpreted by the Tradition—by the "tradition of the Apostles"—and this is what Irenaeus and Origen maintained

9. Ratzinger, "Dogmatic Constitution," in Vorgrimler, *Commentary,* 3.160.

with unmatched eloquence and it is exactly what the Council of Trent meant by *The Gospel*.[10]

When the basic traditional assumptions were questioned, it became necessary to say something about the nature of tradition and how it functioned, in conjunction with the Scriptures, to ensure a Catholic understanding of the Scriptures themselves, as well as of Catholic traditions in a broader sense.[11]

The Council of Trent dealt with the question of tradition in one of its earliest sessions, where it defined the canonical books of the Bible that were said to contain the Gospel of Jesus Christ.

This [Gospel], of old promised through the Prophets in the Holy Scriptures, our Lord Jesus Christ, the Son of God, promulgated first with His own mouth, and then commanded it to be preached by his Apostles to every creature as the source at once of all saving truth and rules of conduct. It also clearly perceives that these truths and rules are contained in the written books and in the unwritten traditions, which, received by the Apostles from the mouth of Christ himself, or from the Apostles themselves, the Holy Ghost dictating, have come down to us, transmitted as it were from hand to hand.[12]

This decree expressed the conviction that Scripture must be interpreted within the Church in the light of tradition. The decree, as Father Congar has pointed out, provided its own terms of reference, which were "to conserve in the Church the essential elements of the Gospel in all their purity."[13] If these essential elements

10. De Lubac, *Exégèse Médiévale*, I.1.57 (my translation).

11. Congar, *Tradition and Traditions*, 48: "There is no doubt that unwritten apostolic traditions exist. Evidence has been provided ever so many times by Catholic apologists from the New Testament witnesses themselves, and the Fathers also often referred to these texts."

12. Council of Trent, Fourth Session, April 1546. The Second Vatican Council quotes verbatim the above passage and adds: "The commission was fulfilled, too, by those apostles and apostolic men who under the inspiration of the same Holy Spirit committed the message of salvation to writing" (*DV* 7).

13. Congar, *Tradition and Traditions*, 157.

were to be preserved, then they would have to be expounded as the Church had always understood them. In this way the apostolic tradition became an essential element in a correct understanding of the Gospel. Trent confined itself to the discussion of apostolic traditions and did not deal explicitly with the question of non-apostolic, or what had come to be called ecclesiastical, traditions.[14]

By the time of the Second Vatican Council four hundred years later, it was thought necessary to go into the question of tradition once again. In his commentary on *Dei Verbum*, Cardinal Ratzinger gives three reasons for this. There was first of all the growth in the idea of tradition as such, which had been developing in secular culture since the beginning of the nineteenth century. Secondly, there was the theological problem of the application of historical-critical methods to the interpretation of Scripture. Finally, there was the growth of the biblical movement, which "was giving rise to a new familiarity with [Scripture] and an ever increasing tendency, both in theology and piety, to go back to it."[15]

There is no doubt that the Council was working with a real problem and trying to fill a real need. Yet in meeting this need the debate over tradition and Scripture altered, and resulted in too little attention being paid to the nature of tradition. Cardinal Ratzinger has written of how the experience of the Second Vatican Council seemed to sweep away the relevance of a great many things that theologians had thought important. "It is probably not an exaggeration to say that it was only the Council that brought home the fact that the classical 'schools' have today become as unimportant as the conflicts between them."[16] He was writing about the antitheses of Thomism, Scotism, Molinism, and the like, and

14. Ibid., 163: "Faithful to its intention of proclaiming the belief of the Church without entering upon any domain where Catholics themselves were divided, the council finally confined itself *exclusively to the discussion of apostolic traditions, written or unwritten.*"

15. Ratzinger, "Dogmatic Constitution," in Vorgrimler, *Commentary*, 3.158.

16. Ibid., 3.161.

he emphasized that Catholic theology had remained alive in other schools and conflicts.

It is not hard to understand what the cardinal is driving at. The divisions between the schools did seem to be irrelevant to much of what was going on in contemporary intellectual life at the time of the Council. On the other hand, it has to be said that the same remark can now be made about the controversies that went on about the Constitution (on Divine Revelation) itself at the time of the Second Vatican Council. To put it bluntly, the arguments in the sixties over the correct interpretation of the decrees of the Council of Trent, and over whether we should speak of one or two sources of Revelation, seem a long way from the life of contemporary Catholicism. Part of the reason for this is the newer understanding of tradition that emphasizes tradition as activity rather than content.

In *Tradition and Traditions,* Father Congar gives a clear statement of the newer view. He begins by saying that "tradition means, in itself, a transmission from person to person."[17] This is, in fact, the first, although not the only, meaning given by the Oxford English Dictionary. "It thus," he continues, "implies a living subject." This living subject, who does the handing over, is the Church. If we ask what is handed over, or what the content of tradition is, we are told that "tradition in this most primitive and general sense requires merely a deposit of some sort. This deposit can include writings, as well as words, actions, rules of conduct and institutions."[18]

Father Congar is calling our attention to the fact that tradition is not merely a doctrine or a teaching, and that any balanced account of tradition must take into account the activity of assimilating, living, and handing over this teaching. Tradition involves the living awareness of God's Revelation in a way that affects the

17. Congar, *Tradition and Traditions,* 196.
18. Ibid.

whole person. We have to practice the Faith if we are to safeguard the Word of God. This is the truth of the new emphasis on tradition as *tradere*. The living of the Faith demands an active and creative appropriation of the tradition of the Church. The handing on of tradition is not the mere passing on of an inert object that has no effect on, and is not affected by, those to whom it is given. Jaroslav Pelikan puts this brilliantly: "Tradition is the living faith of the dead, traditionalism the dead faith of the living."[19] Blondel expresses the same theme in a fuller if less epigrammatic way: "The Ark of the Covenant is faithful practice, and it is there that the secrets of God are to be found; faithful practice is the tabernacle where God perpetuates his presence and his teaching."[20]

Our idea of tradition has to contain this active or living element if "the ancient tradition, teaching and faith of the Catholic Church"[21] are to be adequately conveyed. It may be that this has not always been clearly recognized. Tradition is not merely an abstract collection of unvarying propositions that is handed on from generation to generation. What Eliot said about literature is also true of tradition in the Church:

If the only form of tradition, of handing down, consisted in following the ways of the immediate generation before us in a blind or timid adherence to its successes, "tradition" should positively be discouraged. We have seen many such simple currents soon lost in the sand; and novelty is better than repetition.[22]

It is possible, however, to avoid "timid adherence" without repudiating tradition. Indeed, it can be argued that one of the marks of a living tradition is the presence of self-criticism. A particular tradition, that is, provides both the impetus and the subject matter

19. Pelikan, *Vindication of Tradition*, 65.

20. Maurice Blondel, cited in Geiselmann, *The Meaning of Tradition*, 19.

21. St. Athanasius, from the *First Letter to Serapion*, Second Lesson of the Office of Readings for Trinity Sunday in *LH* 3.584.

22. Eliot, *Selected Essays*, 14.

for a debate on its true nature. Alasdair MacIntyre maintains correctly that any institution, whether it be a university, a farm, or a hospital, will bear with it a tradition of practice or practices. He then goes on to claim that the life of these institutions will partly, "but in a centrally important way," be constituted by "a continuous argument as to what a university is and ought to be or what good farming is or what good medicine is."[23] I think this is to go too far, if he means that the tradition is dead unless it is actually being argued about. But he is surely right in saying that tradition not infrequently requires examination and provides the subject matter and often the methods for this critical awareness.

The contemporary view of tradition maintains that the Revelation conveyed by tradition can best be compared to the living awareness of a person by many different people who constitute some sort of a unity. Such an experience, to be sure, can be expressed in part through language. On the other hand, the richness and complexity of the experience transcend the framework of what can be said explicitly. This position corrects any tendency there may have been to regard tradition as the handing on of a dying or dead series of propositions or statements in the indicative mood.

Newman, as an Anglican, anticipated many aspects of the contemporary theory, and stated in a very fair way what he believed to be the position of the "Romanists":

We see . . . the mistake of asking for a complete collection of the Roman Traditions; as well might we ask for a full catalogue of a man's tastes and thoughts on a given subject. Tradition in its fullness is necessarily unwritten; it is the mode in which a society has felt or acted during a certain period, and it cannot be circumscribed any more than a man's countenance and manner can be conveyed to strangers in any set of propositions.[24]

23. MacIntyre, *After Virtue*, 222. MacIntyre goes on to say, "Traditions, when vital, embody continuities of conflict. Indeed when a tradition becomes Burkean, it is always dying or dead." I would have thought some continuities of conflict are just as hostile to the life of tradition as "timid adherence."

24. *VM* I, lect. 1, sect. 4.

The newer view emphasizes that it is only within the family of believers that we come into a living awareness of the Revelation of Jesus Christ,[25] and that this awareness is much more than propositional. This living awareness is not some sort of deduction from a series of principles or truths, and it has been an important advance to have this clearly stated. In the years since the Council, however, the living, active side of tradition has been emphasized to such an extent that it often seems to be forgotten that tradition also involves the handing on of a reality that is to be understood and lived in terms of the nature of that reality itself.[26] It is tradition, understood in its aspect of a given, which controls and determines authentic development, and this is true no matter how "living" or how "creative" the development may be. This control by the object is the source of the normative and unvarying aspects of tradition.[27]

To provide a complete account as to how the control by the object operates in the development of tradition would be a complex

25. Ratzinger, "Dogmatic Constitution," in Vorgrimler, *Commentary,* 3.182: "Tradition . . . means a fundamental hermeneutical decision, namely that faith is present in no other way than in the historical continuity of the believers and must be found in it and not against it."

26. Congar says, "Tradition is not primarily to be defined by a particular material object, but by the act of transmission, and its content is simply *id quod traditum est, id quod traditur"* (*Tradition and Traditions,* 196). Although one might accept that the active side of tradition is to be emphasized, and even that tradition is not to be defined by "a particular material object," it would not follow that "specific materiality" can be totally eliminated. At the very least, Christian tradition must be *Christian.*

27. The English idealists argued against a view of truth as the copying of a fixed and static reality, yet they also saw that the discovery of truth necessitated the elimination of the purely subjective. For example, Bradley, *Essays on Truth and Reality,* 118–19: "In truth seeking the individual must follow the object. Our understanding has to co-operate in the ideal development of reality, and it has not, like will, to turn ideas into existences. . . . Intelligence of itself does not recreate the given past nor does it procreate entirely the given present or future. And it may be said to wait on and to follow a course of events which it is powerless to make."

operation.[28] Such an account, however, would be indispensable for an adequate theory of tradition. It is quite true, as I have said, that the normative and unvarying aspects cannot be isolated in practice from the living flow of tradition. Yet because tradition must be lived if it is really to be tradition, it does not follow that it is adequately defined by this activity of being lived. What is lived finds its validity in the fact that it is connected either directly or indirectly with the Revelation of God in Jesus Christ. This Revelation introduces the element of objectivity into the living of tradition and sets limits to the creative aspect of this living.

Newman had a great deal to do with focusing attention on the active side of tradition. On the other hand, he was no supporter of creative tradition with no relation to the given aspect of Christian Revelation. In 1835 he published, as one of the *Tracts for the Times,* an essay entitled "The Rationalistic and Catholic Tempers Contrasted."[29] The essay deals in part with the mysterious and unsystematic character of Revelation. Yet, at the same time he warns that, just because of its mysterious character, we have to respect both what has been given to us as well as the way it has been given to us.

We should be very reverent in dealing with Revealed Truth . . . we should avoid all rash theorizing and systematizing as relates to it . . . we should be solicitous to hold it safely and entirely . . . we should be zealous and pertinacious in guarding it . . . we should religiously adhere to the form of words and the ordinances under which it comes to us, through which it is revealed to us, and apart from which the Revelation does not exist, there being nothing else given by which to ascertain or enter into it.[30]

---

28. Such a theory would have to consider what John Coulson calls "the fiduciary use of language," that is, that "language is a living organism whose function is to reconcile the past and present experiences of a community" (*Newman and the Common Tradition,* 4).

29. Republished in 1871 as chap. 2 of *Essays* I.

30. Newman, *Essays* I, chap. 2, sect. 5.

1.3 False tradition

To believe something to be true also involves having some criterion for saying that something else is not true. In other words, a theory of truth also has to provide a theory of what is false. The contemporary emphasis on the lived aspect of tradition does not provide a sufficient criterion for distinguishing the true from the false.

In a very powerful statement of the newer view of tradition,[31] von Balthasar writes that being faithful to tradition does not consist "of a literal repetition and transmission of the philosophical and theological theses that one imagines lie hidden in time and in the contingencies of history."[32] This must be the case if the newer view is the correct one. He then goes on to say that "being faithful to tradition consists much more in imitating our Fathers in the faith with respect to their attitude of intimate reflection and their effort of audacious creation, which are the necessary preludes to true spiritual fidelity."[33]

If we study the past, it is not in the hope [of] drawing from it formulas doomed in advance to sterility or with the intention of readapting out-of-date solutions. We are asking history to teach us the acts and deeds of the Church, who presents her treasure of divine Revelation, ever new and ever unexpected, to every generation, and who knows how, in the face of every new problem, to turn the fecundity of the problem to good account with a rigor that never grows weary and a spiritual agility that is never dulled.[34]

In his desire to shock the timid into a real awareness of the heritage of faith, and to drive home the imperative that this heritage should be made real to the world in which we live,[35] von

31. Hans Urs von Balthasar, *Presence and Thought,* Preface.
32. Ibid., 12.   33. Ibid.
34. Ibid.
35. Von Balthasar's view of this world is not overly sanguine: "[The theologian] belongs to an epoch where the established order, to all outward appearances

Balthasar has emphasized the active side of tradition. But there still remains the question of what we are to understand by the "treasure of divine revelation" that is to be made relevant to our own times. The only answer he gives here[36] is to provide us with an image. It would be a mistake, he says, to imagine tradition as a relay of runners, "each of whom, at the end of his segment of the race, hands off [on?] the 'witness,' the 'message,' a piece of wood, or a written work that, through space and time, is preserved of itself in its immovable materiality."[37]

If there were indeed a witness and a message to preserve, a more correct image would be that of the torch, as in the Olympic races of antiquity. For even while it remains identical to itself, a living flame can lay claim to being protected, at every moment, against a constant succession of dangers and being sustained by a substance that is ever new.[38]

The image is a fine one, but it assumes we already know the flame to be genuine or true. Unless, that is, we are prepared to say that all experiences of the past that are revivified in a telling way are authentic tradition, then we must possess some way of separating the flame that is the light of Christ from the flame that is fed on error. How is it that a living flame "can lay claim to being protected." What protects it? What is "the substance that is ever new" that sustains it?

Once we are satisfied that a given experience of presenting the past to the present is genuine tradition, then the newer understand-

---

still solid, is in reality sapped from within, deserted already by a life that can at any given moment reject it and, transformed, leave it like an empty shell destined to turn to dust at the slightest breeze" (ibid., 9).

36. There is a good deal more that would have to be said in presenting a well-rounded account of von Balthasar's views on tradition. In particular his discussion of *positivity* would have to be considered, and how his own project differs from that of the Enlightenment. *The Glory of the Lord*, "The Medium of the Church," 1.556–570. The passage I have analyzed above shows how something good in itself can be misused if taken in isolation from a theologically sophisticated context such as von Balthasar himself provides us with.

37. Ibid., 11.   38. Ibid.

ing of tradition works beautifully. The trouble is, as Cardinal Ratzinger has said, "not everything that exists in the Church must for
that reason be also a legitimate tradition; in other words, not every
tradition that arises in the Church is a true celebration and keeping
present of the mystery of Christ. There is a *distorting* as well as a
legitimate tradition."[39]

If all living and experiencing of the Christian mystery does not
in fact always result in legitimate tradition, then it follows that
there is something wrong with trying to understand tradition
solely in terms of carrying torches, or of "celebrating." It is because an effort has been made to specify or define the meaning of
tradition solely by its non-propositional, or its lived or immediate
character, that the difficulty has arisen in distinguishing between
legitimate and illegitimate traditions in the Church. In the efforts
to emphasize the living and non-propositional aspect of tradition,
it has not been sufficiently emphasized that it is, as St. Athanasius
said, the "ancient tradition," which was "revealed by the Lord,
proclaimed by the apostles, and guarded by the fathers"[40] that is
at issue. Tradition must involve a living experience of the Church's
heritage, but it is the heritage of the Church, something that comes
from the past, which is lived. Words and propositions alone are
not a sufficient for "revealing," "proclaiming," and "guarding";
nonetheless, they are an essential condition, and without them
there can be neither Revelation, nor proclamation, nor guarding.

Newman in his *Via Media,* written when he was an Anglican
and republished after he had become a Catholic, puts the difficulty
of distinguishing true from false tradition without reference to history in a polemical way.

They [i.e. "Roman Catholics"] profess to appeal to primitive Christianity; we honestly take their ground, as holding it ourselves; but when the
controversy grows animated, and descends into details, they suddenly

---

39. Ratzinger, "Dogmatic Constitution," in Vorgrimler, *Commentary,* 3.188.
40. From the *First Letter to Serapion,* in *LH* 3.584.

leave it and desire to finish the dispute on some other field. In like manner in their teaching and acting they begin as if in the name of all the Fathers at once, but will be found in the sequel to prove, instruct, and enjoin simply in their own name . . . when they have to prove this or that article of their creed, they supersede the appeal to Scripture and Antiquity by putting forward the infallibility of the Church, thus solving the whole question, by a summary and final interpretation both of Antiquity and of Scripture.[41]

Newman came to see that his arguments against the Roman position were not conclusive. Yet as a Catholic he republished the criticisms—showing, I suppose, that he still recognized how tradition can in fact be inadequately understood. Newman wanted to maintain the link between tradition and Church teaching, but he wanted to do this in a way that would maintain the integrity of tradition. He thought that its link with the past ought to be capable of demonstration on historical grounds, and demonstrable in a way that did not logically require the interposition of authority to fill in gaps in the demonstration. He did this because he believed that salvation was inextricably linked with the human life of Jesus Christ and with the Revelation which, in history, the Lord committed to His Church.

Newman's early worries about the Catholic Church and its attitude towards tradition are still very much with us. R. P. C. Hanson, whom Father Aidan Nichols calls "one of the most classically Anglican theologians of recent times," wrote: "Their [Catholics'] religion is a religion which looks to the present, and to the future for its Revelation, indeed one which may confidently expect new revelations and new fundamental doctrines of Christianity to emerge in the future into public gaze. . . . In this insistence it has entirely deserted the whole emphasis and outlook of primitive Christianity, it has reversed the current of original faith."[42]

---

41. Newman, *VM* I, lect. 2, sect. 1.
42. Cited in Nichols, *From Newman to Congar*, 2.

The difficulty may be made clearer by examining the work of another pioneer in the modern theory of tradition,[43] a pioneer who made the necessary distinctions between true and false tradition in terms of their respective relationship to the past. It has been said that J. H. Möhler's book *Einheit in der Kirche (Unity in the Church)*, published in 1825, "was the departure point for the ecclesiological renovation that would end with the Second Vatican Council."[44] Möhler taught that the Christian faith is, above all, faith in the communication of the divine life of the Holy Spirit. This communication is to be found only in the Mystical Body of the Church, which is the dwelling place of the Spirit. It is from the Church, then, that we receive faith, and tradition is the living experience of this Spirit, which is communicated to us through the Church. "Each individual is to receive the holy life extended forth in the Church by a direct imprint in himself. By direct contemplation one is to make the experience of the Church one's own, to beget in oneself holy thought and action, and to develop Christian knowledge in the sanctified mind."[45]

This is a very beautiful expression of how the individual in his own generation assimilates the tradition of the Church. A Catholic spirituality requires both for its theory and for its practice the existence of the community.[46] A great deal of what is contained in the present book could be understood as a meditation on the passage cited from Möhler.

On the other hand, as we have seen, the process of assimilation by the individual at a particular time cannot be all that tradition means. There has to be a reference to what was given in the past. Möhler saw this very clearly.

43. I take Newman to have been the other pioneer.

44. Bouyer, *Church of God*, 93.

45. Möhler, *Unity in the Church*, 85.

46. In another passage, Möhler cites with approval the words of Origen: "The Son of God who dwells in the midst of individuals is grasped in the community of believers" (89).

A proof from tradition is not cited from a doctrine present in a certain generation, but as disciples of the apostles and disciples of their disciples lead back to the first member, that is, to the apostles, *so an example from tradition must go back to the apostolic period. Tradition is thus no unspecified past notion.*[47]

It is only in the Church that individuals realize, or assimilate, the tradition of the Church in any adequate way, but what the tradition of the Church conveys to individuals was revealed by God, or else is ineluctably connected with this Revelation by way of development.[48] It is important to be clear about what is at issue. It is one thing to say that God committed the fullness of His Revelation in Christ to the Church and that it is only in the Church that we find this Revelation and are able to live this Revelation. It is, however, quite a different thing to say that the tradition of the Church is constituted solely by what the community actually experiences at any point in history. To assert the latter is to assert two positions which I believe to be incompatible with Catholicism:

1. Tradition has no constants. That is, if tradition is nothing other than the activity of experiencing by the Christian community, then only what is actually being experienced is part of the tradition. This is incompatible with the belief that tradition is one of the ways in which the *given* of God's Revelation is handed on to us. No matter how great an emphasis a theory of tradition may place on creativity and "spirit-oriented" assimilation, there still has to be a *traditum,* something handed on, which provides the basis or the material for the creative assimilation.

2. Tradition, because it has no constants, cannot be normative. That is, if the teaching of tradition has no roots in the given con-

47. Ibid., 107, my emphasis.

48. Ibid., "The reception of the Christian life principle in each specific individual generation has its source in its link to a spiritual root with and from all earlier Christian generations, back to Christ" (93).

stants of Revelation, then tradition becomes what the community says it is. It is one thing to say that we have access to tradition only through the community. It is, however, a false and dangerous thing to say that the tradition is only what the community says it happens to be at a particular point in history. Tradition develops through history, but unless it bears the marks of continuity with the given of Revelation, then it ceases to be tradition and can no longer serve as a corrective and norm for the Church's spiritual life.

Tradition must, it would seem clear, have some connection with what was given to the Church by God in Christ. An important aspect of the Church's past is connected with the words and propositions used in revealing, proclaiming, and guarding. Cardinal Ratzinger has called attention to "the curious fact" that in its reflections on the concept of tradition

Catholic theology has been tending more and more strongly for about a century quietly to equate tradition with progress and to re-interpret the idea of tradition into the idea of progress, by understanding tradition not as the firmly fixed legacy of the earliest days but as the forward-striving force of the sense of faith.[49]

This tendency has today gained the upper hand. The effort to deepen and enrich the theology of Revelation has led to a situation in which tradition understood as the "firmly fixed legacy of the earliest days" is being wrongly reinterpreted, and as a result tradition no longer serves as a norm for distinguishing what is true and what false in the life of the Church.

This is not a necessary consequence of the new theological trends which influenced the Second Vatican Council. The work of Newman and of Möhler, of Congar and de Lubac, must continue to be the basis of an adequate view of tradition that will give due weight to both its aspects of content and of activity. Yet we must always remember that salvation is inextricably linked with the hu-

49. Ratzinger, *Introduction to Christianity*, 26.

man life of Jesus Christ and with the Revelation that, in history, the Lord committed to his Church. It is through the material aspect of tradition, the *traditum,* that we derive the assurance that we enter into communion with that Revelation.

1.4 The heritage of faith on prayer

The vindication of the idea of tradition in the Church must give due weight to the fact that genuine tradition deals with being "zealous and pertinacious in guarding" the heritage of faith, that is, what was given to the apostles by Christ. This primitive content provides a built in control or standard, which is present in all genuine development. In this book I am concerned with how tradition puts us into contact with the ways the mystery of Christ have been lived by faithful Christians in their life of prayer from the age of the apostles to our own time. The tradition concerning spirituality has developed in the Church through meditation on the Scriptures under the prompting of the Holy Spirit and the guidance of the Magisterium.[50] This tradition has been lived by the doctors and saints as well as by untold numbers of Christians who have prayed and lived their faith.[51] Tradition is thus so closely bound up with the divine and human life of the Church that it possesses a truth value that should be normative for the spiritual life of the Christian.

50. "Prayer cannot be reduced to the spontaneous outpouring of interior impulse: in order to pray, one must have the will to pray. Nor is it enough to know what the Scriptures reveal about prayer: one must also learn how to pray. Through a living transmission (Sacred Tradition) within 'the believing and praying Church' the Holy Spirit teaches the children of God how to pray" (*CCC* 2650). See also, *CCC* 2651.

51. Congar, *Tradition and Traditions,* 173: "The Word of God, with the sacraments of Christ, and the Spirit of Christ, form (the) Church unceasingly, according to the pattern given to it by the incarnate Word. There is no break between the apostolic and the historic moments of this Church; there is no arbitrary distinction between apostolic period and texts, as obviously normative, and the full scope of the Church's life."

It is important at this stage to avoid thinking that the heritage of faith provides us with an object to pray about, while the development, even if authentic, represents nothing more than the human response to this object. The response itself, when it is genuine, is qualified and authenticated by the heritage of faith. That is, the control by the object is present in the process of development itself. This can be seen from a passage from St. Augustine's Commentary on Psalm 144(5).[52] Augustine "dares to say" *(audeo enim dicere)* that, in order that God should be well praised by men, He (God) has praised Himself; and because He has stooped *(dignatus)* to praise Himself, so mankind has found how *(quemadmodum)* it should praise Him.

In the first place, then, Augustine says that God has provided the material or the text for prayer. This material is authoritative and comes from God, and the continuing presence of the authoritative text is part of what the control by the object means. The process of vivifying the text of the psalm through prayer is not a freelance activity, sparked, as it were, by the psalm, and then developed any which way the individual or group using it may fancy. On the contrary, the vivifying of the text and the process of development are controlled by the object itself. Secondly, it is by using the text that we are to praise God; we are to imitate how God praises Himself. This imitation involves more than copying God in using the words of the psalm to praise the Lord. St. Augustine is also teaching that in using the psalm we are entering into the same activity of praising God by which God praises Himself. "God has made Himself lovable, and therefore our hearts are inspired to praise Him," ". . . and His Spirit fills His servants so that they can praise Him. And as His Spirit in His servants praises Him, what is this save to praise Himself?"[53]

52. Augustine, *Enarrationes in Psalmos* 144.1.

53. Ibid.: ". . . et spiritu suo implevit servos suos, ut laudarent eum. Et quoniam spiritus eius in servis eius laudat eum, quid aliud quam ipse se laudat?"

The spirituality of the Church, as it has been passed on over the centuries, has been lived and written about as mankind's response to the Revelation of God in Jesus Christ. But it is the fundamental movement of God to us in Revelation, and His continued activity in the Church and individuals, that provide both the structure and the basic dynamic of the spiritual life. Augustine is giving expression to a traditional theme that prayer is not only our activity and an exercise of our freedom; it also concerns God's activity and God's freedom.[54] Most people would have little difficulty in seeing that prayer is something we do, but the recognition that God plays a part in prayer does not come so easily. Nonetheless, this view of prayer as a response to God, or even as a kind of dialogue between God and man, is an enduring aspect of the Church's tradition concerning prayer.[55]

There is no doubting the inner coherence of this theological position. St. Thomas wrote, in his usual concise way, that "the extrinsic and principal cause of devotion is God."[56] St. Bernard of Clairvaux puts this notion of prayer as a response to God's initiative in a less technical form:

Wisdom cries out in the streets, in the broad and spacious way that leads to death, to call back those who take this path. . . . He calls upon sinners to return to their true spirit and rebukes them when their hearts have gone astray, for it is in the true heart that he dwells and there he speaks,

54. *Christian Meditation,* sect. 3: ". . . prayer is the meeting of two freedoms, the infinite freedom of God with the finite freedom of man."

55. Hans Urs von Balthasar begins his book on prayer with the traditional view that prayer is essentially response. "What do we do, when at prayer, but speak to God who long ago revealed himself to man in a word so powerful and all-embracing that it can never be solely of the past, but continues to resound through the ages?" (*Prayer,* 12). Compare this with *CCC* 2560.

56. St. Thomas Aquinas, *Summa Theologiae* 2a2ae 82, 3. Unless otherwise noted, all references to St. Thomas Aquinas are to this work and translations used are from the earlier translation by the Fathers of the English Dominican Province.

fulfilling what he taught through the prophet: Speak to the heart of Je-
rusalem.[57]

The point that Catholic spirituality is a response to a continuing divine initiative with which we cooperate[58] might become
more accessible if we were to return to the biblical theme of God's
love for Israel, and of Israel's tentative, ungenerous, and back-sliding efforts to return that love. The spiritual tradition of the Church
is a call to return the love of God, a love that is being continually
being poured into our hearts so that with and by means of that
love we can enter into the friendship of God.[59] It is more than a
teaching grasped by our mind but with no impact on our conduct
and our attitude toward life. It contains a message that calls us to
a new way of life, and it is meant to shape and color our attitude
toward existence. This attitude includes, but goes far beyond, the
Christian rules of conduct. Again, while it includes saying our
prayers, it is not limited to techniques or practices of praying. In
the end it is about love: a love for God and our neighbor, and such
a love requires everything we have and are.

Who are your friends, Love?
Not great barons whom You leave aside,
But the poor and the destitute.

Those who to all appearances,
Are of no worth or consequence—to them
You give yourself as if You were straw.

57. From a sermon of St. Bernard used as the second reading for the Tuesday
of the 23rd Week of Ordinary time in *LH* 4.231.

58. *CM*, sect. 6: "There exists . . . a strict relationship between Revelation
and prayer. The Dogmatic Constitution *Dei Verbum* teaches that by means of his
Revelation the invisible God 'from the fullness of his love, addresses men as his
friends and moves among them, in order to invite and receive them into his own
company.'"

59. Galatians 4:6: "God has sent the Spirit of his Son into our hearts, crying
'Abba! Father!'"

The man who goes in search of You
So as to see himself grow in knowledge
Will never savour your presence in his heart.

If it is not lodged in a humble heart
The knowledge that we can acquire ourselves
Is nothing but a mortal wound.[60]

In these words, Jacopone da Todi teaches us that it is love that matters, and that knowledge, in itself, is not the key to friendship with God. Love outruns knowledge, and it is the teaching of the masters of Catholic spirituality[61] that a simple and elementary knowledge of God's Revelation in Jesus Christ is enough to give birth to an overwhelming and joyful love for the world's Redeemer:

Love, where did you enter the heart unseen?
Lovable love, joyful love,
In your plenitude You lie far beyond the reach of thought.[62]

We must remember, however, that a simple and elementary knowledge of God's Revelation in Jesus Christ is not identical with no knowledge at all. We do not have to enter into the dispute as to whether knowledge precedes love, or love precedes knowledge, in order to understand that knowledge of some sort must enter into our love of God. We have no first-hand experience, at the beginning at any rate, of the truths of our faith. Even a very simple truth such as "God loves us" is information which has to be given to us and of which we must have some understanding. We begin

---

60. *Laud* 81.

61. For example, St. Francis de Sales writes: "The will only perceives good by means of the understanding, but having once perceived it she has no more need of the understanding to practise love, for the force of the pleasure which she feels, or expects to feel, from union with her object, draws her powerfully to the love and to the desire of enjoying it; so that the knowledge of good gives birth, but not measure, to love . . . ." (*TLG* VI.4).

62. *Laud* 81.

to love God on the basis of what we have been told about him, and speaking and understanding are intellectual operations.

We pray to a God we cannot see. If we are to pray to this God, who is a being different from ourselves, then we have to know something about who He is, and what He is like. No one was stronger than Newman on the need for a clearly articulated system of belief to serve as the basis for the spiritual life. It is true that the driving force behind his work was the effort to revivify a sense of the presence of God and the reality of the unseen; but he thought this could be done only if we knew something about the God we were supposed to love and were given some clear ideas as to the nature of the unseen. In the *Grammar of Assent,* which sums up a lifetime of thought on faith and reason, he wrote:

We must know concerning God, before we can feel love, fear, hope, or trust towards Him. Devotion must have its objects; those objects, as being supernatural, when not represented to our sense by material symbols, must be set before the mind in propositions. The formula, which embodies a dogma for the theologian, readily suggests an object for the worshipper.[63]

Our knowledge of what God is like comes, for the most part, from what he has told us about himself. The spiritual life, as I have said, takes place within this context of what was revealed about God through Jesus Christ. "The formula, which embodies a dogma for the theologian, readily suggests an object for the worshipper." For the individual, the truths of Faith gradually develop into the objects of his love; but because the object is unseen, he has to have it communicated to him in a way that will require at least a rudimentary use of his mind.

Even if we adopt the new emphasis on the "active" or "living" nature of tradition, an emphasis already expressed by Newman, we should not conclude that tradition is only the communication of a mindless "experience" with no roots in the past. It is intel-

63. Newman, *GA* I.5.1. The work was first published in 1870.

ligible, at least, to say that Revelation is more than the conveying of propositions. But there can be no living awareness of Christ's Revelation which does not include the conviction that what is believed is true, or is the case. And without propositions—or, more generally, language—we cannot affirm truth or deny falsehood.

2 ❦ Living the Tradition

> This spiritual power of life that perpetuates itself and transmits itself in the Church is tradition, the inner, mysterious aspect of the Church that draws back from all scrutiny.
>
> Johann Adam Möhler, *Unity in the Church*, 86

2.1 Notional and real assent

We have seen that tradition understood as the handing on of the heritage of faith must be viewed as an activity. The activity, however, has a content that is rooted in God's Revelation through Christ to His Church. This aspect of the given controls the authentic development of tradition and is the final arbiter of what is true and false in the development.

In the actual, historical, development of tradition it is difficult to distinguish the aspects of activity and content, because they are aspects of an experience that can be only very imperfectly described in terms of living and what is lived. This unity of living experience led Möhler to say that tradition is "the inner, mysterious aspect of the Church that draws back from all scrutiny."[1]

To draw back, however, is not to disappear entirely. It is pos-

---

1. Möhler, *Unity in the Church*, 86.

sible to say something about the development of tradition by using Newman's distinction between notional and real assent, and then applying it to the spiritual tradition of the Church.

In the *Grammar of Assent* Newman argued that our assent to the truths of our faith had to be both notional and real.[2] The distinction between notional and real is not between holding a truth in a superficial and unexamined way, on the one hand, and holding this same truth in a deep and penetrating manner, on the other. A notional assent for him was a description of how the *mind* accepted truth, while a real assent was this same truth brought home to the individual by the "religious imagination" so that it became both personal and practical.

To give a real assent to [a dogma of faith] is an act of religion; to give a notional, is a theological act. [The dogma] is discerned, rested in, and appropriated as a reality, by the religious imagination; it is held as a truth, by the theological intellect.[3]

In Newman's language, the spiritual tradition of the Church is largely concerned with the question of real assent to religious truth. On the other hand, Newman insisted that real assent had to follow on some sort of propositional or notional assent. This follows from his view, already noted, that "knowledge must ever precede the exercise of the affections."[4] We have to be given some sort of statement of the truths of faith, no matter how elementary it may be, if we are to begin the long process of living the tradition in a personal and practical way. This statement is given to us by the notional or doctrinal side of tradition, and the development of the spiritual life is governed, or checked, by and through the notional aspect of tradition; as the spiritual life develops, that de-

2. Newman, *GA* I.5, "Apprehension and Assent in the Matter of Religion." Newman's theory is laid out with clarity in Coulson, *Religion and Imagination*, 46–82.

3. Newman, *GA* I.5.

4. See 1.4.

velopment, too, is governed and checked by and through this notional aspect of tradition.

From this notional perspective, prayer in the Catholic tradition is based on sacred doctrine and centered on the Incarnation. It takes to heart the words of our Savior in St. John's Gospel: "I am the door: if anyone enters by me, he will be saved, and will go in and out and find pasture."[5] St. Bonaventure used these words for his teaching that Christ is both the way and the door to the life of contemplation.[6] The writer of the *Cloud of Unknowing* says, "Whoso entereth not by this door, but climbeth otherwise to perfection, by the subtle seeking and the curious fantastic working in his wild, wanton wits . . . is not only a night thief, but a day skulker."[7] St. John of the Cross teaches the same lesson. It is only by meditation on the life of Christ, and by seeking to imitate the Crucified, that we are able to begin the ascent of Mount Carmel.[8] In more recent times, it has been the message of Newman himself, who preached:

This is the very definition of a Christian—one who looks for Christ; not who looks for gain, or distinction, or power, or pleasure, or comfort, but who looks "for the Saviour, the Lord Jesus Christ." This, according to Scripture, is the essential mark, this is the foundation of a Christian, from which everything else follows.[9]

So far we have outlined some of the themes of tradition concerning spirituality in a notional way. It is, however, more difficult to come to grips with real assents of the religious consciousness

5. John 10:9.

6. See St. Bonaventure, *The Journey of the Soul into God,* chap. 7: "In this passing over, Christ is the way and the door, Christ is the ladder and the vehicle, like the Mercy Seat placed above the ark of God and the mystery hidden from eternity."

7. *The Epistle of Privy Counsel,* chap. 9, in McCann, *Cloud,* 125.

8. St. John of the Cross, *Ascent* I.13: "First let him have an habitual desire to imitate Christ in everything that he does, conforming himself to His life; upon which life he must meditate so that he may know how to imitate it, and to behave in all things as Christ would behave."

9. Newman, *SD,* serm. 19 ("The Apostolical Christian").

as they actually developed. In dealing with real assents we are asking questions about that "inner, mysterious aspect of the Church
that draws back from all scrutiny," of which Möhler spoke. One
way of pointing to the inner and mysterious aspect is to take an
outstanding practitioner of prayer, and to see first of all from an
historical point of view that in fact the person in question was
intimately involved in the development of tradition. Having done
this, we will then be able to determine if there are elements in his
life and teaching that enrich our understanding of both tradition
and the life of prayer.

The life of St. Philip Neri (1515–95), the founder of the Oratory, provides an example of how tradition operates in the life of
the Church. He not only lived the Church's spirituality to a pre-
eminent degree but did so in such a way that he was able to hand
it over to others. Philip was not a great innovator at the level of
theory, yet his own work was remarkably fruitful both in appro-
priating and then in handing on the tradition of the Church; furthermore, because he carried on his work with remarkably little
theoretical framework of his own, he provides us with a clear example of tradition in action.

What has come to us of his teaching, as formal teaching, is
largely derivative:

It was a general maxim of his, especially for the members of his own
Congregation, and for others who are called to minister the Word of God,
that both for prayer and for study they should read chiefly the authors
whose names begin with S., that is, St. Augustine, St. Gregory, St. Bernard and other Saints.[10]

That is as clear a statement of the indispensability of the content, or the material aspect, of tradition as one could hope to find.
St. Philip had a well-trained mind and was deeply versed in the
work of St. Thomas Aquinas. Yet when it came to prayer and the

10. Bacci, *The Life of St Philip Neri,* 176.

spiritual life, he preferred to teach by commenting on the work of others. His method of teaching was a variant on the old practice of *lectio divina*. The Bible[11] was his preferred text, but after the Scriptures, the works of Cassian and the *Lauds* of Jacopone da Todi were among his favorites. In this way Philip opened the minds and hearts of his hearers to a life of the Spirit that stretched from the Gospels to his own time, and beyond his own time to our day. He used what was readily accessible to those he taught, in order to introduce them into a world in which the voice of Christ spoke from heart to heart[12] to all the ages.

2.2 Cor ad cor loquitur

St. Philip was born in Florence in 1515. He lived through most of the sixteenth century and died in 1595.[13] He went to Rome in 1534 (when he was eighteen or nineteen) and spent the rest of his life there. He began as a kind of hermit, living in the city, earning a little money by tutoring, and praying by night in the catacombs. Gradually he began to preach and teach, and he gathered a little group around him to pray and converse about spiritual things.

11. In 1613 Fr. Talpa wrote: "The Institute of the Oratory consists principally in the daily use of the word of God, in a simple, familiar and efficacious manner, and very different from the usual style of preachers; this is the essential part of the Institute as conceived by the Blessed Father [St. Philip]." Talpa was one of the early Oratorians sent to Naples by the saint to found the Oratory there (cited in Ponnelle and Bordet, *St. Philip Neri and the Roman Society of His Times*, 323).

12. *Cor ad cor loquitur*, "heart speaks unto heart." These words from St. Francis de Sales were chosen by Newman for his coat of arms as a cardinal. See below, p. 44.

13. For the life of St. Philip Neri, see Ponnelle and Bordet, *St. Philip Neri and the Roman Society of His Times*; and Capecelatro, *The Life of St. Philip Neri Apostle of Rome*. Both of these books have extensive bibliographies. There are also shorter modern works by Türks, *Philip Neri: The Fire of Joy*; Meriol Trevor, *Apostle of Rome, the Life of St Philip Neri*; and Matthews, *St. Philip Neri*.

Philip was ordained, at his confessor's insistence, in 1551 when he was thirty-six years old. He went to live at the Church of San Girolamo della Carità, where his little group began to grow. This was the beginning of the Oratory. It was the men Philip attracted by his personal influence who constituted the first Oratory. They began to come regularly to pray with him, to go to confession to him, and to listen to discourses on the lives of the saints, the development of the Christian virtues, and Church history. Later, he had some of his followers ordained to help in this work of praying, confessing, and instructing. But it was the larger, secular group of laymen who constituted the first Oratory.

From these modest and unpremeditated beginnings, Philip's influence grew until he was the confessor of popes and cardinals, of dukes, bankers and princesses—but also, and still, of the ordinary people who had been with him in the beginning. In a simple kind of prayer accessible to all, in teaching by example, in the sacraments, and in the love of the *santa communità*, the common life of a community, St. Philip found all that was needed for the beginning of the regeneration of his own age.

The extent and depth of St. Philip's influence on the history of the Church is well expressed in the following passage from Pastor's *History of the Popes:*

Quite unexpectedly, and almost of itself, the sphere of his activities and his influence continued to grow, until in the time of Gregory XIII it included the whole of Rome, and at last the whole Church; until Cardinals and Popes, science and art paid him homage, and what is more, thousands venerated him as the author of their happiness in time and in eternity. By sacrificing all things, and giving up everything for the love of God, he reaped his reward a hundredfold. In the eyes of his friends and contemporaries, and in the estimation of posterity he remains an ideal figure, in whom no defect can be discovered.[14]

14. Pastor, *The History of the Popes*, 19.195–96.

Yet St. Philip and the Oratory did not arrive on the scene like Melchizedek, who had, so the writer to the Hebrews[15] assures us, neither father nor mother nor genealogy. St. Philip drew on a tradition, and it is an aspect of this tradition which I now wish to discuss.

The Counter-Reformation may be said to have begun, somewhat paradoxically, even before Luther pinned his theses on the door of the church in Wittenberg in 1517. This is true, not only because real reform is always internal to the Church, but for a more specific reason. There are good grounds for arguing that the circle around St. Catherine of Genoa (1447–1510),[16] which grew into the Oratory of Divine Love, may be taken as the beginnings of the Counter-Reformation. Ten years before the sack of Rome (that is, about 1517), St. Catherine's disciple Ettore Vernaccia planted the Genoese foundation in Rome. The little Church of SS. Silvestro and Dorotea was the scene of the exercises of this group which soon included some of the outstanding humanists and ecclesiastics of the day. In particular, it included "the seraphic" Gaetano da Thiene, and "the high-handed mystic"[17] Pietro Carafa, who was to become Pope Paul IV. The sack of Rome in 1527 by the imperial troops dispersed the Roman group, but it caused the spread of the Oratory of Divine Love over many parts of Italy, and its influence for good was incalculable.

There is still a certain mystery about this Oratory of Divine Love. Part of the reason was the secrecy of the members about the charitable work they were engaged in. Vernaccia's daughter did not know of her father's membership in the Oratory, much less the crucial role he played in its development, until after his

15. Hebrews 7:3.

16. For the life of St. Catherine of Genoa and the work of the Oratory of Divine Love, see da Genova, "Catherine de Gênes," in *DS* 2.290–321; and von Hügel, *Mystical Element*.

17. The epithets are from Ponnelle and Bordet, *St. Philip Neri*, 75.

death. Yet without being able to trace its course exactly, Pastor sees in this society the cradle of the Counter-Reformation.

Like most things that are really good the Reformation of the sixteenth century grew out of small beginnings. It grew silently at the foot of the Curia, till at length it embraced those who bore the dignity of the Papacy. A generation later St. Philip began his work in Rome. From a very modest and humble beginning amongst the poorest and the most neglected, Philip's work, under God, developed into the instrument for the regeneration of Rome.[18]

Baron von Hügel has written of his preference for "that ampler pre-Protestant, as yet neither Protestant nor anti-Protestant, but deeply positive and Catholic, world, with its already characteristically modern outlook and its hopeful and spontaneous application of religion to the pressing problems of life and thought."[19] St. Philip in many ways seems to belong to "that ampler pre-Protestant . . . but deeply positive and Catholic world," and he brought much that was best in the tradition of the Church into the world of the Counter-Reformation.[20] Yet in doing this he avoided tying the tradition down to the forms of the sixteenth century, and so lived the tradition in a way that made it more accessible to those who came after him. This can be seen from the cases of Goethe and Newman.

In his *Italian Journey*, Goethe reserved his only kind remarks about the saints for Philip. Goethe thought that Philip had broken out of what he called a "domestic piety" and achieved a "universal" one.[21] It would be a little unkind to say that by "universal"

18. Pastor, *History of the Popes*, 7.10–11.

19. Von Hügel, *The Mystical Element of Religion*, preface to the first edition.

20. John Coulson writes: "What is especially significant is that, in adopting Philip Neri as his patron, Newman was enabled to move behind the Tridentine curtain to that remaining element of Renaissance humanism which Philip and his Oratorians so fleetingly represent" (*Newman and the Common Tradition*, 98).

21. Goethe, *Italian Journey*, 309. The entry is for May 26, the feast of the saint.

Goethe meant capable of appealing to Goethe, but the fact is, Philip was the only saint "to sneak into the heart of Goethe."[22]

The holiness Goethe saw embodied in Philip is not really so singular as the German supposed. Rather, the fact of the matter is that Goethe's description points up in an able way just how traditional the sanctity of St. Philip was:

[St. Philip] sought "to conquer" the imperious traits of a natural leader, "to disguise the shining brilliance of his being through self-denial, abstention, philanthropy, humility, and abasement. The thought that by appearing a fool in the eyes of the world he might truly gain insight into God and things divine, and train himself in this knowledge, this became the inspiration of his endeavours."[23]

If Philip managed to get through to Goethe, then it is not surprising that Newman came to see Philip as the living embodiment of a lived and renewed tradition. Newman, who became a member of the Oratory during his stay in Rome in May 1847 and introduced it into England, called Philip a "man of primitive times"[24] because of the saint's love for the Church of the martyrs. Yet it was this same St. Philip who, three hundred years after his own death, was able to captivate and inspire Newman for the whole of his Catholic life. In *The Idea of a University,* Newman wrote: "I can say for certain that, whether or not I can do anything at all in St. Philip's way, at least I can do nothing in any other."[25] In "The Mission of St. Philip" he expressed his devotion to the saint, as well as his determination to follow in his footsteps:

Would that we, his children of this Oratory, were able—I do not say individually, but even collectively, nor in some one generation, but even in

22. Von Balthasar, *The Glory of the Lord,* 5.147.

23. Cited in von Balthasar, *The Glory of the Lord,* 5.405.

24. Newman, *MD,* "Litany of St Philip": "Vir prisci temporis—man of primitive times." The Latin and English versions of the litany are both by Newman himself.

25. Newman, *Idea,* pt. I, disc. 9, sect. 10.

that whole period during which it is destined to continue here—would that we were able to do a work such as his! At least we may take what he was for our pattern, whatever be the standard of our powers and the measure of our success. And certainly it is a consolation that thus much we can say in our own behalf—that we have gone about his work in the way most likely to gain his blessing upon us, because most like his own.[26]

In St. Philip, Newman found, at the beginning of his Catholic life, someone who taught and handed on the authentic tradition of the Church about the life of prayer.

In 1879 Newman, toward the end of his Catholic life, was in Rome to be made a cardinal. He found he had not only left his family coat of arms at home in Birmingham, but had also forgotten to verify the text of the new motto he planned to add to them. He wrote to his friend Hutton: "Do you recollect in the Vulgate or in A Kempis, the words 'Cor ad cor ⟨cordi⟩ loquitur'?"[27] It turned out that the text was from St. Francis de Sales, and that Newman had used it many years earlier.[28] In a striking way Newman's choice of his motto illustrates the force of a living tradition. St. Francis de Sales frequented the Roman Oratory during his years in Rome and was a close friend of several of St. Philip's earliest disciples.[29] Among these was Cardinal Francesco Maria Tarugi, who was known in his own time as *dux verbi* (which I suppose might be translated as a peerless exponent of the word

26. Newman, *OS,* serm. 12, sect. 7.

27. *LD* xxix, April 25, 1879.

28. In a letter to Bishop Moriarty in "University Preaching," *Idea,* pt. II, 6. The citation from St. Francis reads: "Quantumvis ore dixerimus, sane cor cordi loquitur, lingua non nisi aures pulsat." *Oeuvres de Saint François de Sales,* Paris 1834, III, Sermons I, p. 29; Annecy edition, XII, 1902, p. 321, "On a beau dire, mais le coeur parle au coeur, et la langue ne parle qu'aux oreilles." See *LD* xxix, 108, note 2.

29. He may even have met St. Philip on his first visit in 1592. He also went to Rome in 1597, and again in 1603 in connection with his appointment as a bishop. Later St. Francis founded an Oratory in his diocese at Thonon.

of God), "because of his great eloquence and the abundant fruit which he produced in his hearers."[30] Tarugi used to say: "The word which issues forth from the mouth reaches to the ear; the word which comes from the heart does not stop until it reaches another heart."[31] The source of the expression may very well have been St. Philip himself. In any case it is clear that the idea of a simple preaching that touched the heart was common coin at the Oratory and that St. Francis shared it with, if he did not learn it from, the circle around St. Philip. Centuries later the expression, and all it carried with it, resonated in the heart of Newman, even though he had forgotten its source. Philip had become for Newman the bearer of a tradition that stretched from the catacombs to nineteenth-century England.

2.3 How St. Philip taught

We have seen that St. Philip drew on the past in a way that did not tie him to the sixteenth-century Counter-Reformation. The unstructured teaching and simple life of this "man of primitive times" spoke directly to his own age and to those that followed. Now we have to examine how St. Philip taught.

Shortly before he died, St. Philip ordered all his personal papers, writings, and letters to be destroyed. Furthermore, he saw to it that this was in fact done, and almost nothing remained except for a few letters and three sonnets. As he published no books, we have to rely entirely on second-hand information and the example of his life if we want to find out what he taught.

This is not as serious as it might at first appear, since the tradition of the Church as it makes itself known in the life of prayer is not to be found in the first instance in books about prayer. It is to be found in the lives of people who pray. A great deal of prayer

30. *The Excellences* I.3.
31. Ibid.

is learned by experience and by imitating others. Sometimes those who do know something about prayer write about it, and the writings of these people also become a part of the tradition.

Secretum meum mihi: "My secret is my own." These words from Isaiah[32] were often used by St. Philip when asked about his own life of prayer. Yet no one has ever doubted that he was one of the greatest of contemplatives in a century that saw a splendid flowering of the spiritual life. St. John of the Cross, St. Teresa of Avila, St. Ignatius, to mention only the most well known, were all his contemporaries. But he, unlike them, left no doctrine or technique of the spiritual life. I do not think this was the result merely of modesty or of temperament. The whole question of teaching, and especially of teaching about prayer, is a difficult one. In his *Seventh Epistle,* Plato says that it is impossible to teach directly about important things. In this letter he is talking about philosophy as the love of wisdom, but his words apply equally to teaching about prayer: "It is not something that can be put into words like other branches of learning; only after long partnership in a common life devoted to this very thing does truth flash upon the soul, like a flame kindled by a leaping spark, and once it is born there it nourishes itself thereafter."[33]

Plato teaches here that the only way truth can be learned is by long association between teacher and pupil, and the depreciation of the written word repeats in stronger terms his earlier suggestions in the *Phaedrus.*[34] In view of Plato's own extensive writings,

32. Isaiah 24:16, in the Vulgate.

33. Paragraph 341. It is often claimed this letter is a forgery, but as Walter Hamilton observes: "If it is a forgery, it is a forgery on a scale and of an elaboration otherwise unknown among forged letters" (*Phaedrus and the Seventh and Eighth Letters,* 106).

34. E.g. *Phaedrus,* 275: "Then it shows great folly . . . to suppose that one can transmit or acquire clear and certain knowledge of an art through the medium of writing, or the written word can do more than remind the reader of what he already knows on any given subject."

the denial that he has written or will write a message may seem strange. But his work does consist in dialogues, not in a systematic exposition of the theory of forms. Lingering around all his work is the sense that the most important things cannot be said, and that it is only by a living experience in which love plays an indispensable role that we come to know things as they really are.[35] For Plato the most important object of knowledge is the Form of the Good. But the function of this Form is not only to produce the other forms, but to make them knowable to us. Intelligibility is conferred by the light of the Good itself. When St. Augustine reworked this material into Christianity, he taught that the action of God is required if the truth is to become known. Real assent to truth requires an illumination of the human soul by God.[36]

St. Philip shared Plato's distrust of the written word as a means for communicating the living truth. Nothing could have been more foreign to his character than a desire to be regarded as a master in the spiritual life with a doctrine to propound and a technique to impart. One can well imagine the irony with which he would have greeted some of the more solemn treatises on prayer. It must not be imagined that this in any way implies that St. Philip was a simpleton or an uneducated buffoon. Nor, most certainly, does it mean that he had nothing to teach about prayer. He was a

35. "Written words are the helpless victims of men's ill-will, and encourage inferior exposition at second hand. Writing can easily become a kind of lying, something frivolously pursued for its own sake, in fact an art form. True understanding comes suddenly to trained thinkers after sustained and persistent discussion; and there is little danger of a man forgetting the truth once he has grasped it since it lies within a small compass" (Iris Murdoch, *The Fire and the Sun, Why Plato Banished the Artists*, 23).

36. Rist, *Augustine*, 78: "Even if we have a certain awareness within us, it needs to be lit up by the Good, that is, for Augustine, by God, so that we can 'see' what is in front of our eyes, whether those eyes be physical or mental. As a Platonist, Augustine sees this illuminating light not as a power within ourselves, but as the light of God himself . . ."

well educated, highly civilized, and insightful man who found no small amusement in many aspects of the human situation. He has been compared—and quite rightly compared—to Socrates.[37] Like Socrates, Philip delighted in deflating pompous people who took themselves too seriously. Yet he loved them and he wanted them to love God the way he did. Pretensions of whatever sort—intellectual, moral, social, but most of all spiritual—Philip saw as obstacles to the growth of the gifts of the Holy Spirit in the individual. The obstacles had to be removed. Cutting people down to size in order that they could grow was a large part of Philip's apostolate. It is perfectly clear that St. Philip was the first victim of his own irony and scepticism about human motives and pretensions.

There was, indeed, a truth to be communicated, but the flame had to be enkindled. To convey the truth to his followers in a way that would touch their hearts and change their lives, there was first the ministry of the confessional. But in a more public way, Philip developed the practice of extemporary preaching on the Bible and other books he regarded as conveying the fundamentals of the Christian life. One of the principal exercises of the Oratory as it developed was this "speaking on the book" *(il ragionamento sopra il libro),* an improvised talk that sprang from the reading of some inspiring text. In Philip's view, "speaking on the book" left the way open for Holy Spirit to infuse its power into the speaker. The absence of a prepared discourse meant

37. The comparison to Socrates was made in Philip's own lifetime by Cardinal Valier: "Truly he is to be called a Christian Socrates, who despising all external things [is] an exceedingly bitter enemy of vices, a constant cultivator of virtues, a master of sincerity, a propagator of true instruction, teaching humility continuously, not only by words but by example, opening out his heart to all with profoundest charity, instructing some, assisting others with beneficial reminders, commending all to the Most High with his holy prayers and preserving unfailing joy in pious exercises of this kind" (*Philippus sive de Christiana Laetitia Dialogo,* 7–8) (my translation).

that a living connection was set up between the speaker and his hearers.[38]

In 1588 St. Philip dictated a letter to the Fathers of the Oratory in Naples, in which he expressed his joy that they had been speaking there "on the book":

> . . . in accordance with the ancient usage of the Oratory, when they did so *in spiritu et veritate et simplicitate cordis,* and when they left the field to the Holy Spirit, that He might infuse His power into the mouth of the speaker, without all that profound study, that premeditation, that analysis of authors, such as the men of the Sorbonne are wont to employ.[39]

Certainly, the practice seems to have worked for a time, although even before the end of his life, he was complaining that the preaching at the Oratory had lost its original fire.

Today we may be more prepared to accept at least the idea of a speaker being moved by the Holy Spirit than St. Philip's contemporaries seem to have been. The enemies of the early Oratory sometimes complained about the unorthodoxy of the talks. The critics were in the end silenced because their accusations were false. Nonetheless, the criticisms remind us of the truth that Catholic preaching involves not merely being moved by the Holy Spirit, but being moved by the Holy Spirit to speak the revealed truth. It is here we see the wisdom of St. Philip, who wanted to combine both the element of the truth conveyed by tradition as well as the freedom of those who have become the dwelling place of the Holy Spirit. I have outlined the practice of speaking on the book and have emphasized the extemporary, "freelance" aspect of the practice. We now have to see the other half of the practice: that is, that the speaking was a speaking on a text.

Ragionamento sopra il libro was an inspired variant or develop-

---

38. See Cistellini, *San Filippo Neri e la congregazione Oratoriana,* 1.78–90.

39. The letter was actually written by Fr. Nicolò Gigli, Philip's secretary, on December 23, 1588. It is cited in Ponnelle and Bordet, *St. Philip Neri,* 203.

ment of *lectio divina*, which was an older and a common practice in the Church. St. Teresa says that anyone who has difficulty with formal meditation and the use of the imagination should read slowly from a book.[40] She thought that this contact with the Scriptures, the writings of the Fathers of the Church, or the lives of the saints would make up for the meditation we were unable to make. Reading would provide us with the truths of our faith, which we have to assimilate so that they become a second nature to us. Once they become a real part of ourselves, they should affect our life with God as well as the way we treat other people. St. Teresa insists that meditation, in this very general sense of continuing to appropriate in an ever-deeper way our knowledge of Jesus Christ, must be a constant element in our life of prayer.[41]

The advice to take up reading if we cannot meditate would have appeared strange to earlier writers. For them, reading came first. Reading not only provided the indispensable basis for prayer; it was itself prayer. In Chapter 48 of the *Rule* St. Benedict says that the brethren must be occupied at stated hours in *lectio divina*, that is, in reading the Bible.[42] For St. Benedict and the monastic tra-

---

40. St. Teresa of Avila, *Life*, 4: "Anyone unable to make use of this method [that is, meditation] . . . should occupy himself frequently in reading, since he cannot find instruction in any other way. . . . Reading is . . . necessary for him, however little it may be, as a substitute for the mental prayer which he is unable to practise."

41. St. Teresa, *IC* vi. 7: "You will also think that anyone who enjoys . . . favours will not engage in meditation on the most sacred humanity of our Lord Jesus Christ, because by that time he will be wholly proficient in love . . .

"I cannot conceive what they are thinking of; for, though angelic spirits, freed from anything corporeal, may remain permanently enkindled in love, this is not possible for those of us who live in this mortal body. . . . The last thing we should do is to withdraw of set purpose from our greatest help and blessing, which is the most sacred humanity of our Lord Jesus Christ."

42. *Rule of St. Benedict*, chap. 48: "Idleness is the enemy of the soul. The brethren, therefore, must be occupied at stated hours in manual labour, and again at other hours in sacred reading."

dition, this *lectio* was the sum total of non-liturgical prayer. A great deal of attention had always been given to understanding this *lectio*. In a twelfth-century work, the *Ladder of Monks*, Guigo II distinguishes four stages in spiritual exercises. These are: reading, meditation, prayer, and contemplation. "Reading seeks for the sweetness of a blessed life, meditation perceives it, prayer asks for it, contemplation tastes it."[43] From Guigo's text we learn that meditation, prayer, and contemplation are all to be understood in relation to the reading, partly because reading often meant an audible verbalizing of the words.[44] This verbalizing provided matter for the other forms of prayer, which were all regarded as ways of assimilating this matter in a progressively more complete way, and "matter" was described in a fairly literal way:

Reading, as it were, puts food whole into the mouth, meditation chews it and breaks it up, prayer extracts its flavour, contemplation is the sweetness itself which gladdens and refreshes. Reading works on the outside, meditation on the pith: prayer asks for what we long for, contemplation gives us delight in the sweetness which we have found.[45]

The images of putting food in our mouth and being refreshed make it clear that the words spoken and heard by the reader remain as an integral part of meditation and the other forms of prayer. Or, to put the matter the other way around, we can say that prayer is a kind of reading; it is a reading in which all the elements of our nature are involved. We have to speak and hear the text, which means using our body in an obvious sense, and then our memory files the text away so the intelligence can understand its meaning.

43. Guigo II, *The Ladder of Monks*, chap. 3.
44. See Leclercq, *The Love of Learning and the Desire for God*, 24: "In the Middle Ages, as in antiquity, they read usually, not as today, principally with the eyes, but with the lips, pronouncing what they saw, and with the ears, listening to the words pronounced, hearing what is called the 'voices of the pages.'" The evidence for this does not seem watertight, however. See Burnyeat, "Reading Silently.'"
45. Guigo II, *Ladder*, chap. 3.

Finally, the will strives after fruition of the text and seeks to put it into practice.[46]

Lectio divina, as it was understood at the beginning, was the reading of the Bible and only the Bible, and so we find the phrase *sacra pagina* (sacred page) often given as a synonym. The practice has its roots in Judaism and the early Church,[47] but the first clear statement of its nature is found in Origen.

Do you then, my son, diligently apply yourself to the reading of the sacred Scriptures. Apply yourself, I say. For we who read the things of God need much application, lest we should say or think anything too rashly about them.[48]

The necessity of applying oneself to the Scripture draws attention to the fact that *lectio divina* is a serious business and involves the whole person. It was the analysis of applying oneself with full attention which led to the distinguishing of the *lectio* into the reading itself, meditation, prayer, and contemplation. These distinctions are to be found in Origen. In the same letter he continues, first with a discussion of what came to be called meditation:

And applying yourself thus to the study of the things of God, with faithful prejudgments such as are well pleasing to God, knock at its locked door, and it will be opened to you by the porter, of whom Jesus says, 'To him the porter opens'. And applying yourself thus to the divine study, seek aright, and with unwavering trust in God, the meaning of the holy Scriptures, which so many have missed.[49]

46. Leclercq, *Love of Learning,* 26: "For the ancients, to meditate is to read a text and to learn it 'by heart' in the fullest sense of this expression, that is, with one's whole being: with the body, since the mouth pronounced it, with the memory which fixes it, with the intelligence which understands its meaning and with the will which desires to put it into practice."

47. See Bouyer, *A History of Christian Spirituality,* I, chap. 1; and idem, *Introduction to Spirituality,* 45–55.

48. Origen, *Letter to Gregory Thaumaturgos,* sect. 3, in The Ante-Nicene Fathers 4.394.

49. Ibid.

He then goes on to emphasize that prayer is essential if we are to be successful in this meditation, and, finally, that the fruit of the *lectio* is contemplation:

Be not satisfied with knocking and seeking; for prayer is of all things indispensable to the knowledge of the things of God. For to this the Saviour exhorted, and said not only, "Knock, and it shall be opened unto you; and seek, and ye shall find" but also, "Ask, and it shall be given unto you."[50]

By serious reading of the Bible we are saved from earthly desires and concerns with worldly matters and are brought little by little to put on the divine nature. The purpose of the reading is to immerse oneself in the text, which serves as the matter not only for reading but for meditation, prayer, and contemplation. The *lectio* is not a means to other sorts of prayerful activity, but an end in itself.[51]

The tradition of spiritual reading, to which St. Teresa draws our attention, grew out of the *lectio divina,* but it represents a development in several ways. In the first place, as the term indicates, spiritual reading is no longer a question of *sacra pagina,* but of any solid book of "mystical theology" or "spiritual discussion." Secondly, the study of Scripture becomes a question of study, a subject for the classroom and the study, and separated from prayerful reading. Finally, intelligence and the understanding are distinguished from, if not opposed to, the development of a taste or love *(gustus, affectus)* of God's presence.[52]

50. Ibid.

51. In the words of J. Alvarez de Paz: "Lectio is whenever we study the pages of Sacred Scripture, not only so as to know, but so that we may advance by the spirit and knowing the will of God we may accomplish it in deed" (cited in Sieben, "De la *lectio divina* à la lecture spirituelle," in *DS* 9.487) (my translation).

52. Ibid.: "We call it spiritual reading, when we study mystical books and spiritual tracts, in which we seek not only knowledge of spiritual things but much more to taste and love [them]" (my translation).

In a very general way it can be said that the development of spiritual reading was brought about by a desire to make the spiritual life more accessible to people living in the world. *Lectio divina* in the Benedictine sense required education and the structured existence of the monastery. If the only sort of prayer was praying with the Bible, and this required a fairly high degree of education and leisure, then it followed that either prayer would have to be closed to most people or its foundations would have to be simplified. It was the friars, and then the founders of the *devotio moderna,* who were responsible for trying to make the practice of prayer more available to the laity.[53] The work of the Jesuits carried on this process.[54]

St. Philip's method of teaching was another sort of development of *lectio.* In speaking on the book, the speaker expounded a given element of tradition and, at the same time, allowed scope for its living and creative aspect. The text provided the basis for and a control over the discourse, while the improvised and immediate character of the talk ensured that it became a living development of Christian truth. Philip's own discussion of the Jacopone's *Laud* "The Five Ways in Which God Reveals Himself" is an instance of teaching by commenting on a book. It was Jacopone, not St. Philip, who was the inventor of the distinctions used in the *Laud,* but "there can be no doubt that when he in his turn explained them, he spoke with the book in hand, in accordance with the custom he had himself inaugurated. Thus Philip's sermons, which were few in any case, were but commentaries."[55]

53. For a summary of this development, see Sieben, "De la *lectio divina* à la lecture spirituelle," in *DS* 9.487–96.

54. Sieben, "De la *lectio divina,*" in *DS* 9.494: "The Jesuits seem to have been the first to use the expression 'spiritual reading' (*lectio spiritualis*)."

55. Ponnelle and Bordet, *St. Philip Neri,* 576.

2.4 *What St. Philip taught*

It would be wrong to draw the conclusion that Philip had nothing to communicate, or that he did not know where he stood, or that his influence consisted essentially in the removing of false ideas. Assuredly, his irony was directed against humbug, pretension, false thinking, and self-deception. But his technique was directed toward removing everything that stood in the way of his disciples being nourished by the spiritual tradition which was, and is, the Church's heritage. If the message of Socrates was "know thyself," then the message of St. Philip is "know Jesus Christ." A truly Christian spirituality must be based on Jesus Christ, "who was put to death for our sins and raised up for our justification."[56] It is this Jesus Christ whom St. Philip sought to make better known and better loved. It is true that this can be said about any saint. St. Philip, however, was content to efface himself before the tradition of the Church, so that the tradition of the Church could shine all the more brightly through him.

One of the texts St. Philip used in communicating the tradition of the Church was the *Lauds* of Jacopone da Todi. The poetry of this radical Franciscan, which typified so much of the medieval longing for reform in the Church, colored the minds of both St. Philip and St. Catherine of Genoa. The *Lauds* express the desire for a reform based on the Franciscan love for Jesus Christ and him crucified. It was a reform based on love for the Church as the living but wounded Mystical Body of Jesus Christ. The reform they sought to bring was the witness of the joy of a life given over and taken up into the love of God. The life of prayer that went with this reform was open to all, but especially to the poor and the simple; for Christ himself had thanked the Father that he had "hidden these things from the wise and understanding, and revealed them to babes."[57]

56. Romans 4:25.
57. Matthew 11:25. Cistellini cites Talpa: "At the heart of everything for Philip

Prayer in itself is not complicated or esoteric, and it is open to all. The ability to pray has little to do with an intellectual awareness of what people today call "spirituality." Anyone whose life is based on a sense of the presence of Christ in his Church will pray without any need of theory. Indeed, many of those whose prayer is most profound and who possess a real knowledge of what divine intimacy means have very little knowledge about the theory of prayer. Often they have an instinctive repugnance for talking or speculating about the spiritual life. It is as though they are aware that thinking about prayer may distract them from its practice, and may even become a substitute for it.[58] The absence of theoretical knowledge does not mean that it is always easy to pray, but it does mean that the life of prayer in the Church is wider and deeper than whatever sort of theorizing may be in vogue at the moment.

Jacopone da Todi[59] (123?–1306) entered the Order of the Friars Minor during the last quarter of the thirteenth century, when the conflict between the Franciscan Spirituals and Conventuals was raging. He came from a rich and aristocratic family and had been married previously. His wife died, it is said, in an accident; after finding a hair shirt on her body, he turned his back on his former life. He spent several years as a kind of freelance preacher, and deliberately turned himself into "what is low and despised in the world"[60] because he believed in an uncompromising way that "the foolishness of God is wiser than men, and the weakness of God

---

there is the conviction that the spiritual life, [usually] looked on as something difficult, should become so familiar and ordinary that it would become pleasant and easy for every sort of person" (*San Filippo Neri*, 1.109) (my translation). Or, as Newman said in his Hymn to St. Philip: "Thus he conducts by holy paths and pleasant" (*VV*), "St. Philip in His School."

58. See De Guibert, *The Theology of the Spiritual Life*, 360–63. "The Reading of Mystical Works."

59. For the life of Jacopone de Todi, see Peck, *The Fool of God*.

60. 1 Corinthians 1:28.

is stronger than men.''[61] Later he became a zealous and imprudent member of the Spirituals. He entered into open rebellion against Pope Boniface VIII, and was excommunicated. In 1298 he was captured, then sentenced by the pope he had attacked to perpetual imprisonment in an underground cell. In the Year of Jubilee 1300, Jacopone begged for the lifting of the sentence of excommunication so that he could at least receive the sacraments. His plea was ignored. Finally, he was released by Benedict XI (Boniface's successor) in 1303. He died three years later in peace at a small friary in Umbria.

Von Balthasar calls Jacopone "the only true penitent fool in the West—apart from the Russians.''[62]

The saints follow in the footsteps of Jesus, who was despised, abused, thought to be mad [Mark 3:21] and possessed [Matthew 12:24; John 7:20; 8:48] and yearn, for the sake of Jesus, to be regarded as fools. In their abandonment to God's every command, the finger of their yearning points in this direction, and they know that, as the imitation of Christ, it could be pleasing to God.[63]

Jacopone's work consists of a series of ninety-three religious poems, which go in English under the name of *Lauds*.[64] The words "praises" or "canticles" might also serve as a translation of the Italian *lauda* (*laude* in the plural). They have been called "the most powerful religious poetry in Italy before Dante's time," and they have not lost their force even today.[65]

On the face of it there could not be two figures more dissimilar than Jacopone da Todi and St. Philip Neri. The one was a radical Franciscan who took part in open rebellion against the pope and

61. 1 Corinthians 1:25.

62. Von Balthasar, *The Glory of the Lord*, 5.146.

63. Ibid., 5.143.

64. The first printed edition of the *Lauds* was edited by Francesco Bonaccorsi, the Florentine religious humanist, in 1490.

65. Hughes and Hughes, *The Lauds*, xix.

was excommunicated and imprisoned for his pains. The other lived in the heart of the Rome of the Counter-Reformation, and was beloved and honored by popes and cardinals. Jacopone lived on the margins of the "official" or "hierarchical" Church and belonged, according to a modern author, to a medieval "counter-culture."[66] Philip, on the other hand, was a Florentine of the High Renaissance, who rejoiced in the arts, especially music, and made no effort to rebel against the society or the Church in which he found himself.[67]

The influence of Jacopone in the period just before the Reformation, and later, during the Counter-Reformation, is of singular importance. The tradition of the Church is shared by those whose forms of life may be very different,[68] and both St. Catherine of Genoa and St. Philip were influenced by, and treasured, the *Lauds* of Jacopone. Furthermore, since the Oratory of Divine Love (which grew up around St. Catherine) and the Oratory (which St. Philip founded) were both of enormous importance in the period under question, so the spirit of Jacopone, and the tradition he enshrined, found a home and had an influence in the heart of the Catholic reform movement.

66. Peck, *The Fool of God*, xii.

67. St. Philip, Newman says, "lived in an age as traitorous to the interests of Catholicism as any that preceded it, or can follow it." Yet Philip saw that the mischief was to be met: "not with argument, not with science, not with protests and warning, not by the recluse or the preacher, but by means of the great counter-fascination of purity and truth. . . . He preferred to yield to the stream, and direct the current, which he could not stop, of science, literature, art and fashion, and to sweeten and to sanctify what God had made very good and man had spoilt" (*Idea*, pt. I, disc. 9, sect. 9).

68. Outram Evennett calls the spirit of St. Philip and the Oratorians "modishly Franciscan"! The passage runs as follows: "St. Philip Neri and the warmer spirit of the Oratorians—not indeed indulgent but somehow modishly Franciscan—represented a variation (of the new tides of spirituality) that found a wide response in the Rome of Sixtus V, Clement VIII and Paul V which St Philip did so much to convert" (*Spirit of the Counter-Reformation*, 41).

The evidence for St. Catherine's interest in the *Lauds* is to be found in Baron von Hügel's monumental *The Mystical Element of Religion*. After an exhaustive analysis of the *Lauds* in relation to Catherine's doctrine, he writes:

Jacopone it is, then, who furnished Catherine with much help towards that rare combination of deep feeling with severely abstract thinking which, if at times it somewhat strains and wearies us moderns who would ever end with the concrete, gives a nobly virile, bracing note to even the most affective of her sayings.[69]

Philip possessed a copy of the *Lauds,* and in 1558 Giambattista Modio, Philip's penitent, published a new edition for use at the Oratory. In the preface he clearly designates Philip as the inspiration of the work: "having been written by the command of him who has so very much influence over me," and the *Lauds* are known to have been of central importance in the preaching at the Oratory.[70]

The affinity is not really so difficult to understand. Both Jacopone and Philip were ready to put into practice the words of St. Paul, even to the point of being thought mad, in order to find Christ:

For whatever gain I had, I counted as loss for the sake of Christ. Indeed I count everything as loss because of the surpassing worth of knowing Christ Jesus my Lord. For his sake I have suffered the loss of all things, and I count them as refuse, in order that I may gain Christ, and be found in him . . .[71]

In their efforts to "gain Christ" they appropriated the tradition of the Church, they lived it, and they handed it on.

69. Von Hügel, *Mystical Element*, 110.

70. See Ponnelle and Bordet, *St. Philip Neri*, 204–5, 208–12, where the evidence for St. Philip's love for the *Lauds* is discussed at length.

71. Philippians 3:8–9.

PART II. On the Lord's Appearing

Show me where my Lord is, I have heard he loves me;
Tell me where to find Him, I can wait no more.
Long it is He waits for me in sorrow.

Jacopone da Todi, Laud 42

Although ever since Luther we have become accustomed
to call the Bible "God's Word," it is not Sacred Scripture
which is God's original language and self-expression, but
rather Jesus Christ. As One and Unique, and yet as one
who is to be understood only in the context of mankind's
entire history and in the context of the whole created cosmos, Jesus is the Word, the Image, the Expression, and
the Exegesis of God.

Hans Urs von Balthasar, The Glory of the Lord, 1. 29.

3 ❧ The Drawing of This Love and the Voice of This Calling

> The Lord appears to me in this life in five ways:
> He who ascends to the fifth has scaled a great height.

3.1. Conversion and development

We have seen that the *Lauds* of Jacopone were among St. Philip's favorite writings and that he used them in his talks at the Oratory. In the Introduction I said I would use *Laud* number 46, "On the Lord's Appearing," a *Laud* St. Philip himself used in "speaking on the book," to illustrate and comment on the spiritual tradition of the Church. In this *Laud* Jacopone speaks of the different ways or modes in which God appears to the believer. He begins by saying:

> The Lord appears to me in this life in five ways:

And in the next line he continues:

> He who ascends to the fifth has scaled a great height.

On the face of it, the lines seem to be talking about different things; the first is concerned with the Lord's appearing, while the second seems to refer to the progress of the individual Christian. The second verse of the poem strengthens this impression of a double movement:

The first is the state of fear, the second healing love;
The third manifestation is of tender sustenance,
Followed by fatherly love
And lastly by conjugal love, the love of the bridegroom.

In the above verse the Lord's appearing is described in various ways, and Jacopone's reactions are said to be fear and love. There is no carelessness or contradiction on Jacopone's part, for he is teaching in his own way that the spiritual life is a two-way street. Not only does it involve our efforts and our prayer, but, more importantly, these efforts and this prayer have to be seen as a response to the God who first goes out to us.[1] The writer of the *Cloud of Unknowing* wrote of this first step on God's part as the "drawing of this love and the voice of this calling."[2] St. John of the Cross, teaching the same doctrine, says: "First it must be known that, if a soul is seeking God, its beloved is seeking it much more."[3] He goes on to say:

When, therefore, the soul reflects that God is the principal agent in this matter and the guide of the blind self, Who will take it by the hand and lead it where it could not of itself go (namely, to the supernatural things which neither its understanding nor its will nor its memory could know as they are), then its chief care will be to see that it sets no obstacle in the way of the guide, who is the Holy Spirit, upon the road by which God is leading it.[4]

In this chapter I want to discuss the idea of conversion as an experience in which God calls us into a living awareness of his

1. See 1.3.
2. *Cloud,* chap. 2: "What weary wretched heart and sleeping in sloth is that, the which is not wakened with the drawing of this love and the voice of this calling?" The author is actually speaking about the beginning of the contemplative life, but the phrase (cited in the text) admirably describes the process of conversion from the side of the divine initiative.
3. *LFL,* III.27.
4. Ibid.

friendship and we respond. Our response, however, though it initiates the Christian life, does not complete it. Thus we should also consider the idea of the development of our response and try to see what we can make of the traditional doctrine that the spiritual life develops through different stages.

3.2 *The voice of this calling*

In one of his Lauds, Jacopone wrote:

You, Love, are the hook
With which I have been caught,
The desire of my hungry heart.[5]

These lines make two points. First of all, they say that God is the desire of the hungry heart and, secondly, that we have been hooked by God. Only by God's action on us we can find and keep the object of our heart's real love.

The truth that God is the desire of the hungry heart is not easy to argue for nowadays. One reason for this is the general unwillingness to think about human life in terms of ends or goals. Even when this unwillingness is overcome, few now assume that one final goal will emerge as the object of everyone's striving.[6] It is taken for granted that the result of an effort to determine what people really think important will reveal a wide variety of opinion.[7] It is also held, furthermore, that it will be impossible to argue that one or another end *ought* to be pursued by everyone. Various sorts of relatively final ends will be found to characterize different sorts of people, and that is about all we will be able to say.

5. *Laud* 81.

6. Anscombe, *Intention,* #21: "Can't a man just do what he does, a great deal of the time? He may or may not have a reason or a purpose; and if he has a reason or purpose, it in turn may just be what he happens to want; why demand a reason or purpose for *it*?"

7. See, for example, Taylor, *Sources of the Self: The Making of the Modern Identity.*

The Christian can argue that to put our search for happiness or satisfaction in pleasure, material goods, the fruits of ambition, or even the quiet achievements of scholarship, will not completely satisfy the longing of the mind and heart for some sort of absolute. He may contend that the insatiable need to know, the fathomless capacity of the will to love, and our going out to the inexhaustible mystery of the beautiful and the sublime all point to a reality beyond anything this world can provide. This movement from different aspects of creation to the affirmation that only God will satisfy us is useful and legitimate. It does not, however, appear to be an argument that moves people nowadays. At best it is only a suasion to belief, because the starting points of the process will not be recognized as starting points unless we know that they lead somewhere. Unless, that is, we somehow apprehend that there is a God who created everything there is, both visible and invisible, we will not be able to understand these experiences as anything more than descriptions of man's condition. The truth that only God will satisfy is not like a major premise of an argument, based on reason, which serves to show that people who do not accept the reality of God are either fools or wicked, and probably both. On the contrary, the truth that it is God who is "the desire of my hungry heart" is the affirmation of a living faith in the reality of God.

In his sermon "On Conversion," St. Bernard tells us that it is the power of God and not the voice of the preacher that converts men. And what St. Bernard says about the effect of preaching is true about any experience that leads us to God.

For who dare compare the sayings of men with what God is said to have said? The Word of God is living and effective (Heb. 4:12). His voice is a voice of magnificence and power (Ps 28:4). "He spoke and they were made" (Ps. 148:5). He said "Let there be light, and there was light" (Gen. 1:3). He said "Be converted" (Ps. 19:3), and the sons of men have been converted. So the conversion of souls is clearly the work of the divine voice, not of any human voice. Even Simon son of John (Jn. 21:15), called and appointed by the Lord to be a fisher of men, will toil in vain all night and catch nothing until he casts his net at the Lord's word. Then he can catch a vast multitude (Jn. 21:5ff; Mt.4:19).[8]

Neither St. Bernard nor anyone else who wrote about prayer in the tradition would maintain that a true analysis of human experience will fail to show that man needs God. But the vivid, personal realization that *my* experience reveals a need and a desire for God is itself God's gift.

The lines of Jacopone express this very well. That he has been caught on the hook of God's love is not the result of Jacopone's own efforts. God first loved Jacopone, and the poet strives to respond to the pull of this love. We hear an echo of the words of St. John: "In this is love, not that we loved God but that he loved us and sent his Son to be the expiation for our sins," and "We love, because he first loved us."[9]

Our response to this love of God for us is supposed to be one of love for Him. "You shall love the Lord your God with all your heart, and with all your soul, and with all your mind, and with all your strength."[10] This love that we are commanded to give to God is not something of which we are capable if we rely only on the strengths and capacities of our own nature. Left to ourselves, we are not in fact capable of loving God above everything else. This is the teaching both of our faith and of experience.

St. Thomas Aquinas teaches:

In Himself God is supremely knowable, though on account of the feebleness of our knowledge, which has to depend on things of sense, we do not find him so. Likewise he is supremely lovable considered as the object of eternal happiness, but again not for us, because our affections are naturally inclined to what we see.[11]

8. St. Bernard, "On Conversion," chap. 1, sect. 2.
9. 1 John 4:10 and 19.
10. Mark 12:31.
11. 2a2ae 24, 2 ad 2.

We may suspect, or even be convinced, that there is a God, and we may believe that only he will make us happy, but we do not seem to be able to do very much about putting these suspicions or convictions into practice.

The situation is not a new one. The words of St. Paul in the *Letter to the Romans* describe an experience familiar to all: "I can will what is right, but I cannot do it. For I do not do the good I want, but the evil I do not want is what I do."[12] Part of our nature seems to pull us toward the God we dimly recognize as the goal of all our seeking, but we seem incapable of following the path that leads to happiness for any length of time. We see our good, we see what would make us happy, but our own actions prove we cannot act consistently in a way that would obtain that happiness for us.

It would seem to follow from this that our inclination to love God is useless. We are faced with an impossible situation. Our nature seems to crave something it cannot attain. Underneath the restless search for pleasure, for money, for achievement, for power, honor, and recognition, even underneath the desire to help others and do our duty, under all this there is a kind of secret, hidden knowledge that without the love of God none of this will satisfy. Yet we do not seem to be able to love God in a real and effective way. What then is the point of all this confusion and struggle, this search for happiness in so many different places? What is the point of wanting to love God, and of our apparent inability to do so?

Here we have to remember the other side of the relationship. God has not left us to the resources and strengths of our own nature. "God has sent the Spirit of his Son into our hearts, crying, Abba! Father!"[13] says St. Paul, and, as a result, we too are able to call God our Father. God gives himself to us, so that we may be able to give ourselves back to him.

12. Romans 8:18–19.
13. Galatians 4:6.

It is clear that if we are to be able to cry "Abba Father" then we will need help from God to cleanse our minds and strengthen our wills. This special help is called actual grace. Cardinal Journet defines actual grace in the following way:

Grace—we are speaking here of *actual grace*—is the divine impulse which produces in us acts of free adherence to God, of free acceptance and consent. God comes to me to draw me to himself. I can interrupt or destroy this divine movement; or else I can let God act in me and take possession of my free will and make it assent, *without violating it.*[14]

It is actual grace that moves us from the state of being aware that only God will satisfy us, and yet being unable to act on this perception. Actual grace seeks me out in sin and brings me to a state of friendship with God. This movement, through which we become friends of God, is called justification.

The Council of Trent stated in a clear way the traditional teaching that becoming a friend of God (or justification) does not come about because of the merits of the person concerned.[15] It does not result from advantages of birth, background, or even of moral or intellectual attainments. Rather, it comes about from what the Council called a "predisposing grace of God through Jesus Christ."[16] This "predisposing grace," which the Council terms *a calling (vocatio),* is necessary so that "they who by sin have cut themselves off from God, may be disposed through His quickening and helping grace to convert themselves to their own justification by freely assenting to and cooperating with that grace."[17]

At first sight, some of this may seem unnecessarily compli-

14. Journet, *The Meaning of Grace,* 17.

15. Session VI, The Decree on Justification, *passim,* and Canon 1: "If anyone say that man can be justified before God by his own works, whether done by his own natural powers or through the teaching of the law, without divine grace through Jesus Christ, let him be anathema."

16. Session VI.

17. Ibid.

cated. But it is important to realize that, as Jacopone writes in the next verse of his *Laud*, it is "the Lord God in his power" who "raises my soul from the dead." We can refuse his friendship, but we cannot create it. Without the action of God's grace on our minds and hearts, we can neither know nor love God in a way that will bring us back to Him and so satisfy our own hunger for love and completion.

When we talk about grace, we are confronted with two aspects that are not easy to reconcile. We have seen that actual grace is called a divine impulse. It follows from this that one component in any theory about grace will be that of God's action on the human mind and will. On the other hand, as it is we human beings who are to do the knowing and loving, we also have to take account of human freedom. Any doctrine of grace has to take account of both God's action and human freedom. Furthermore, any doctrine of grace that is in error about the relationship of these components will be the source of error concerning both charity and the life of prayer.

In the history of Christian thought there have been two extremely influential errors. They have been influential not only because they were formulated by well-known thinkers, but even more importantly because they represent ways of dealing with the relationship between God's sovereign will and man's freedom, which we recognize as answering to our own experience. These theories, that is, may have got it wrong, but they have it wrong in ways that matter. They are dangerous because, while they do illumine experience, they illumine it with a false light.

One of these views sees man as taking the first step toward God. To illustrate this view, Cardinal Journet[18] used the image of the little monkey who sees a snake in his path, and, to save itself,

18. Journet, *The Meaning of Grace*, 19–20. "I remember coming across the same problem stated in India under a different imagery. Salvation, it was said, comes about either in the way of the kitten or the little monkey."

leaps into its mother's arms. The mother then lifts it safely out of danger by swinging into a tree. In this image, the little monkey makes the first move—it is frightened, and leaps to where help is to be found. In another image, we are like people at the bottom of a well, and we have no way of getting out. We stretch out our arms, then someone (God) takes them and pulls us out of the well. Here again, the first movement is on our part—we stretch out our arms, which are then seized by one stronger than we are.

On the face of it, the view that it is we who make the first step toward God appears to respect human dignity and freedom. Man's unaided affirmation of the existence, the truth, the unity, and the beauty of God is taken as the supreme example of his integrity in seeking the truth about existence. And man's first turning to God to ask his help is then regarded as the outstanding and unequivocal affirmation of human dignity.

But Pelagianism (and that is what we are talking about) makes our salvation primarily a matter of a moral and human initiative. Our love for God becomes something of which we are the cause. Thus it is our own merit in recognizing that we are in danger or need which results in our *vocation* or calling. As a result, it will be those who have earned it, the moral, or those lucky enough to have been brought up in the right way, who will be given the chance to be saved. But this is to put the cart before the horse: goodness and the actions that lead to salvation are the result of our friendship with God, not its cause. It is the mercy of God that is the cause of our justification, not our own works.

Consider God's love for an unfaithful Israel: "I have loved thee with an everlasting love and therefore have I drawn thee, taking pity on thee."[19] Our Lord repeated this lesson in the words found in St John's Gospel: "No one can come to me unless the Father who sent me draws him."[20] Or again, we read in St. Paul that "it

19. Cf. Jeremiah 31:3.
20. John 6:44.

was not by the works of justice, which we have done, but according to his mercy he saved us."[21]

It is possible, however, to go too far in this direction; there are some who emphasize the divine action to such an extent that no place is left for human activity. Here Cardinal Journet uses the example of a kitten which, when it is in danger, is so terrified it does nothing at all. The mother must come to the rescue, take the kitten by the scruff of the neck, and snatch it out of harm's way. In this case the mother does everything, the kitten nothing.

This position has the merit of ascribing to God the first place in our justification. This was the strength of the position of the early Protestant Reformers. In trying to give to God the glory that is His due, they emphasized an authentically Christian note in their theory about our *vocation*. On the other hand, they left no room for the human response to God's call.

On the Catholic view, our being raised from the dead requires our acceptance of the grace of God through an act that is our own. If the restoration of our relationship to God is to include an authentically human dimension, then we have to be more than passive recipients of God's mercy. We are to respond to God's initiative by an act that is a truly human one. If we are going to be saved by God, we have to return his love by loving him. Being loved is not the same thing as loving, and we are not like Cardinal Journet's kitten.

When we are raised from the dead, when we are justified, we are established in a relationship of charity with God. The establishment of this relationship depends on the grace of God, which we are free to refuse. Consequently, as the Council of Trent puts it:

. . . while God touches the heart of man through the illumination of the Holy Ghost, man himself neither does absolutely nothing while receiving that inspiration, since he can also reject it, nor yet is he able by his own

21. Titus 3:5.

free will and without the grace of God to move himself to justice in His sight.[22]

It is clear, then, that neither the monkey nor the kitten will do as an image of the beginning of our life of friendship with God. To what, then, shall we liken this beginning? St. Francis de Sales presents us with another lesson from the animal kingdom. He says there is a kind of bird called an *apode;* these have extremely short legs and feeble feet.[23] Their short legs and feeble feet are of no use in helping to launch themselves, and the only way they can get into the air is to wait for a gust of wind, or a breeze, which they then use to start flying. If the wind does rise, and if they make use of their wings "to correspond with this first start and motion which the wind gives them, it also continues its assistance to them, bringing them by little and little into flight."[24]

We are like these strange birds, flapping around on the ground and unable to fly. It is by the mercy of God that the wind is sent which enables us to begin to live in a new element. He sends us the favorable wind "of his most holy inspirations, which, blowing upon our hearts with a gentle violence, seizes and moves them, raising our thoughts and moving our affections into the air of divine love."[25] This first stirring or motion, which God causes in our hearts to incite them to their own good, is effected *in us,* but not *by us.*

The inspiration comes suddenly, and it is clearly not from ourselves. These are the two points on which St. Francis, and they are two points we should all take to heart if we are to begin to understand, in the measure it is possible, the mysterious beginnings of our turning to the life of charity. The promptings of grace are not necessarily dramatic, and they can be refused. Often the moment we say "yes" to God comes after a struggle that has been

22. Session VI, chap. 5.
23. These birds do exist and belong to the swift family.
24. St. Francis de Sales, *TLG* II.9.
25. Ibid.

more intense than the actual moment of conversion. Yet the earlier struggles seem to have left us on the ground—desiring God perhaps, desiring to live a Christian life maybe, but nothing seems to have happened. We were like the poor apode, flapping our wings, stumbling around, but getting nowhere.

The conversion of St. Augustine, for all its drama and the artistry with which it is recounted, teaches the same lessons. Augustine had learned the faith, he struggled with the flesh so that he could live as he sensed he really wanted to, and yet he could neither believe nor live as he should.

> I said mentally, Lo, let it be done now, let it be done now. And as I spoke, I all but came to a resolve. I all but did it, yet I did it not. . . . and the very moment in which I was to become another man, the nearer it approached me, the greater horror did it strike into me; but it did not strike me back, nor turn me aside, but kept me in suspense.[26]

One day he went into a garden, threw himself onto the ground, and begged God to end his agony. "How long? How long? Tomorrow, and tomorrow? Why not now? Why is there not this hour an end to my uncleanness?"[27]

Then Augustine heard a child's voice crying out, "Take up and read, take up and read." He was not sure whether it was a child's game, or even if it was a real child—none of that mattered. He took up the New Testament and opened it at the passage in St. Paul where the Apostle says to put on the Lord Jesus Christ, and make not provision for the flesh, to fulfil the lusts thereof.[28] And then, suddenly, the struggle to accept the love of God, and all that that entailed, for him was over:

> I grasped, opened, and in silence read that paragraph on which my eyes first fell—Not in rioting and drunkenness, nor in chambering and wantonness, not in strife and envying; but put ye on the Lord Jesus Christ,

---

26. *Conf* VIII. 11.   27. *Conf* VIII. 12.
28. Romans 13:14.

and make not provision for the flesh, to fulfil the lusts thereof. No further would I read, nor did I need; for instantly, as the sentence ended—by a light, as it were, of security infused into my heart—all the gloom of doubt vanished away.[29]

Augustine's conversion was from paganism to Christianity. But whenever a Christian turns away from sin and error, the same pattern is repeated to this extent: the preliminary struggle, no matter how brief or how long, no matter how fierce or how little it may seem to cost, is like the efforts of the apode who tries to fly, but cannot. It is only with the wind of grace that we fly aloft and turn to Christ.

But thou, O Lord, art good and merciful, and thy right hand had respect unto the profoundness of my death, and removed from the bottom of my heart that abyss of corruption. And this was the result, that I willed not to do what I willed, and willed to do what thou willedst.[30]

God's grace moves us in countless ways—through a bad conscience, or through music, or through the beauties of nature. Sometimes it may be something more obviously religious, like the liturgy or a homily or reading about a saint. The grace may even come when we are reading *about* religion. It often comes to those who in a conscious way are looking for truth about the meaning of life, or searching for a goodness that they suspect is somehow hidden in the wear and tear of existence. For some, it has come in the search for a beauty that is, as Plato said, "everlasting, not growing or decaying, or waxing and waning."[31]

But God's grace comes as an accompaniment to almost any sort of experience. It shows itself as a realization of otherness. This is a common experience that is difficult to describe. It is an awareness that whatever occupies the center of my consciousness does not add up to everything I am experiencing. An example from

29. *Conf* VIII. 12.   30. *Conf* IX. 1.
31. *Symposium* 211.

daily life may make this clearer. Suppose you are concentrating on a book, and someone enters the room behind you. You are vaguely aware that there is something qualifying your awareness of the reading of the book, for it is a part of your experience. On the other hand, while it is part of your experience, it does not really enter into what it's normally like to read a book. In a similar way, the first pull of God, or the first uneasiness with a situation which may indicate the workings of grace, often comes quietly and as an almost unremarked aspect of an ordinary situation.

God's grace moves us like the wind blowing on the feathers of the apode—it now has the chance to fly, and our soul now has the chance to rise and turn to God. Grace enables us to make an act of living faith in God. This in turn leads us to hope that the promises God has made are really for us, and we begin to love God as our good. We begin to have sorrow for our sins, and the desire to do better. Contrition and penance, a deepening realization of how awful sin is, lead us to that love of God which loves him just because he is lovable above everything else.

3.3 The drawing of this love

"On the Lord's Appearing" speaks of the succession of ways or modes in which God appears to the believer and also about the different responses that his appearing evokes. These reactions to the succeeding modes point to the development that takes place in the spiritual life; I want now to say something about this development.

One of the constants of the Christian tradition is that the life of prayer involves a development. From the Gospels to the Second Vatican Council, the goal of the Christian life has been seen in the words recorded in St. Matthew's Gospel: 'You, therefore must be perfect, as your heavenly Father is perfect.'[32] No matter how we

---

32. Matthew 5:48.

are to understand this perfection,[33] it seems self-evident that we are not perfect and there must be some sort of activity that leads us from our present condition to the perfection required by the Gospels. This idea of a development in the Christian life is part of the most ancient tradition of the Church. St. Irenaeus writes:

For the Uncreated is perfect, that is, God. Now it was necessary that man should in the first instance be created; and having been created, should receive growth; and having received growth, should be strengthened; and having been strengthened, should abound; and having abounded, should recover [from the disease of sin]; and having recovered, should be glorified; and being glorified, should see his Lord.[34]

In the history of Christian spirituality there has been a serious effort to discern and describe this development which culminates in the vision of God in heaven. One result of this effort is the tradition that characterizes the gradual ascent to perfection by three stages: the purgative, the illuminative, and the unitive. This tradition in the form we know it[35] goes back to the Pseudo-Dionysius and finds its roots in the philosophy of Neoplatonism. It sees the goal of Christian perfection as a mystical experience in which the soul is united to God. The progress to this goal begins with an ascetical training whose aim is to purify the soul in order to make it a worthy dwelling place for the Holy Spirit. The word "ascetical" comes from the Greek *askein,* meaning to practice or exercise in order to acquire a skill, especially an athletic skill.[36] In

33. Passmore, *The Perfectibility of Man,* gives a very readable, if irreverent, survey of the idea of perfection from Plato to Norman Brown.

34. Irenaeus, *Against Heresies* IV.38.3, in The Ante-Nicene Fathers 1.522.

35. Bouyer, *Introduction to Spirituality,* 244: ". . . the first definite division into three stages was made by Evagrius Ponticus, and then taken over by the majority of writers. They did not usually adopt these three stages under precisely the form they took with Evagrius, but rather under the form they assumed a little later with Pseudo-Dionysius."

36. See Aumann, *Spiritual Theology,* 14.

the ascetical life, the individual by his own efforts tries to bring his life into conformity with the demands of the gospel.

Faith at this stage is what Origen calls "faith pure and simple,"[37] which means that faith is accepted and used as a basis for the ascetical life. On the other hand, the object of faith seems to be very much an object, in the ordinary sense of the term, and remains over and apart from the individual. Furthermore, the law of God, experienced as something imposed from the outside, often seems to predominate. Faith and the law provide the believer with a plan for reorganizing his life, but he does not experience their truth. In the illuminative way, he begins to have an experience or foretaste of the truth of faith. Faith now becomes a quality of his being and the life of prayer becomes increasingly dominated by an awareness of God's action rather than his own. When this action of the Holy Spirit becomes the object of our direct awareness, then the soul has passed to the unitive way. In the unitive way, the will of the individual and the will of God are so united that like two candles fused together[38] they give but one light.

Another description of the journey to Christian perfection also has three stages—the way of beginners, of proficients, and of the perfect. This is the scheme St. Thomas prefers; he emphasizes that the stages on the ladder of perfection are determined by their relation to charity.[39] At the beginning, the life of a Christian is largely occupied with fighting those elements in himself which pull him away from God. Later, his life is dominated by those aspects in his makeup which help him to put God first. Finally, his relationship to God is best characterized not by what he himself does, but by what God does to and for him.

---

37. See Bouyer, *Introduction to Spirituality,* 262.

38. The example is from St. Teresa, *IC* VII.2.

39. 2a2ae 24, 9: "In the same way various stages can be marked according as growth in charity leads a man to fix his attention on different things."

For, to begin with, he must devote himself mainly to withdrawing from sin and resisting the appetites, which drive him in the opposite direction to charity. This is the condition of beginners, who need to nourish and carefully foster charity to prevent its being lost. A second stage now follows, when a man's preoccupation is to advance in virtue. It is the mark of those who are making progress, and who are principally concerned that their charity should grow and become strong. The third stage is when a man applies himself chiefly to the work of cleaving to God and enjoying him, which is characteristic of the perfect who *long to depart and to be with Christ.*[40]

The Latin word translated here as *stage* is *studium*. A *studium* can also be translated as something like "focus of attention" or "main concern." I do not think anything rigid or fixed is indicated either in Thomas's use of *studium* or in his discussion of our growth in charity. A focus of attention does not eliminate everything else. For example, concentrating on a problem of trigonometry does not eliminate our knowledge of arithmetic, nor does it mean that the time and energy spent in early life on learning to add and subtract was a waste of time. In a similar way, when Thomas says that the primary concern of the perfect is to cleave to God, he does not mean they are to forget particular acts of charity and give up fighting what militates against them. On the other hand, their charity is expressed by actually living the first commandment of loving God before everything else.[41]

It is worth pointing out that neither classification was developed and adopted merely in the interests of theological theory. The two classifications are both attempts to deal with elements in the life of prayer that have forced themselves on the attention of those who have been knowledgeable about the spiritual life. Sometimes this knowledge is the result of reflection on their own experience;

40. 2a2ae 24, 9.
41. 2a2ae 24, 9 ad 3: The perfect also make progress in charity, but it is no longer their chief preoccupation, for now their primary concern [their *studium*] is to cleave to God.

sometimes it derives from trying to help others. In either case, the different views of development should be looked on as attempts to describe enduring aspects of human experience. They may not be the best descriptions in principle, but they seem to be the best anyone has as yet come up with. I think that part of the suspicion with which they are often regarded stems from their being used in a prescriptive manner; that is, it is almost as though not only man's response, but even God's call, is looked on as having to conform to these patterns. Such a view is bad theology, and bad psychology.

In a well-known and enormously influential essay, Karl Rahner argues that the two classifications depend on different views of Christian perfection and that they are not two different ways of discussing the same phenomena.[42] He concludes, in an acerbic way, by dismissing both. The first is found wanting because it views perfection as a mystical experience, the other because it really says nothing useful:

We have traditionally, therefore, two different and separate divisions or stages. Of these, one is problematical because it takes it in varying degrees too much for granted that the goal of the spiritual life consists in a mystic state of union with God and because it moreover considers this mystical state to be predominantly (at least fundamentally) a higher *knowledge*. The other division is no less problematical, for it really means precious little due to the fact of its being so formal and hence empty.[43]

42. Rahner, *Theological Investigations*, 3.8. The essay was first published in 1944. The extent of its influence may be gauged by considering two articles in the *DS*, one on "Commençants" by Pierre Pourrat, P.S.S., published in 1953 (*DS* 2.1143–56), the other on "Progrès-Progressants" by Hein Blommestijn, S.J., published in 1986 (*DS* 12–2.2383). The author of the first article is happy with the traditional scheme, while the second quotes Rahner's article and remarks: "What was in principle an analysis of a dynamic process of transformation became more or less a theoretical and static system for ordering in a successive manner the ideal evolution of the spiritual life" (my translation).

43. Rahner, *Theological Investigations*, 3.9.

I think a good deal of this is too swift to be altogether convincing.[44] The great interest, however, in Rahner's article is not
what he dismisses but what he retains of the tradition. He accepts,
first, that the search for a way to Christian perfection is a valid
enterprise and, second, that this way will be divisible into stages:

There is first of all the fact that in some sense or other, and in some form
or other, there must be something like a way to Christian perfection, a
way which is formed by or divisible into different stages; for unless this
is presupposed the continual and always renewed attempt to define these
stages in greater detail as found in the whole history of the Christian religion—becomes absolutely incomprehensible and absurd.[45]

His search for a substitute for the traditional classifications has
two steps. First, he wants to argue against the use of a doctrine
common to Plato, Aristotle, and much of Christian tradition: that
the moral virtues presuppose training and habituation.[46] I think
Rahner is just wrong about this, and the acceptance of his point
of view has had disastrous effects.[47] We may think that the Aris-
totelian view of the moral life demands the acceptance of too much
metaphysical baggage, but we then have to ask what has been put
in its place. The answer seems to be, not very much. Perhaps the
concept of virtue was sometimes used in a way that left little room

44. It is not adequate, for example, to say about *The Cloud of Unknowing* or St.
John of the Cross that the summit of the Christian life is a Neoplatonic *gnosis*.
They both teach that the only union with God that is possible in this life is through
a will inflamed by charity in a cloud of unknowing—or in a dark night of the
spirit. See below, chaps. 6 and 7.

45. Rahner, *Theological Investigations*, 3.10.

46. Aristotle, *NE*, II.1. 1103 a 14–18: ". . . intellectual virtue in the main owes
both its birth and its growth to teaching . . . while moral virtue comes about as
a result of habit, whence also its name *ethike* is one that is formed by a slight
variation from the word *ethos* (habit)."

47. There have been many books over the last decade that have described the
baleful effects of abandoning the concept of virtue and have argued for a return of
its use. See for example MacIntyre, *After Virtue*.

either for the creativity of the individual or for God's action, but this is no reason to abandon the idea altogether.

The second move in Rahner's argument is, however, a great deal more interesting. He argues that we should not think of development toward perfection as consisting in different stages, each one of which is marked by different *sorts* of acts. Rather, we ought to view the road to perfection as a growth in intensity and depth of the same sort of acts. The development is determined by our response to the real situations of ordinary life. A beginner in the spiritual life, for example, may make a pure and selfless act of love for God, and a person much further along the road of Christian perfection may make the same sort of act. What differentiates the two acts is not the nature of the act, but its intensity and depth. Furthermore, the intensity and depth of the acts result in part from the longer and wider experience possessed by the person who has been fully living his Christianity in a personal way within his own particular situation. Rahner has substituted an elevator concept of development in place of the image of passing from one locality to another. In other words, development is not marked by a number of entirely different sets of acts determined by their place in a series of clearly marked stages.[48]

To develop Rahner's new emphasis would require, as he himself says, first of all a statement as to how it is that man gradually develops a capacity to commit himself more fully in and through acts that, from an external point of view, may not differ very much. Secondly, he would have to show how this capacity is to be fitted into, as Rahner puts it, "the typical chain of the situations of human life." I think both of these requirements serve as a

---

48. I do not really understand the root of Rahner's difficulties with the classifications found in the tradition. It is possible that he has viewed them from the standpoint of Descartes's isolated self, and then found them wanting. But neither the Greek Fathers, nor St. Thomas, nor St. John of the Cross worked with this view. See Kerr, *Theology after Wittgenstein*, 10–14, where he goes after Rahner's use of the cognitive subject as the basis for his (Rahner's) theological work.

healthy corrective to a view of Christian development interpreted as a mechanical passing from one *studium* to another.

On the other hand, traditional spirituality was aware that perfection was not a matter of adding pieces of new material to an already-existing structure. St. Thomas, in an important article in one of his questions on charity, asks whether charity grows by addition.[49] He replies in effect that charity does not grow by one bit of charity being added to another.

In spite of what some assert, there is no way in which charity can increase by adding one charity to another. . . . The only way for charity to grow is for its subject to participate more and more in charity, that is, more and more to be roused to its act and brought under its sway. . . . Charity grows, not by one charity being added to another, but by being intensified in its subject, which is to say that it increases as to its essence.[50]

Furthermore, although growth in charity may be described by different *studia*, the masters of the spiritual life knew that these *studia* set no limits to God's action. St. Teresa, for example, taught that the beginner may be further ahead than someone well practiced in the ascetical life:

I will tell you, then, that God is sometimes pleased to show great favour to persons who are in an evil state and to raise them to perfect contemplation, so that by this means He may snatch them out of the hands of the devil.[51]

Conversely, St. John of the Cross expressly holds that the trials of contemplatives often resemble the difficulties of those struggling with the first steps in Christian virtue:

For to some the angel of Satan presents himself—namely, the spirit of fornication—that he may buffet their senses with abominable and violent temptations, and trouble their spirits with vile considerations and rep-

49. 2a2ae 24, 5.
50. Ibid.
51. *Way of Perfection*, chap. 16.

resentations which are most visible to the imagination, which things at times are a greater affliction to them than death.[52]

We can conclude from this that there is or should be some development in the Christian life and this development is marked by different focuses of attention.[53] On the other hand, this development should be understood as taking up everything that has gone before, and earlier concerns may become, once again, the center of attention when least expected.[54]

In Jacopone's five ways of the Lord's appearing, we have an account of one such development. The changes are brought about by Christ's different ways of appearing to the human soul, and by the believer's response to these. The intense personal quality of the poem reminds us that we are dealing with a set of experiences which the poet has tried to capture for others in his *Laud*. Yet, the fact that he can write about these in a way that will be understood shows he is in possession of a vocabulary that is both rooted in, and partly formative of, Christian experience. This means that his account describes a development of the Christian consciousness as such, from its first uncertain beginnings in the life of grace to the consciousness of the love of God in the unitive way.

---

52. *DN* I.14.1.

53. Benedict J. Groeschel, in *Spiritual Passages,* has given a serious and contemporary attempt to understand the three ways in terms of the psychological development of the human being. The last section of his book is entitled "Doctrine of the Three Ways—Alive and Well."

54. Father Faber puts this very well when he says, "We are not told by the saints to be patient with our sins, but with our sicknesses, those sicknesses of the soul under which sanctification consists not in the cure, but in the combat" (*Spiritual Conferences,* 397).

In the first stage the Lord God in His power

Raises my soul from the dead;

Putting to flight the demons who bound me in error,

He touches my heart with contrition.

4.1 The God who frees us

In this verse Jacopone relates how God takes hold of the human soul and turns it around to Himself. God frees us from futility, from sin and despair, and gives us the means to turn away from our destruction. We have seen that this calling, and this turning, are what we mean by justification or conversion. God knocks at the door of our heart, and we, on our part, must remove the obstacles to that door being opened. The matter does not, however, seem that way to us. We imagine that turning to God is a matter of a new insight, or of a little more effort on our part, and not the gift of God. Yet the truth is that our turning to God is possible only because God in His love has called us to turn to Him and live, and that He has also given us the grace to respond.

Conversion requires God's grace, as "the drawing of this love,"[1] to allow us to assent to God's revelation. This revelation, brought to us by Scripture and tradition and proclaimed by the

1. The phrase is from *Cloud,* chap. 2; see 3.1.

Church, is "the voice of this calling"[2] for me, here and now. Left to ourselves, without both the drawing and the voice, we alternate between periods of despair over our situation and an even more persistent practice of our vices. We may even be frightened by our situation, but it is a fear that only adds to our torment. There is as yet no saving fear of the Lord. Effective sorrow for sin and contrition for having offended God are not something of which we are capable when left to ourselves. It is true, as Jacopone says, that our hearts must be touched with contrition. But the touch is the touch of God and not our own doing.

We may sense that we need and want God, but we seem to be able to do little about it. God appears remote and inaccessible, and sometimes we seem more than half convinced he does not exist. We are made miserable by the thought of God's absence, yet we do not really desire His presence. Our conscience rebukes us, but we have no effective desire to turn away from sin.

The prayer of the person whom God is calling begins with a prayer of petition. In its confusion and in its need, the soul seeks God's help in a simple and unstructured appeal from the heart.

4.2 Putting to death the demons who bound me in error

When, in the early decades of the nineteenth century, Newman preached his sermon "The Religion of the Day,"[3] he took it for granted that the Devil was behind this religion of the day. He says this religion "has taken the brighter side of the Gospel—its tidings of comfort, its precepts of love; all darker, deeper views of man's condition and prospects being comparatively forgotten. . . . This is the religion *natural* to a civilized age, and well has Satan dressed and completed it into an idol of the Truth."[4] Much of modern

2. Ibid.
3. Newman, *PS* I, serm. 24.
4. Ibid.

thinking about man has been based on ignoring "all darker, deeper views of man." The Christian view that man is born alienated from God, from other people, and from himself, and that this alienation is the result of sin, has not found much favor with the opinion-makers who have helped to form modern consciousness.

The concept of original sin is the common opponent against which all the different trends of the philosophy of the Enlightenment join forces. In this struggle Hume is on the side of English deism, and Rousseau of Voltaire; the unity of the goal seems for a time to outweigh all differences as to the means of attaining it.[5]

Yet the belief in original sin has always been a doctrine of orthodox Christianity, and it remains so to this day. In an apostolic exhortation, entitled *Reconciliation and Penance,* in 1984, Pope John Paul II wrote:

However disturbing these divisions may seem at first sight, it is only by a careful examination that one can detect their root: it is to be found in a *wound* in man's inmost self. In the light of faith, we call it sin: beginning with *original sin,* which all of us bear from birth as an inheritance from our first parents, to the sin which each one of us commits when we abuse our own freedom.[6]

In the *Apologia,*[7] Newman argued that the evil of this world is so incongruent with the existence of a good God that, if we want

5. Cassirer, *The Philosophy of the Enlightenment,* 141. The German edition was published in 1932.

6. *RP,* sect. 2.

7. Newman, *Apo,* chap. 5, first published 1864 (Image Books, New York, 1956). Newman begins the passage by saying: "Did I see a boy of good make and mind, with the tokens upon him of a refined nature, cast upon the world without provision, unable to say whence he came, his birth-place or his family connexions, I should conclude that there was some mystery connected with his history, and that he was one, of whom, from one cause or another, his parents were ashamed. Thus only should I be able to account for the contrast between the promise and condition of his being. And so I argue about the world."

to hold onto the reality of God,[8] we are forced to assume something like the Fall.

> . . . *if* there be a God, *since* there is a God, the human race is implicated in some terrible aboriginal calamity. It is out of joint with the purposes of its Creator. This is a fact, a fact as true as the fact of its existence; and thus the doctrine of what is theologically called original sin becomes to me almost as certain as that the world exists, and as the existence of God.[9]

There is nothing in the history of the twentieth century to support the idea that improved educational and social conditions will automatically result in human beings who are morally better.

On such a view the history of the twentieth-century Europe should have been one of moral progress and enlightenment. The SS, the concentration camps and gulags, not to speak of the millions of the aborted and the callousness towards the starving "Third World," have demonstrated the shallowness of that kind of optimism. . . . In particular, in this century we have seen star instances of an Augustinian *libido dominandi,* of a sheer lust for power at its crudest: power, said Goering, is my fist on your throat.[10]

John Rist has written, "Augustinian reflections on the conditions of human beings often look more plausible than his suggestions about the origins of those conditions."[11] Rist instances, by way of example, the notion of a specific "original sin," and seems to think it possible to question the theory "erected on the observations" without denying the observations themselves.[12] For the

---

8. Nicholas Lash writes: "Within the Christian as within the Jewish tradition the structure of discovery is from the experience of God as redeemer to the confession of God as Creator, not the other way round" ("Production and Prospect," in McMullin, *Evolution and Creation,* 274). This is certainly what Newman thought.

9. *Apo,* chap. 5. 10. Rist, *Augustine,* 292.

11. Ibid., 293.

12. John Rist writes that "Augustine would [that is, Augustinus Redivivus] be quite happy to fight in his corner against modern optimism about the present state of human nature, and to insist that, even if one could not tell by observation

purposes of this book the truth of the "observations" is enough. That is, it suffices that prayer take place within a belief in the fallen condition of the human race without having a definite theory as to how this condition came about. The Psalmist said: "Turn away mine eyes, from beholding vanity."[13] But many contemporary Christians say, "Turn away my eyes, from beholding the human condition." No amount of "positive thinking" will alter the spectacle that Newman paints, although the acceptance of the reality of original sin depends on faith in Christ's revelation.[14]

Given a damaged human nature, there is also the question of the context, or environment, in which we have to operate. Throughout the whole of his sermon "The Religion of the Day," Newman keeps before us the sinister figure of the Father of Lies, "whose aim is to break our strength, to force us down to the earth—to bind us there."[15] Satan is portrayed as an intelligence that has created the religion of the world so "as to serve his purposes as the counterfeit of truth."[16]

---

that it is 'fallen,' it certainly behaves *as if* it were fallen" (*Augustine,* 293). Is this really enough? I am not as optimistic as Professor Rist seems to be that biblical exegesis can provide a way to preserve "the observations" without the "theory erected on them."

13. Psalm 119:37, in the Authorized version.

14. *RP,* sect. 2: "In the light of faith, we call it sin: beginning with *original sin.*"

15. *PS* I, serm. 24.

16. Ibid. Kenelm Foster, O.P., notes in *Angels* (volume 11 of the Blackfriars *Summa*) that the name *Satan* is derived from the Hebrew word for "adversary," and continues by pointing out that traditionally Satan or the Devil is viewed as a personal being who consciously knows and wills. He is a fallen angel, that is a nonhuman, created spirit. Finally, he is preeminent in evil and is the supreme enemy of God. Our belief in the existence of the Devil is based on the Bible, and especially on the New Testament. It is also part of the defined teaching of the Church, and both the Fourth Lateran Council and the Council of Trent had important things to say about the existence and nature of the Devil and of evil spirits (*Summa,* app. 2, "Satan").

Newman's analysis of "the religion of the day" is as applicable to our own time as it was to the first half of the nineteenth century. But what are we to say about his belief in the Devil, who is supposed to have helped create this religion? Is it really necessary for a proper understanding of our faith, and of the obstacles it encounters, to accept the existence of a powerful, malign intelligence bent on our destruction? Surely, it could be argued, as it is often not only argued but assumed, that the belief in Satan and lesser demons is all part of a world view that we have outgrown. It is true, so the upholder of "the religion of the day" maintains, that the writers of the Bible, and many up to our time, may have believed in a real Devil, but this belief has no necessary connection with the peace and reconciliation that Christ's saving death has brought to us.[17]

Those who argue in this way are often reacting against the attribution of every temptation and every sin to the Devil's direct agency. And, on the face of it, this attribution seems to be wrong on two counts.

In the first place, as St. Thomas says, it can be argued that the world and the flesh are adequate explanations for most of the sins that are committed.

For as Origen says, even if there were no demons men would still have a desire for food and for sexual love and so on, and from these desires, unless they are controlled by reason, many disorders arise. This is all the more true if we assume that human nature is corrupt. Now it is in the power of free will to control these desires and to keep them in order, and

---

17. For example, in *The World Order* (volume 15 of the Blackfriars *Summa*), M. J. Charlesworth remarks: "Although this New Testament view of the demons is coloured by primitive imagery it seems clear that it implies the real (and not just symbolic) existence of personal evil spirits. One might ask, however, just how *central* the belief in the existence of demonic powers is to the Christian? Put in another way, if it should turn out that the demonic powers were not real, would the essentials of the Christian's religious faith be affected (as surely they would be if Our Lord's Resurrection turned out not to be true)?" (15.73n).

thus there is no necessity to derive all sins from the instigation of the demons.[18]

With this argument of St. Thomas in mind, we might go on to argue that it is unnecessary to bring in the Devil in order to account for wrongdoing. We could say that if we are looking for some explanation of mankind's sinful behaviour, it would seem better to stick with what we clearly recognize as the sources of wrongdoing—the world and the flesh—than to introduce an additional principle of explanation that, in the nature of things, we have difficulty in using and that may in fact be superfluous.

Secondly, if the Devil is in some way directly implicated in all wrongdoing, the Evil One is not a useful principle of explanation. If everything sinful is the immediate result of the Devil's action, then there is no point in worrying about the varieties and degrees of the sins of worldliness and of the flesh. If we attribute all sin directly to the Devil, we will have an overall hypothesis or explanation that could be true, but we will not be in possession either of an adequate description of the sinful situation or of its proximate explanation. If a man falls off a cliff, it may be quite true to say that the force of gravity caused his body to fall to the earth. On the other hand, if you are a policeman and suspect foul play, you will be much more interested in knowing what the man was doing at the edge of the cliff and why he fell over. In a similar way, while it is true that the devil is the cause of all sin, there are times when it does not help much to say so.

St. Thomas maintains that the world and the flesh are indeed sufficient to show up men's weakness; it follows that we must not ignore or gloss over their power to keep the soul in bondage. On the other hand, these two principles of the explanation of human behavior are not sufficient to describe all the forces at work in the human situation. Thomas says Satan exists and uses the world and

18. 1a 114, 3.

the flesh to test and seek out men's weakness, but his use of them for our downfall is insufficient to satisfy his malice.[19]

This teaching of St. Thomas does not underestimate the power of the world and the flesh to lead us into sin. Their capacity, however, to do harm is not sufficient to exhaust the malevolence of the Devil and his evil spirits. To the mindless dynamic of worldliness and the flesh pulling us down and keeping us away from God there is added the intelligence of an enemy who desires our ruin. It is the office of the Devil to tempt. He uses the obvious means, and indirectly he is the cause of all sin.

Thus, to understand the causes of temptation, we have to avoid two extremes. We must not, on the one hand, attribute all sin immediately to the devil. On the other hand, we must never forget that we have to take the devil into account if we are to have a complete picture of the causes of evildoing. The teaching of the present pope, in *Reconciliation and Penance,* reasserts this traditional view:

Clearly, sin is a product of man's freedom. But deep within its human reality there are factors at work which place it beyond the merely human, in the border area where man's conscience, will, and sensitivity are in contact with the dark forces which, according to St. Paul, are active in the world almost to the point of ruling it.[20]

If the teaching of St. Thomas, of Newman, and of the pope is true, then it is clear that the existence of the Devil is not a peripheral question. It is not peripheral because to leave the Devil out of consideration or to deny his existence is to miss an important element operative in individual lives and in the development of history. It is clear that the religion of the day, which Newman excoriated, finds the belief in Satan to be an embarrassment. It is an embarrassment because it is at odds with the temper of academic society, which nowadays so colors our understanding of

19. 1a, 114, 1 ad 3.
20. *RP,* sect. 14. The pope refers to Romans 7:7–25 and Ephesians 2:2, 6:12.

Christianity. But perhaps this ability of Satan—to disguise his presence to the learned and to reveal it to followers of black magic as well as to the readers of paperbacks sold in every drug store—is another triumph of the Father of Lies.

In his sketch of the life of St. Martin of Tours,[21] Newman concludes with an account of an appearance of Satan to St. Martin. Satan appears as Christ, robed in power and majesty, and demands to be worshipped. Martin keeps silence but finally he says: "I will not believe that Christ is come, save in that state and form in which He suffered, *save with the show of the wounds of the Cross.*"

Newman then throws down his challenge to "the religion of the day" and says that Christ comes not in pride of intellect or reputation for philosophy.

These are the glittering robes in which Satan is now arraying. Many spirits are abroad, more are issuing from the pit; the credentials which they display are the precious gifts of mind, beauty, richness, depth, originality. Christian, look hard at them with Martin in silence, and ask them for the print of the nails.[22]

Jacopone, in "Christ's Lament over the Sinner,"[23] has our Lord reproach fallen man in the following way. The verses sum up neatly the three main sources of temptation.

In flight from Me you have let flesh deceive you,
You abased yourself for pleasure,
Mindless of what is to come.
Flee no more, My son, or you will stumble.

The world puts on a gladsome face
To persuade the unwary of its goodness;
Its emptiness and falsity it carefully conceals, knowing
That as you approach Me, I raise you up and crown you.

21. *Vita Beati Martini* 25, quoted in *HS* II.10.9.
22. *HS* II.10.9.
23. *Laud* 26.

> Demons, too, are watching your every move,
> Intent on blocking your return to that lofty state
> (The loss was yours, and the fault as well)
> From which with bloody violence they made you fall.

The soul seems to be caught for good in the Devil's toils and it is tempted to despair. Who will "put to flight the demons who bound me in error"? How will I ever be reconciled to God? The answer is found in St. Paul: "But God shows his love for us in that while we were yet sinners Christ died for us. Since, therefore, we are now justified by his blood, much more shall we be saved by him from the wrath of God."[24]

Yet knowing this as an abstract truth is not enough. If we are to be justified by the blood of Christ and brought to God, we will have to be given the grace to cry with Jacopone:

> You did not spare Him whom You loved so dearly;
> Why then be indulgent with me?
> Catch me on your hook,
> Like a fish that cannot get away—
> That will be a sign that you love me.
> Do not spare me: I long to be drowned in Love.[25]

4.3 *He touches the heart with contrition*

It is God who raises us from the death of sin, and it is God who puts to flight the demons who use the world and the flesh to bind us in error. It is also God who touches our heart with contrition so that we can turn to God and live.

We have seen that justification involves a turning to God in faith after the Lord has given us the grace to turn to Him. Along with the turning there has to be a hatred of the sin that has caused our alienation from God and a forgiveness of this sin by the Father.

---

24. Romans 5:8–9.
25. *Laud* 83.

This hatred of sin and its forgiveness is what Jacopone means by the Lord touching our hearts with contrition.

God calls and justifies in a single instant, but from our perspective the process of justification seems often to be drawn out over a long period of time. That is, the act of faith, which is the response to God's calling, is frequently the result of a struggle that may take years, as in the case of St. Augustine. Similarly, the process by which the person grasps in a real way his own sinfulness as an offense against the God who loves him can be long and complex.

The person who is trying to answer the call of God often has no difficulty in recognizing that his behavior is incompatible with the answer he wants to make to the call. Yet he does not grasp in a real way that it is the behavior itself, what he is actually doing, that is keeping him from God. The behavior is known, but it is not properly understood or properly categorized. Somehow or other, like the younger son in our Lord's parable of the Prodigal Son, the man must come to his senses—he must go back into himself[26]—and admit in a real way the seriousness of his actions.[27] He must become aware that what he is doing is sinful and relate this awareness to the mercy of God. This recognition will not be forced on man by God, any more than he will force man to turn to Him. Jacopone imagines the mercy of God grieving over man's condition and taking counsel with her children as to the best means of bringing man to God:

Mercy grieved to see man fallen to such a low estate,
For with him were lost all his descendants as well.
Gathering her children about her she deliberated

26. Luke 15:17.

27. Luke 15:17–19: "But when he came to himself he said, How many of my father's hired servants have bread enough and to spare, but I perish here with hunger! I will arise and go to my father, and I will say to him 'Father I have sinned against heaven and before you; I am no longer worthy to be called your son.'"

How she would come to his aid.
They decided to send a messenger
To tell despairing man he would not perish;
Lady Penitence was chosen to bring the news.[28]

The plan at the beginning is to awaken in man's heart a sorrow for having offended God. This sorrow will be met by the mercy of God, and man will come back to the Father. Penitence, however, quickly perceives that she is not up to doing what is asked of her. Penitence requires contrition,[29] or sorrow for past sins, and there is no room for contrition in the heart of the man who has turned his back on God. So, in order to awaken in man a sorrow for his sins which will turn him to God, "Contrition sent instead her three sons to scour man's heart and prepare a place."

The first to appear was Fear, who troubled the heart of man
And cast out arrogant and false Security.
Fear was followed by Shame,
That man might recognize his wretchedness and deformity;
And in his train came Grief overwhelming,
For the offenses man's sin had given to God.[30]

Fear, shame, and grief are said to be the sons of contrition; they can be seen as derivative or the result of contrition if the sinner already has some sense of sorrow for the God he has offended. On the other hand, fear, shame, and grief can also be looked on as emotions that are capable of stirring us up to contrition. Sin brings with it its own consequences, including a hardened conscience,

28. *Laud* 43.

29. Jacopone here is not distinguishing between penitence and contrition. Strictly speaking, contrition is less than the virtue of penance. "*Penance is to deplore past sins,* and, while deploring them, not to commit again, either by act or by intention, those which we have to deplore" (2a2ae 84, 10, ad 4). The underlined words refer to contrition, the aspect of deploring past sins, and that is less than the intention not to do them again.

30. *Laud* 43.

which lulls men into a false security, hides from them their real wretchedness and deformity, and removes any sense that sin offends God.

We tend to say that people have a bad conscience when they have done something wrong, but often this is not the case. Conscience, at least in the sense of judging this or that particular act to be wrong, seems relatively easy to stifle. On the other hand, because sin is disordered behavior, it does have consequences in the natural order that are verifiable in experience. Among these consequences are, as Jacopone says, fear, shame, and grief.

Fear, shame, and grief, as the result of behavior that is objectively sinful, are often not recognized as being related to the sin that has brought them about. Yet if sin remains unacknowledged, it leads to disordered living, which, as likely as not, will bring the sinner to the psychiatrist's office. It may not be the case that all mental illness is the result of sinful behavior. It is true, though, that sinful behavior is conducive always to unhappiness and often to mental disorder.

The sinner has to learn that the source of his unhappiness is in fact the sin he refuses to recognize. Pope Pius XII said that the sin of the twentieth century "is the loss of the sense of sin."[31] That is part of the trouble. We hear it said that even to talk about, much less to emphasize, the traditional themes of Catholic personal morality either betrays a small-minded, petty, unimaginative, ungenerous, and uncreative spirit, or on the other hand manifests a Pelagian attitude, which puts all the emphasis on man's own activity. One's efforts to tell the truth, to be chaste, to do one's job properly, and to avoid detraction are not, so it is often said, actually wrong; it is just that they do not matter very much. They do not matter much, so it is said, either because they are far removed from the real forces that move life, and especially political life, or else they do not matter because God has mercy on whom he will

31. Quoted in *RP*, sect. 18.

and we are not justified by what we do. And so the false conclusion is drawn, that to emphasize personal sin is to miss the real problems that face mankind in today's complex and often difficult world.

It is quite true that to think about nothing but sin would reduce us to despair. St. Teresa of Avila made this point in the sixteenth century.[32] On the other hand, leaving sin out of our efforts to understand the human condition—who we are and where we are going—is a mistake that has serious consequences. These consequences apply not only to the afterlife but to this world as well, because the sense of sin is closely related to our sense of the reality of God and of His love for us. Without an awareness of the God who ever was, and is, and is to come, we lose our grasp on the foundation of our liberty and integrity as human beings, and of the unique and irreplaceable value of each human life.

"The loss of the sense of sin is . . . a form or consequence of the denial of God," wrote Pope John Paul II, "not only in the form of atheism but also in the form of secularism."[33] The sense of sin, then, is united to our awareness of the reality of God. Losing the sense of sin has meant atheism in practice and with it, as the pope says, secularism. Atheism and secularism have abolished the particularly Christian view of the dignity of man in the face of existence.

In the gospel, personal sin and our sense of wrongdoing, the reality of God, and the dignity of man are all linked together. They are not peripheral or neurotic concerns, in the light of either time or eternity. Jacopone had a greater sense of the nature of Christian

---

32. *IC* I.2: "For although, as I say, it is through the abundant mercy of God that the soul studies to know itself, yet one can have too much of a good thing, as the saying goes, and believe me, we shall reach much greater heights of virtue by thinking upon the virtue of God than if we stay in our own little plot of ground and tie ourselves down to it completely."

33. *RP*, sect. 18.

existence than do those who have cooperated with the opinion makers in their efforts to remove sin and the reality of God from the Catholic consciousness.

Fear, shame, and grief have to be recognized as the consequence of sin and then identified as the appropriate reactions to the state of alienation from God. How exactly this is to happen will vary from person to person. If the vague foreboding that often seizes people who are in a state of sin can be identified as fear of God and of His punishments, then we have the beginning of one of the ways back to God. This is what has been called *servile fear*. Servile fear is often taken as the first response to a dawning awareness of the seriousness of sin. On the face of it, this does not seem to be the most common experience nowadays. This is not to say that fear, grief, and shame are not all present in a confused and undefined way. On the other hand, to be afraid of God's punishments requires a lively belief in God. Furthermore, this faith has to be in a God who not only is capable of punishing but also is prepared to mete out punishment to the wrongdoer. It is quite clear that the God of Christian revelation is in fact a God who is both capable of punishing and prepared to punish. In the age in which we live, however, there is no tradition of understanding experience in terms of fundamental Christian notions such as God, sin, and judgment. This means there is no Catholic vocabulary which people find ready at hand to describe their unhappiness. As a result, while the raw material of servile fear is certainly present, it is not explicit enough to be described in this way.

Yet God still calls the sinner to Himself. That is the fact of the matter, but he calls in many ways and with many voices, and who can number them? Jacopone's fear, shame, and grief describe elements common to many of the ways of God's calling. The experience of these emotions is often confused and hardly recognized for what it is. Yet, through the mercy of God, it is enough. The Lord touches the heart of the sinner, and he turns to God in what he now recognizes as fear, grief, and shame.

My lament comes late,
And late are the tears
I shed for the loss of You.
How can you dwell on this,
O my heart,
Without turning to ashes?

How can you turn your back on Love,
Love that grieves for you?
Deny your heart
To the One who suffered for you?
Put aside all concern with yourself
And weep over the dishonour you have done Him![34]

4.4 *Beginning to pray*

Christ compares God to a good shepherd who goes looking for his lost sheep. Jacopone compares Him to a fisherman who seeks to hook his fish and finally land him. In both cases the image reminds us that the first movement in our conversion away from sin and to God comes from God. The Lord goes out to us, and like the ungainly apode, we have to cooperate with the wind of God's grace if we are to leave the ground and begin the long flight home to our Maker.

One of the first effects of God's grace is contrition. God in His mercy touches the heart and suddenly we are seized with pain and confusion on account of our condition. We may hardly recognize what is wrong, yet, allied to a deep sense of the mercy of God there is also the experience of fear, shame, and grief for what we are and for what we have been.

This first experience of the mercy of God has to be met on our part with an effort to turn ourselves to Christ in a deep and serious way. We have to learn to take account of this confused sense of our own unworthiness in a manner that will not push us into despair but

34. *Laud* 11.

will lead us to respond to the mercy of the Lord. One of the ways we do this is through the practice of prayer, and at the beginning of our conversion prayer is dominated by the prayer of petition.[35] We need help and we should ask for it. This will always be true as long as we live, but it is especially true in the difficult and disordered beginnings of our response to God. Our behavior and our reactions are not consistent. At times we may have a sense that God is all-important, and then we try to rearrange our lives in accordance with His demands. At other times, the whole business of religion may seem both useless and disagreeable. Furthermore, because we are not sure where we really stand, it seems as though there are no fixed points in our world. Some days it appears as though faith is the answer to everything, and other days faith seems both false and harmful. At some periods we sense that it is only by submitting to the law of Christ that the unrest and unhappiness of our hearts will be stilled. At other periods we seem to be certain that if we do not give free expression to lust, ambition, and every other sort of desire, then we will never realize our potential and become who we really are. We are talking here not about a purely intellectual debate but about how people actually behave. The beginning of a serious Christian life is often accompanied by both wildly fluctuating convictions and radically inconsistent behavior. God's approach produces reactions on our part, and not all of them are admirable.

In this condition we have to ask for help in a simple way. A short verse from one of the psalms is often appropriate. "O give me understanding that I may learn thy commandments,"[36] would

35. The vocabulary of supplication in the New Testament is rich in shades of meaning: ask, beseech, plead, invoke, entreat, cry out, even "struggle in prayer." Its most usual form, because the most spontaneous, is petition: by prayer of petition we express awareness of our relationship with God. We are creatures who are not our own beginning, nor the masters of adversity, nor our own last end. We are sinners who as Christians know that we have turned away from our Father, Our petition is already a turning back to him. *CCC* 2629.

36. Psalm 119 (118) 73.

be an excellent example. A short line from one of the saints, such as St. Philip's expression, "My Jesus, if you help me not, I am ruined,"[37] would be equally appropriate. There is nothing complicated or difficult about this practice. It requires nothing but the recognition of our poverty and the humility to ask for assistance. Indeed, this asking for things in a simple and unplanned way is often the only prayer we are capable of in this condition.

When St. Thomas comes to consider the nature of prayer, he asks whether prayer is primarily a question of thinking or of willing.[38] He begins, in his usual way, by giving reasons opposed to the position he wants to establish, in this case by stating some of the reasons we might think prayer is essentially a matter of willing. When we think about praying, he says, we realize that it seems to be a kind of desiring or a wanting. We may pray for grace to avoid a temptation, or for better health, or for peace with someone from whom we are estranged, but all these fall under the heading of desire, and desiring or wanting pertains to the appetitive and willing side of our nature.

Furthermore, the final goal of all our striving is to be united with God in heaven, and union with God is a union of love. Therefore, at the basis of all our prayer, there should be the desire to be united with God. Now love is an appetitive act, and so once again it seems that prayer is essentially a matter of the will and not the intellect.

St. Thomas does not, of course, want to deny that prayer involves desire, nor does he want to deny that union with God is something that involves our whole being. He wants to say, however, that prayer is not formally or essentially willing. The reasons for this are somewhat technical, but in arguing his case he leaves us with some very practical counsels. Prayer, he says, is not primarily willing, because praying is both a speaking and a reason-

37. Bacci, *The Life of St Philip Neri*, I.178.
38. 2a2ae 83, 1.

ing. He cites Isidore of Seville, who says that "to pray is to speak," and Cassiodorus, who maintains that "prayer is spoken reason." So, there are two things here. First of all, prayer involves speaking, and, secondly, prayer is said to pertain to the reason.

Language is an essential part of our rationality and our humanity. Respect for language and the capacity to use it are part of the glory of our human nature. This does not mean that we possess an adequate theory of language,[39] and indeed controversy about language has become a central issue in the twentieth century. There are those today who would argue that the secret of human nature is to be found in man as a "language animal"[40]; whether or not this position is correct, it does point up the truth that Thomas's concern for language is not old fashioned or "traditionalist" in the bad sense.

Thomas is telling us that prayer involves the wonderful instrument of language, and it would be self-defeating to try to suppress it. It is quite true that St. Paul speaks of the Spirit interceding for us "with sighs too deep for words,"[41] but that does not means we are to begin our prayer by trying to imitate the Holy Spirit. If we begin by ignoring our humanity, we are in great danger of ending up as less and not more than human.

Secondly, prayer is spoken *reason*. The reason of which St. Thomas speaks here is practical reason. Practical reason means reason used not merely to recognize something that is already the case, for example, that two and two are four, but reason used to discern the correct thing to do in a particular set of circumstances.

39. See Taylor, *Philosophical Papers: Human Agency and Language*, 1. 216: ". . . in an age of great scientific advance, and after spectacular progress in so many fields, human language appears to us much more enigmatic than it did to the men of the Enlightenment."

40. See Taylor, *Philosophical Papers*, 1.217, where he deals with the question "How did we slide to the sense that the secret of human nature was to be found in man as a 'language animal' (to use George Steiner's phrase)?"

41. Romans 8:26.

We may know that it is right to give money to the poor, but it another thing to know, here and now in this particular situation—I may be a family man out of work—that it is right to give money to this particular person. I have to determine by the use of my practical reason what I have to do in these particular circumstances. No book of rules, and no amount of theoretical knowledge, can provide this information. It has to be my practical reason, judging as the man of practical reason would judge, which determines or creates what is right for me to do.[42]

Now sometimes practical reason brings about what it wants directly, as when it decides I should reach into my pocket and give the man the money. Sometimes, however, it acts indirectly, as when I ask someone else who is my equal or superior to give the man the money. This asking is a request or petition. St. Thomas quotes St. Augustine, who says "prayer is petition," and St. John Damascene, who says that "to pray is to ask fitting things from God."[43] So, if praying is asking, and asking is an exercise of practical reason, then praying is an act of reason.

In sum, we should realize that the end or goal of our praying is that we may be united to God, and this union is a union of love, which involves both mind and heart. Also, prayer involves the use of language; the language we use when we pray ought to be carefully considered and treated with respect. Since language matters, it should not be disdained as though it were some kind of obstacle to real intimacy with God. In addition, prayer is said to consist basically in petition, that is, in asking God for what is good for

42. Aristotle said that *practical wisdom* "is a true and reasoned state of capacity to act with regard to the things that are good or bad for man" (*NE* VI.5, 1140b5). Alasdair MacIntyre comments: "It [i.e. practical wisdom] is the virtue of practical intelligence, of knowing how to apply general principles in particular situations. It is not the ability to formulate principles intellectually, or to deduce what ought to be done. It is the ability to act so that principle will take a concrete form" (*A Short History of Ethics*, 74).

43. 2a2ae 83, 1.

us, both spiritually and temporally. Finally, prayer is essentially an
act of our practical reason, in which we ask God to bring about
what we have determined is for our own good. Practical reason,
we have seen, does not act in accordance with a book of rules.
This means that prayer, even the fundamental prayer of petition,
is a living, free, and spontaneous act of the person praying. Each
time we pray, we go out to that beauty forever new and forever
old,[44] and our prayer should be a response to God who is endlessly
creative and demanding, and yet the same yesterday, today, and
forever.[45]

The use of the prayer of petition is often neglected today. People
have a sense that it is an irrational activity, or that it is in some
way unspiritual and hardly Christian, or they feel it is not compatible with the mentality of sophisticated modern man. We have
become accustomed to thinking that to put God at the center of
our world view is to demean our human dignity. The use of the
prayer of petition displays, so we feel, a cowardice in the face of
the difficulties of life and reveals a childish dependence on God,
which is unworthy of free men. The imperative as we see it, that
we should respect the autonomy of our humanity, is part of the
cultural legacy of the Enlightenment.[46] The conceptual difficulties
with asking things from God publicized by the Enlightenment are
not intrinsically foolish, and most people have from time to time
felt the force of one or another of them. It is worth trying to un-

44. *Conf.* X.26: "Late have I loved you, O Beauty so old, and so new. Late
have I loved you!'

45. Hebrews, 13:8.

46. Pelikan, *The Christian Tradition*, 5.60: "When applied to the Christian tradition and its doctrines, the Enlightenment represented what has been called the
''revolution of man's autonomous potentialities over against the heteronomous
powers which were no longer convincing,'' namely, the heteronomous authority
of the church and of its dogma and ultimately of the objective authority of Scripture
and of transcendent revelation itself.'' The reference is to Paul Tillich's *Perspectives
on 19th and 20th Century Protestant Theology.*

pack what is contained in these attitudes. There are two questions to be asked. First, is it foolish to pray? Second, is it Christian to pray?

One of the oldest and most obvious objections to prayer is that it is a pointless occupation. If God is a conscious being who is all-powerful and directs the universe, including all human activity, as He sees fit, then what effect could prayer possibly have? Or, if God is not that sort of being, then perhaps it is blind necessity that governs everything, in which case there is obviously nothing to be gained in praying that anything should change. Or again, some people say that we have an unworthy conception of God if we think His will can be altered by anything we could do.

St. Thomas sums up these objections and then answers them by pointing out that it is an aspect of God's Providence that some of the things that happen should be brought about through prayer. God's Providence does rule all things; we do not change it by prayer, but prayer is a constitutive element in bringing about what God's Providence has decreed.[47]

Our prayer of petition is one of the means God uses for bringing about the realization of His purposes. We are not telling God what He does not know; we are not trying to alter His will, and yet at the same time we are acknowledging that God's Providence rules all things and that the universe is not governed by iron necessity or blind chance. The use of the prayer of petition establishes

47. 2a2ae 83, 2: "In order to throw light on this question we must consider that Divine Providence disposes not only what effects shall take place, but also from what causes and in what order these effects shall proceed. Now among other causes human acts are the causes of certain effects. Wherefore it must be that men do certain actions, not that thereby they may change the Divine disposition, but that by those actions they may achieve certain effects according to the order of the Divine disposition: and the same is to be said of natural causes. And so it is with regard to prayer. For we pray, not that we may change the Divine disposition, but that we may obtain by asking (impetrate) that which God has disposed to be fulfilled by our prayers, in other words that by asking, men may deserve to receive what Almighty God from eternity has disposed to give, as Gregory says."

and deepens our relationship with a God we believe to be personal. In this prayer we open our heart to God and ask for what we need in a simple and uncomplicated way. As we begin to learn about ourselves through recognizing what we need and through a growing sense of our own weakness and dependence, so at the same time we begin to know the merciful God who is the giver of all we need.

It might, however, be the case that the prayer of petition is not an irrational activity, yet it might still be true that it is not a particularly Christian one. People often say today that it betrays an unspiritual and even a magical frame of mind to ask particular things from God. The truly spiritual person should pray to be united to the will of God, so it is said, and what is the point of telling God a lot of things He must know already? Some might say that we are treating God as though we were children who expected everything we wanted from a kind of super Santa Claus. To do this, so it is maintained, is surely to display a very unworthy conception of God and very little respect for ourselves.

Even if our prayer is not an asking for unworthy objects, there always remains the suspicion that we are trying to bend God's will to our own. Would it not be a better indication of our belief in God's Providence merely to pray that God's will should be done and forget about praying for anything definite?[48] This view is only strengthened when we remember that it is often very difficult to know exactly for what we should pray. St. John Damascene says that "to pray is to ask fitting things of God,"[49] and it would follow

48. The attitude is not a new one. St. Teresa discusses it in the *Way of Perfection* in a passage that is included in the Office of Readings of *The Liturgy of the Hours,* for the Wednesday of the 13th week of Ordinary Time. "O Eternal Wisdom, between you and your Father that was enough; that was how you prayed in the garden. You expressed your desire and fear but surrendered yourself to his will. But as for us, my Lord, you know that we are less submissive to the will of your Father and need to mention each thing separately . . ."(3.431).

49. Quoted, 2a2ae 83, 1.

that it would be wrong to pray for what is not fitting. Further-more, we read in Romans, "we know not how to pray as we ought."[50] We might well conclude that it is impossible for us to ask for what is fitting, and Scripture seems to support this view. "You ask, and receive not: because you ask amiss."[51] If we cannot be sure of asking for things that God wants us to have, then it would appear to be better to leave the whole matter entirely in His hands and forget about the prayer of petition.

In answer, it should be remembered, first, that our Lord taught His disciples to ask definitely for those things contained in the petitions of the Lord's Prayer. Again, the writer of the Letter to the Hebrews writes of Jesus "that he always lives to make inter-cession . . ."[52] In response to the objection that only God knows what is good for us, and so we cannot pray for what we really need, St. Thomas reminds us first that the passage from Romans also includes the promise that the Holy Spirit will help us in our infirmities to ask for what is fitting. His main point, however, is that there are some things we cannot use badly and these must be prayed for unconditionally:

There are certain goods which man cannot use in an evil manner and which cannot have bad results, such as the blessings by which we are sanctified and merit bliss. For these the good pray absolutely, as it says in the Psalms, Show us thy face and we shall be saved (79,4), and again, Lead me into the path of thy commandments (118,35).[53]

The purpose of the prayer of petition is not to bend the will of God, but to pray for what we need in conformity with His will. It is His will for us that we should pray in this way. In the prayer of petition, we grow gradually into a sense of the reality of our dependence on God and develop the confidence to ask Him for what we need. The simple, familiar business of asking for what we require, if we are going even to begin to live the Christian life,

---

50. Romans 8:26.   51. James 4:3.
52. Hebrews 7:25.   53. 2a2ae 83, 5.

is the foundation of our response to the call of God. It is through the prayer of petition that we begin to relate ourselves in a real way to the God who was before all things and is in all things.

One of the marks of genuine growth in prayer is a deepening sense of confidence in God. Modern man is afflicted with anxiety, that is, with a sort of fear that seems to have no definite object. Our attempts to pray and lead a good life sometimes seem to make existence more complicated. Our efforts to respond to God often bring confusion and suffering, but they do gradually develop in us a heightened awareness of the reality of God and of His care for us. This new sense of the presence of God is the best antidote for that formless fear and unease that we call anxiety.

This anxiety, as well as suspicion, pessimism about the future, and a distrust of human motives, often seems rooted in a particular sort of temperament, but no one is entirely exempt from these experiences. Little can be done to change first reactions or moods. On the other hand, the practice of the prayer of petition gradually develops a confidence in God that is based on a growing realization of His loving Providence. This confidence runs deeper and is more enduring than either temperament or moods.[54]

54. 2a2ae 83, 9: "Prayer is not offered to God in order to change his mind, but in order to excite confidence (fiducia) in us. Such confidence is fostered principally by considering God's charity towards us whereby he wills our good (hence we say 'our Father') and to indicate this excellence which is powerful to fulfil his charity, 'who art in heaven.' "

5 ❧ The Healer

> The reawakened and still fragile soul
>
> Is then visited by the Healer,
>
> Who nurses and comforts
>
> And strengthens with Sacraments.

5.1 The sacraments and meditation

In this verse Jacopone speaks about the converted soul that has begun to live the life of grace. Although the soul has been raised from sin and despair, it is all too prone to fall back into its former state. It has made a start in giving itself to God, yet it is still very weak. Conversion leaves all the acquired natural habits and tendencies unchanged. The pull of the world, of the flesh, and of the Devil remain. And, to make matters worse, faith, hope, and charity often seem very weak. The soul may even wonder if it has made a mistake. This is a state in which the soul easily slips away from God.

One of the most attractive and helpful aspects of the *Confessions* of St. Augustine is that he makes no bones about how difficult things were for him after he was converted. There was no question of a "personal decision for Jesus Christ" and then living a trouble-free life ever afterwards. There remained the pull of the senses, the pull of past habits, and the effects of original sin.[1]

---

1. See for example, *Conf* X.28.

The newly converted are in for a struggle if they are to remain in friendship with God. They have brought too much of their old life with them to be anything but spiritual invalids. They have need of a healer to begin the cure of their nature wounded by the consequences of the Fall and of their own sins. It is the sacraments which are Christ's appointed means to begin this cure. At this stage, the sacraments appear mainly as the means of forgiving, reconciling, and strengthening the soul for its battle against all the forces that are trying to pull it back to where it started. "Woe is me!" cried St. Augustine, "Lord, have pity on me. Woe is me! Lo, I hide not my wounds; thou art the physician, I the sick; Thou merciful, I miserable."[2]

A serious sacramental life must be accompanied by a life of personal prayer. The practice of meditation is an indispensable element in trying to strengthen and steady our response to the call of God. The link between meditation and the sacraments is part of the heritage of the Counter-Reformation, and it is a link that should be maintained.[3] In this sort of prayer we try to appropriate the truths of our faith (with our intellect) so that they affect our behavior, and in this way both the intelligence and the will are involved in Christian meditation. The truths of our faith have to be entered into so deeply and grasped so firmly that they become a sort of second nature to us.

---

2. *Conf* X.28.

3. Evennett, *Spirit of the Counter-Reformation*, 40: "There was in fact a necessary and close connection between the personal discipline involved in regular periods of mental prayer and the new fervour for the sacraments of Confession and Communion. These two aspects of counter-reformation piety—the efforts of personal *ascèse*, the 'disciplined life of religious regularity,' and the recourse to the covenanted channels whence flowed divine Grace *ex opere operato*—are seen once more to come together."

5.2 *The Christian's warfare*

We have seen that the soul has to be touched or influenced by God in some way before it can begin to live the Christian life. But it is one thing to receive God's grace, and it is another thing to be able to live this new life with zest and confidence. St. Teresa, who compared the journey of the soul to God to a progress through the rooms of a wonderful castle, says that these souls have hardly got into the front door. Eventually they do manage to enter the first rooms at the lowest floor, but they bring so much of their old life with them that they are unable to appreciate the beauty of the castle or to find any peace in it.[4] They are, she says, no longer paralyzed by sin, but they can hardly move their spiritual faculties. They have lived so long in sin that they have become accustomed "to living all the time with the reptiles and other creatures to be found in the outer court of the castle."[5]

Living with reptiles describes the state of many people who have just begun to pray. They have been moved by God to seek him, and they do respond. Often the response itself seems generous. On the other hand, they are, as Jacopone says, fragile, and their spiritual health is precarious. The newly awakened soul believes it has given itself over to God, and it may even think its troubles are over. It has found God, said it is sorry for having sinned, and the future may seem like plain sailing. But as it settles down to living the life of a Christian, it begins to see that its response to God is half-hearted, desultory, and timid. Like Lot's wife, it spends a lot of time looking backwards.[6]

How, then, is the newly converted going to improve the nature of his response? The answer is simple even if it is not easy to do. The new convert has to begin to live what St. Francis de Sales called the devout life. St. Thomas defines devotion as "nothing

4. *IC* I.1.   5. Ibid., I.1.
6. Genesis 19:26.

else but the will to give oneself readily to things concerning the service of God."[7] In our efforts to lead a devout life we have to remember that here, as in every other phase or aspect of the spiritual life, it is God who makes the first move. God is with us and active from the very beginning of our life of devotion. On the other hand, we have little or no experience of this truth. All we are aware of is the courtyard of the castle and the messy, fascinating, poisonous nest of serpents and reptiles that seem to afflict us not only in the everyday circumstances of life, but also when we try to pray. If we are going to live a devout life, it follows that we are in for a battle, and there is no doubt that at certain periods the element of struggle is in fact uppermost in the life of a Christian. Cardinal Newman alluded to this when he said:

To change our hearts is to learn to love things which we do not naturally love—to unlearn the love of this world; but this involves, of course, a thwarting of our natural wishes and tastes. To be righteous and obedient implies self-command; but to possess power we must have gained it; nor can we gain it without a vigorous struggle, a persevering warfare against ourselves. The very notion of being religious implies self-denial, because by nature we do not love religion.[8]

The image of the Christian life as a battle in which we follow in the army either of our Lord or of the Devil is one especially dear to many of the saints of the Counter-Reformation.[9] It is wrong, however, to think of it as new with them, or as belonging essentially to their period. It is found in St. Paul, in Cassian,[10] and in St. Thomas, and it is also found in Jacopone, who describes this

7. 2a2ae 82, 1 sed contra.

8. *PS* VII, serm. 7 ("The Duty of Self-Denial").

9. E.g., St Ignatius of Loyola, *Spiritual Exercises*, "A Meditation on the Two Standards," sects. 137–48, in Keane, *Spiritual Exercises*, 50–52.

10. See *The Conferences of John Cassian* IV. 12 ("The Conference of the Abbot Daniel"), where he describes the "free will of the soul" which stands in an intermediate position somewhat worthy of blame, and neither delights in the excesses of sin nor acquiesces in the sorrows of virtue."

warfare in one of his Lauds. He imagines a dialogue between the
will that seeks God and the will of the flesh that seeks its own
satisfaction.

> Suddenly I find myself thinking
> Of a woman I used to know—soft,
> Rosy-hued, elegant, a model of grace.
> I feel sick with longing for her;
> I wish I could speak to her.
>
> Let me reward you for that mad fantasy:
> For the whole winter now you'll go
> Without a cape and without shoes.
> And then we'll scourge you
> Until the flesh comes off in strips.

Finally the will of the flesh gives up as the Christian decides for
God:

> Too much, too much! You've won, I'll complain no more.
> Besides, what good has it done me? From now on,
> All I'll ask is not to transgress God's law.
>
> Good! Keep your word and I'll see to it
> That you'll not suffer any more.
> Now to our common joy we'll both be saved.[11]

It is quite true that the image of the Christian's warfare is not
much in vogue today. It is also true that the image of the battle
has its dangers. But this does not mean we can leave it out of account altogether. St. Thomas says, as we have seen, that at the
beginning of our spiritual life we must be concerned with withdrawing from sin and resisting the appetites.[12] People may have
thought in the past that this was the sum total of the spiritual life.
If so, they were wrong about this, but people today are just as

11. *Laud* 3.
12. 2a2ae 24, 9 sed contra. See above, 3.3.

misguided in teaching that the struggle against sin has no place in the life of a Christian.

We are all familiar with this struggle, or at least we ought to be. When we begin to be serious about trying to please God, we find that we are in for a war with ourselves. When we first sense in ourselves a desire to live a life which is more hard-working, more patient, and more chaste, we find that the greatest obstacles to doing what God wants us to do are not outside ourselves. On the contrary, it would be truer to say that while in one sense we really do want to be industrious, patient, and chaste, there is another and very real sense in which it would be true to say that we do not want to be hard-working, patient, and chaste. There is the will of God for us that the rational will wants to follow. But in addition there is the will of the flesh which seeks to entice our rational will into following the suggestions of our fallen human nature. This means that at the beginning of our conversion we are faced with very serious and hard struggles. And the struggle is a civil war; it is a war in which we have to fight against ourselves.[13]

The struggle against sin in this difficult but obvious fashion is largely a matter of the first *studium*. After that, people generally settle down into either virtue or vice. The virtuous find it progressively easier to yield to the divine will, and the vicious give way without resistance to the will of the senses. The struggle, in other words, leads to a truce. It may be a truce based on the fact that we have smothered our higher nature. Or it may be a truce based on having won at least a few of the first rounds in the battle with the will of the flesh. In neither case, however, have we reached the end of the story. There is always time for another conversion even if we have all but given up the struggle. On the other hand,

13. Cf. Scupoli, *Spiritual Combat,* chapter 12: ". . . as it is reason which constitutes us men, we cannot be said to will any thing which is willed by the senses unless we be also inclined thereto by the superior will. And herein does our spiritual conflict principally consist."

even if we have won the first few rounds, there still remains the constant warfare against ourselves, which has to be continued against less obvious, but even more dangerous, sins.

5.3 Spiritual convalescents and imperfect cures

Jacopone presents Christ as the Healer who brings the sacraments, which will gradually make us over into the image of the beloved Son of God. Healing is not always a definitive cure. Nor, furthermore, does a definitive cure always leave the former invalid in perfect health. The sacraments heal, but there is always the possibility of turning away from God. This is true even after a lifetime of trying to imitate Christ. It is only the one who perseveres to the end who will be saved,[14] but, as the Council of Trent teaches, we cannot be sure of this perseverance, and we must pray for it daily.[15] Again, even though we may be restored to friendship with God through the sacraments, we bear with us our history, our half-eradicated sins and weaknesses, and the terrible weight of original sin, which constantly pull us away from our own good. The newly converted soul, though full of enthusiasm and energy, is an invalid and too liable to fall once more into sin. He badly needs a healer who will give him the strength and grace to become a friend of God. It is important at this stage to realize that a fall into sin is not the end of everything. For, although we must not rashly presume on God's grace, we have also to remember that God forgives the penitent sinner again and again.

We are, all of us, called to put on Jesus Christ. We are to live our vocation as Christians in the grace and love of Jesus Christ, so that the Father may see in each one of us the image of His dearly beloved Son. That is our calling as people baptized into the saving death and resurrection of Jesus Christ. Yet, without the action of

14. Matthew 10:22.
15. *Council of Trent* VI, canon 13; also VI, canon 16.

Christ who is the good physician, we will have neither the courage nor the strength to cooperate with His grace.

It may be objected that to regard the sacraments as the means of healing the individual's relationship with God is to fall into an individualistic attitude that ignores a great deal of the richness of recent sacramental theology. This sacramental theology, which was developed in the years leading up to the Second Vatican Council, was concerned with amplifying and giving new perspectives to truths that were accepted by all Catholics. For example, the truth that the sacraments confer grace *ex opere operato,* that is, that grace is made available to the recipient by the power of Christ operating through the sacraments, was common teaching. Building on the basis of these accepted truths, many theologians tried to amplify sacramental theology by enriching it with positions that had been elaborated by the Fathers of the Church but had been overlooked or undervalued during the course of the centuries.[16]

The new sacramental theology held that the proper context for thinking about the sacraments is to realize, first of all, that they are the mystery of Christ's death and resurrection lived out in the action of the Church. Furthermore, this mystery is made real to us in and through the Church. Then, secondly, we have to see our own participation in the sacraments as an aspect of something much bigger than ourselves. It is through the sacraments that the Church as the body of Christ is built up and gradually brings God's plans to realization.

16. The spirituality of the Counter-Reformation, which did so much to form Catholic spirituality for nearly four hundred years, was personal and sacramental, but not liturgical: "It is not invalid to recognize in the dominant spirituality of the Counter-Reformation certain powerful and distinctive traits. Broadly speaking, its genius took individual rather than corporate or liturgical expressions" (Evennett, *Spirit of the Counter-Reformation,* 41). Nonetheless, it is a great deal easier to point out what was inadequate in the achievements of the Counter-Reformation than it is to emulate its creativity.

Not only do the Fathers believe that the sacraments communicate grace *ex opere operato* (a later term)—not only do they believe the Body and Blood of Christ are given to us objectively in the Eucharist, in such a way that the words "This is my Body, this is my Blood" are to be understood in a sense that is obviously mysterious but, at the same time, absolutely real—but, according to their interpretation, there is a great deal more: the whole mystery of Christ, the mystery of His death and resurrection, and the mystery of our salvation in its eschatological fullness.[17]

After the Council, the way seemed open for a sacramental theology and a sacramental practice that reflect the wider horizons of this new perspective and help to remove the view that the sacraments were only for the individual's perfection in complete isolation from the rest of the Church. In this way the Church as the blessed community willed by Christ for the salvation of all would resume its proper place at the center of the hearts and minds of faithful Catholics.

The worship of the Church ought to have been at the center of this revival, and it seemed as though this would be the case. The first major document of the Council concerned the Liturgy.[18] This document seems to have been implemented by people possessed of a dry, didactic, exclusively verbal view of worship. But worship is not a purely verbal business. The attempt to enlarge our perspective on the sacraments, taken together with an approach to liturgy that has been exclusively verbal and has forgotten that liturgy involves symbols and action, has certainly had a profound and noticeable effect on Catholic thought and practice. Whatever may be chalked up in favor of the liturgical reform—and opinions about this differ wildly—it has certainly been bought at a very high price. The price has been the loss of a sense of the objective reality of Christ's action in the sacraments, which has led to an obvious change in attitude toward the Blessed Sacrament itself.

17. Bouyer, *Church of God,* 12–13.
18. The Constitution on the Sacred Liturgy (*Sacrosanctum Concilium*).

This is so manifest that it requires no documentation. The truths that were formerly accepted by all regarding the operation of the sacraments *ex opere operato* and of Christ's real substantial presence in the Eucharist have been replaced, rather than enhanced, by the larger eschatological perspectives. The new perspectives, which should have brought with them a deeper understanding of the operation of Christ's power in the whole Church through the sacraments and of His real presence not only in the Eucharist but in all the sacramental actions of the Church, have instead introduced a subjectivism about the sacraments that is in danger of reducing them to nothing but memorials of the Paschal Mystery.

As a result, the community, interpreted often in a naturalistic way, has become all important. For example, baptism has become merely incorporation into the (Christian) community, and the Eucharist has become only a memorial activity in which we remember in faith and look forward in hope. The new (or revived) elements, upon which we were supposed to learn to concentrate, have replaced almost completely the foundation on which they rest. This foundation is the reality of Jesus Christ present in the sacraments through His action in the Church.

We have to return to the sober realism of Catholic sacramental theology and practice. Unless we do this, the Christian foundations of the eschatological and community aspects of the sacraments will collapse into something indistinguishable from embryonic political parties or pressure groups or social clubs. Jacopone says that Christ appears as the Healer who nurses and comforts and strengthens with sacraments. That may not be the whole of sacramental theology, but it is one of its indispensable aspects, and that fact must be reasserted.

It is true that we have to see the individual and his response to the Lord's appearing within an enriched appreciation of the different elements we have been discussing. On the other hand, if we are to avoid turning people into units in a collective called the Church, we have to remember that the drama of redemption is made real in individual people who live the life of Christ in His Church. To try to reduce Christianity to movements or groups is to miss the point of the parable of the lost sheep. The Shepherd goes looking for one particular sheep; God calls each one of us by name. Newman in an early sermon gives a powerful and a timely lesson in this personal aspect of the sacraments:

> In truth, our Merciful Saviour has done much more for us than reveal the wonderful doctrines of the Gospel; he has enabled us to apply them . . . but how should we bring home his grace to ourselves? . . . how secure the comfortable assurance that he loves us personally, and will change our heart, which we feel to be so earthly, and wash away our sins, which we confess to be so manifold, unless he had given us Sacraments— means and pledges of grace—keys which open the treasure-house of mercy.[19]

5.4 Mortification

Mortification does not get a very good press nowadays. It seems connected in many people's minds with a crabbed and warped view of human nature. Yet it is very much an aspect of any sane Catholic spirituality, and its justification is to be found in the mystery of redemption itself. Our Lord redeemed us from our sin by His Passion and death. Through the death of the sinless lamb, we sinners are restored to friendship with God. Yet if we are to enter more deeply into this friendship with God, we must make the saving Passion and death of our Lord more real to ourselves by meditating on Christ's saving work. Furthermore, if this meditation is to be real and effective, it must be accompanied by mortification. We have to try to put to death those things in ourselves which lead us away from our Lord, His Law, and His Passion. We have, in addition, to learn to give up our excessive attachment even to good things that get in the way of a closer union with God. St.

19. *PS* III, serm. 20 ("Infant Baptism").

Philip used to say that the true preparation for prayer is the practice of mortification:

. . . for to desire to give ourselves to prayer without mortification is like a bird trying to fly before it is fledged. Hence, when one of his penitents asked him to teach him how to pray, he replied, "Be humble and obedient, and the Holy Ghost will teach you."[20]

It is important to understand that mortification is not merely an ascetical practice which we undertake in order, as it were, to get ourselves into good spiritual shape. In the most important sense, it is an effort to conform ourselves to a deeper spiritual movement that characterizes all of God's redeeming work.[21]

"Come," says the Prophet, "let us return to the Lord; for he has torn, that he may heal us; he has stricken, and he will bind us up."[22] This pattern of wounding in order to heal, the mysterious rhythm of killing in order to bring to life, is woven into the fabric of both the Old and the New Testaments. Our own acceptance of suffering and our own efforts to die to ourselves have to be seen within this larger context of God's dealing with mankind. In the book of Deuteronomy, for example, we find the following passage:

See now that I, even I, am he,
and there is no God beside me
I kill and I make alive;
I wound and I heal;
and there is none that can deliver out of my hand.[23]

Or, again, from the book of Tobit:

For he afflicts and he shows mercy;
he leads down to Hades and brings up again,
and there is no one who can escape his hand.[24]

20. Bacci, *The Life of St Philip Neri*, 1.180.
21. See Charles Morel, "Mortification" in *DS* 10.1791–99.
22. Hosea 6:1.
23. Deuteronomy 32:39.   24. Tobit 13:2.

This work of God, this wounding in order to heal, this killing in order to bring to life again, reaches its summit in Christ. St. Peter tells us that Christ died for our sins, the righteous for the unrighteous, that he might bring us to God. He then goes on to say "being put to death in the flesh but made alive in the spirit."[25] Christ was the supreme example of God's unfathomable way of dealing with us, which is to kill in order to make alive and to wound in order to heal. Because of Christ's love for us, we all benefit from His work. "He himself bore our sins in his body on the tree, that we might die to sin and live to righteousness. By his wounds we have been healed."[26] There is, since the Passion and death of Christ, a redemptive value in accepting the will of the God who wounds in order to heal. This is shown in a pre-eminent way in the life of Christ, but each one of us has to imitate the acceptance by Christ of His Father's will.

Since, therefore, Christ suffered in the flesh, arm yourselves with the same thought, for whoever has suffered in the flesh has ceased from sin, so as to live in the flesh no longer by human passions but by the will of God.[27]

We are to arm ourselves with the thought of Christ's suffering so that we can share in His victory over sin and live no longer by human passions but by the will of God. In Catholic thought, this effort to cooperate with the pattern of suffering and of healing, of dying and of resurrection, which we find in the Bible, provides the framework and the dynamic for our own practice of mortification. The author of the *Imitation of Christ* wrote about the need to cooperate with God's way of healing through suffering in the following way:

Behold, then, how in the cross all things stand; and how, in dying to the world, lies all our health; and that there is no other way to life and true inward peace but the way of the cross, and the way of daily submission

25. 1 Peter 3:18.   26. 1 Peter 2:24.
27. 1 Peter 4:1.

of the body to the spirit. Go wherever you will, and reap whatever you desire, and you will never find, above you or beneath you, within you or without you, a more high, a more excellent, a more sure way to Christ than the way of the Holy Cross.[28]

The word *mortification* is not in the Gospels, but is to be found in St. Paul. The thought, of course, comes from our Lord: "Truly, truly I say to you, unless a grain of wheat falls into the earth and dies, it remains alone; but if it dies it bears much fruit";[29] or the equally well known passage from St. Luke: "If any man would come after me, let him deny himself and take up his cross daily and follow me."[30]

The Greek word for mortification is to be found in St. Paul in numerous places, where, for example, he says that we are always "carrying about in the body the death of Jesus, so that the life of Jesus may be manifested in our bodies."[31] We are to carry about in our body the putting to death of Jesus, that is, we are to mortify ourselves, so as to participate in the death of the Lord. Yet we do this only in order that we too may share in His life.

We may say, in summing up, that the meaning of *mortification* depends on a tradition that begins with the Old Testament and flowers in St. Paul. It receives its clear meaning and power from the death and life of Christ. Any personal effort of ours to follow Christ in His suffering should be seen as a submission to the will of God, and as a cooperating in the work of our Maker. We must always keep before our minds and hearts that the purpose of mortification is to configure us to Christ, in whom the work of God finds its highest and most perfect expression. The Spirit we have received in baptism prompts us, and it sustains our own personal efforts to persevere in putting to death the works of the flesh, so that we may live the life of God.

From all this it follows that mortification is not essentially a

28. *Imitation* II.12.   29. John 12:25.
30. Luke 9:23.   31. 2 Corinthians 4:10.

technique for depriving ourselves of God's gifts, nor of making ourselves suffer. The purpose of mortification is to subdue something in us that is hostile to what God wants of us and for us. This principle of hostility St. Paul calls the flesh. It is what a man becomes when the created spirit no longer submits itself to the divine Spirit, and in consequence no longer imposes a spiritual life on the body. Father Bouyer even suggests that the word *flesh* was chosen precisely to signify that it is not a living body that St. Paul had in mind, but rather the entity deprived of the breath of life that we call a corpse.[32] By our disobedience we give free reign to the physical appetites of our body and so become dead to the spirit.

Mortification is the effort, with God's help, to bring the flesh to heel so that the Holy Spirit may reign in us. It is undertaken in faith because we hope and trust in what God has promised us but we do not as yet possess. Often it may seem we deny ourselves for no reason. But this willingness to undertake the ventures of faith (as Newman put it[33]) distinguishes mortification in the Catholic sense of the word from Stoicism or spiritual athletics. That is, we risk what we have for something unimaginably greater.[34] In the *Lectures on Justification* there is a long passage in which Newman binds together the doctrinal and the ascetical aspects of mortification in a clear and compelling way. He concludes by saying:

You hear men speak of glorying in the Cross of Christ, who are utter strangers to the notion of the Cross as actually applied to them in water and blood, in holiness and mortification. They think the Cross can be theirs *without* being applied—without its coming near them—while they

32. Bouyer, *A History of Christian Spirituality,* I.79.

33. *PS* IV, serm. 20 ("The Ventures of Faith").7

34. 2 Corinthians 4:16–18: "So we do not lose heart. Though our outer nature is wasting away, our inner nature is being renewed every day. For this slight momentary affliction is preparing for us an eternal weight of glory beyond all comparison, because we look not to the things that are seen but to the things that are unseen; for the things that are seen are transient but the things that are unseen are eternal."

keep at a distance from it, and only gaze on it. . . . [but] Christ's Cross does not justify by being looked at, but by being applied; not by as merely beheld by faith, but by being actually set up within us, and that not by our act, but by God's invisible grace.[35]

5.5 Meditation

The activity of making real to ourselves the person and the message of Jesus is called meditation. It must be emphasized that meditation, as understood in the Catholic tradition, uses our natural capacities of thinking, willing, and imagining.[36] There is nothing supernatural or mysterious in the activity of meditation. It is an ordered or planned movement from one idea to the next for the purpose of assimilating the content of our Faith in a deeper way. This effort at assimilation is undertaken in order that our fitful and unstable relationship to God may be strengthened and steadied.[37]

There are many different forms of Christian meditation. Blessed

35. *Jfc* lect. 7, sect. 6 ("The Characteristics of The Gift of Righteousness"). See also *PS* VIII, serm. 8 ("The Yoke of Christ"): ". . . till the words 'yoke' and 'cross' can stand for something pleasant, the bearing of our yoke and cross is something not pleasant; and though rest is promised as our reward, yet the way to rest must lie through discomfort and distress of heart."

36. Abbot Chapman wants to go even further and says that meditation is not prayer at all. "Of course you can meditate—anybody can. Only you can do it with a pencil in your hand, or a pipe. It is not prayer, though it is useful, and even necessary. Spiritual reading or study of theology, if made devoutly, is most fruitful meditation" (*Spiritual Letters*, 36). This makes sense only if we restrict the meaning of prayer to contemplative prayer, but the passage does have the merit of emphasizing that methods are not the essence of meditation.

37. Meditation engages thought, imagination, emotion and desire. This mobilization of faculties is necessary in order to deepen our convictions of faith, prompt the conversion of our heart and strengthen our will to follow Christ. Christian prayer tries above all to meditate on the mysteries of Christ, as in *lectio divina* or the rosary. This form of prayerful reflection is of great value, but Christian prayer should go further: to the knowledge of the love of the Lord Jesus, to union with him (*CCC*, 2708).

Edith Stein gives a simple account of meditation; as she describes it, meditation must continue to be an aspect of Christian prayer:

The activity of the mind by which it assimilates the contents of faith is called meditation. Here the imagination looks upon the events described in the Gospel, seeks to exhaust their meaning and considers with the understanding their general significance and the demands they make. The will is thereby inclined to love, resolving henceforth to live in the spirit of faith.[38]

Meditation, no matter how complex it may be, seems to comprise the three movements sketched above. In the first place there is a consideration of some incident in Christ's life, or some truth of faith. We do this in a way that will focus on the incident or truth itself (and not on ourselves), so that we can grasp it more deeply. Secondly, we try to apply this truth to our own lives and see what personal lesson can be derived from the consideration. Finally, the will is brought directly into play, and we resolve to act in a way that is more in harmony with our faith.[39]

The individual effort to deepen the awareness of the reality of Christ's truth and of the particular demands it makes on us begins to solidify a personal grasp on the reality of the spiritual world and its implications for us. This developing awareness begins to provide the will, or the desiring, needing part of our nature, with a counterpoise to the immediate attraction of the moment.[40]

---

38. Stein, The Science of the Cross, 85.

39. The third movement of meditation often has to do with the effort to reform our life, and St. Francis de Sales calls it the "particular resolution." See below, 5.6.

40. It is historically inaccurate to identify meditation with the Exercises of St. Ignatius. The Exercises represent a form of meditation that emphasizes mental effort and the principle of activity and struggle. The predominance of the Jesuit form of meditation obscures the distinctive approach to meditation to be found in de Bérulle and the French School, the Carmelites, the Capuchins, St. Francis de Sales, and St. Philip Neri. Outram Evennett maintains: "The intensive and exclusive concentration on formal discursive meditation with its mental efforts, and on the principle of activity and struggle—of which the Jesuits were the supreme and the

5.6 *Thinking and doing*

Meditation involves the use of our faculties. The Almighty has gone out to us in His mercy and touched our hearts with His grace, and we have turned to Him. Yet our awareness of God now seems to come in fits and starts, and our own behavior as Christians lacks steadiness. Our convictions wax and wane with whatever we may be experiencing at the moment; as a result, we are not very effective in fighting the war against the world, the flesh, and the devil. The battle is, as Newman put it in another context, a night battle. We do not know God except in a superficial and emotional way; we do not know our enemies; and we do not know ourselves. There is noise, there is confusion, there is backsliding, and there is very real moral and mental suffering.

Through meditation we begin to stabilize our relationship with God, as we assimilate the truths of revelation. We educate ourselves, with God's help, to know God, to rejoice in Him, and to live for Him. Meditating about God can be likened to remaining ready for the return of an absent friend or partner. First of all, we keep his memory alive by thinking about him, by reading his letters, and by remembering what we have promised to do in his absence. Aristotle said that living with someone else is necessary for the exercise of the virtue of friendship. Absence may sometimes make the heart grow fonder, but after a while it usually makes the heart grow cold. That is also true of our dead. One way of helping to keep alive the memory of an absent friend is to do what we have undertaken for him in his absence, and more generally to lead the sort of life which will make it possible to resume the partnership when he returns. By exercising our imagination, our memory, our intellect, and our will, we

***

extreme champions—was questioned in a running undertone of dissatisfaction by upholders of a more contemplative doctrine of prayer, not only in Spain, but elsewhere too" (*Spirit of the Counter-Reformation,* 40).

deliberately keep alive and even strengthen our end of the relationship.

Meditating about our new-found faith in God follows the same pattern. God is not with us in any way perceptible to our natural powers, but by the use of these powers we try to keep His memory alive. That is, we do not see Him, or touch Him, or hear Him. So, in order to retain our grasp on God, we must deepen our hold on the reality of the world of our faith. It is through an ordinary use of the intellect, the will, and the imagination that we begin to do this.

Through our meditation we acquire a treasure house of structured experiences on which to fall back when the reality of the world seems to overpower us. St. John of the Cross says that even in spiritual things we should take advantage "of the sweetness and the pleasure which come from sense; for, if the desire is fed with pleasure in spiritual things, it becomes detached from pleasure in sensual things and wearies of things of the world."[41] In becoming familiar with God and the truths of our faith, we gradually grow to love them deeply enough to influence our choices and behavior. Through the use of our ordinary capacities we learn gradually to do the will of God.

It is sometimes implied that to insist on some form of meditation even at the early stages is to show a want of regard for the freedom of the individual in his approach to God.[42] I think this argument has to be treated with respect. People are very different, and the way God gradually awakens a person's heart and soul to turn to Him varies from one soul to the next. For this reason there must be a real element of freedom in each one's approach to God. St. Teresa puts it this way:

41. *LFL* (2d redaction) III.32.

42. Cf. *LFL* (1st redaction) III.51: "God leads each soul along different roads and there shall hardly be found a single spirit who can walk even half the way which is suitable for another."

It is very important that no soul which practices prayer, whether little or much, should be subjected to undue constraint or limitation. Since God has given it such dignity, it must be allowed to roam through these mansions—through those above, those below and those on either side. It must not be compelled to remain for a long time in one single room—not, at least, unless it is in the room of self-knowledge.[43]

On the other hand, St. Teresa herself insists time and time again that years of meditation, especially on the person of Jesus Christ, is the usual gateway to contemplation. In this she is at one with St. John of the Cross and the tradition of Catholic mysticism. Freedom must be preserved, but this is no blanket dispensation from the ordinary, run-of-the-mill progression that is the lot of most people.

An emphasis on meditation is quite compatible with a knowledge of, and a respect for, more contemplative kinds of prayer. It is not a question of imprisoning people in a form of prayer that may be unsuitable to them. Yet we have to develop a personal awareness of the truths of our faith. Without this awareness there can be no living relationship with Christ, who loves us and redeems us. Meditation is how this awareness is usually developed. The writer of *The Cloud of Unknowing,* one of the most severely apophatic mystical books on prayer ever written, insists that we begin with meditation on the life and teaching of Christ. Thus he writes:

. . . whosoever man or woman weeneth to come to contemplation without many such sweet meditations beforehand of his own wretchedness, the passion, the kindness, the great goodness, and the worthiness of God, surely he shall err and fail of his purpose . . . the lower part of the contemplative life lieth in good ghostly meditations, and busy beholding unto man's own wretchedness with sorrow and contrition, unto the passion of Christ and of His servants with pity and compassion, and unto the wonderful gifts, kindness, and works of God in all His creatures, bodily and ghostly, with thanking and praising.[44]

43. *IC* I.2.
44. *Epistle of Privy Counsel,* chap. 9.

In the *Interior Castle* St. Teresa says that people have tried to talk her out of practicing meditation. The reason they have tried to do this has a curiously modern ring. They argue that rather than trying to talk to God we should try to listen to him. They have tried to convince me, she says, that we should contrive not to use our reasoning powers, but to be intent upon discovering what the Lord is working in the soul. "For my part I confess my lack of humility, but their arguments have never seemed to me good enough to lead me to accept what they say."[45]

Her reasons for refusing to accept the view that prayer at the beginning means essentially listening and not meditating are based both on reason and on her own experience. In the first place, until we are called to contemplation, there are many things for us still to do.

> If we are not quite sure that the King has heard us, or sees us, we must not stay where we are like ninnies, for there still remains a great deal for the soul to do. . . . The Lord wishes us to make requests of him and to remember that we are in his presence, for he knows what is fitting for us . . . penances, works of charity and prayers . . . We can practice for ourselves, as far as our miserable nature is capable of them.[46]

Furthermore, as St. John of the Cross also teaches,[47] the effort to still the understanding just does not work. "If the understanding did nothing it would experience much greater aridity and would grow more restless because of the effort caused by the cessation of thought."[48]

Secondly, she says that the effort to stop the understanding from working is painful, and all the interior activities should be gentle and peaceful. The soul should not try to force God's hand; it

45. *IC* IV.3.   46. Ibid.

47. [If we turn aside from meditation too soon, the soul will have no occupation], "but will be wholly idle, and there would be no way in which it could be said to be employed" (*Ascent* II.14.7).

48. Ibid. The rest of the discussion in this section is based on *IC* IV.3.

should resign itself insofar as it can to the will of God. Here St. Teresa is arguing that trying to make ourselves be quiet, or to make the mind a blank, produces not peace but disquiet. It may be true that meditation is sometimes hard work, but it is work done in conformity with our human nature, and it helps to develop our awareness of Christian truths and Christian living. Trying to force ourselves not to think is a subhuman activity that produces uneasiness, confusion, and often enough physical symptoms such as headaches.

The third reason for meditating and not trying to force a state of quietude is that the very effort the soul makes in order to cease from thought will only awaken thought and cause it to think a great deal. Focusing our attention on trying to be still, besides being subhuman, is also regressive behavior. It is introspective in a bad sense, for the self concentrates on its own efforts to be still. This activity brings neither self-knowledge nor knowledge of God.

The fourth reason is that prayer, on the Christian view, is concerned, not with our interior states, but with the reality of God and of His demands on us. The pleasing thing in God's eyes, she says in a very characteristic way, is our remembering His honor and glory and forgetting ourselves and our own profit and ease and pleasure. "And how can a person be forgetful of himself," she asks, "when he is taking such great care about his actions that he dare not even stir, or allow his understanding and desires to stir even for the purpose of desiring the greater glory of God or of rejoicing in the glory that is His." She continues: "God gave us our faculties to work with, and everything will have its due reward; there is no reason, then, for trying to cast a spell over them—they must be allowed to perform their office until God gives them a better one."[49]

We have seen that the beginning of a serious Christian life involves a struggle against the world, the flesh, and the Devil. The

49. Ibid.

effort to fulfil the law of Christ involves us in something like a civil war with ourselves. The prayer that helps to integrate the way we live with the moral demands of Christianity is meditation. There is more to meditation than an effort to be moral, but this is one of its facets. It is said that the Devil finds work for idle hands. Certainly he finds work for idle minds. The purpose of our prayer at this stage is to help us to withdraw from sin and resist the appetites. This requires that we use our heads to see our own lives in relation to the law of God. Then, we have to use our wills to try to keep this law. To induce a state of quietude by natural techniques is perfectly compatible with living an immoral life and even with refusing to admit the existence of Christian norms.

The final movement of meditation is often described as a decision to do some particular action that will bring us closer to living according to Christ's will for us. St. Francis de Sales calls this decision a resolution,[50] and it is this resolution which is directly applicable to Christian morality in an obvious way.

His argument for the necessity of a particular resolution in connection with meditation runs as follows. First of all, we consider some incident in the life of Christ, or some of His words, in order to move the affective part of our nature. One purpose of deliberately stirring our affective nature is to help us "to expand our hearts" as much as possible. For example, a meditation on our Lord's first words from the cross ("Father forgive them, for they know not what they do") will, he says, "doubtless excite in your soul a holy desire to imitate Him, namely, a desire to pardon your enemies and to love them."

This generalized sentiment of forgiveness and love, however, is not enough for effective Christian living. We have to bring our general reflections and generous desires into relation with the particular circumstances of our daily lives and decide to do something

---

50. *IDL* II.6 ("Of Affections and Resolutions"). This is how St. Francis describes the third part of meditation.

specific. Unless we do this, the prayer remains almost literally "up in the air," or abstract, and will have little effect on our lives. "You must not dwell upon these general reflections . . . without determining to reduce them to special and particular resolutions for your own correction and amendment" is how St. Francis puts it. It is by actually doing things, or not doing things, that we begin to develop steadiness and firmness in responding to the demands of Christian living. The resolutions that the saint encourages us to make are thus the way the general moral and religious principles of our faith are made effective in our own lives. It is clear that a prayer of meditation that culminates in a resolution is particularly suited for the beginnings of a serious effort to live the Christian life.

Growth in the love of God means growth in doing what He wants us to do. He wants us to love Him and to show that love by trying to develop a life in which the Christian virtues will be more and more evident. It may be the case that Catholics, possibly in reaction to what they understood as justification by faith, used to talk too much about the virtues in relation to the spiritual life. Trying to force God's hand and to imitate Christ by our own un-aided efforts is a Pelagian rather than a Catholic enterprise. Insofar as Catholics had really fallen into this way of thinking and acting, some sort of redress was necessary.

The years after the Second Vatican Council saw a determined effort to avoid an overly ascetical and even Pelagian approach to the spiritual life. It was often emphasized that it is the *Church* that is holy. The holiness of an individual is a participation in the holiness of the Mystical Body. It is the Church which is indefectibly holy, and it follows from this, as one writer puts it, "that the holiness of the individual is always a mere participation in the holiness of the Church, proclaiming to the world, as it must, the holiness of the Church."[51] This is a fine statement of an important

51. Wulf, "The Call of the Whole Church to Holiness," in Vorgrimler, *Commentary*, 1.263.

truth about the Church. It is in and through the Holy People of
God that the holiness of the individual is born, is nurtured, and
is perfected. The same writer then goes on to say: "Christian holiness is not primarily—much less exclusively—moral perfection,
heroic human virtue, but primarily and in the deepest sense the
glory and the love of God given to the redeemed without any
merit on their part."[52]

That is theologically correct, but views like this have been
badly used. Even though we receive the holiness of Christ not
directly but through the Church and its sacraments, nevertheless
it is individuals who receive it. Reacting against the fear of Pelagianism on one side, we have fallen into yet another way of thinking which is itself almost indistinguishable from the most extreme
ex opere operato thinking that the Council set out to correct. It often
seems to come across that, because it is the Church that is holy,
then it hardly matters what we do.

Even to speak of the quest for holiness is nowadays to invite
derision. Catholics seemingly have more important priorities to
keep them occupied. At first, after the Council, people argued
that, since the Church was holy, then it was presumptuous and
betrayed the mentality of a bookkeeper to worry too much about
how *I* behave. It was felt that fresh perspectives were opening up.
In these new, great, splendid, and wide-open spaces it seemed almost blasphemous to try to restrict the free spirit of man within
the narrow, petty, and inward-looking confines of a moral view
of life. It was thought, and it was said, that mature and responsible
Christians should have a broad view of things and should not concern themselves with the personal striving and the personal fail-
ures of people obsessed with an individualistic and law-oriented
morality. Perhaps, it was often added, it even shows a lack of trust-
ing faith to be concerned with what *I* do or don't do.

The new perspectives have done their work, and they seem

52. Ibid.

hardly adverted to any longer, much less questioned. Yet without an effort to live the moral law, to draw away from sin, and to practice the virtues, we are in the gravest danger of becoming self-serving hypocrites who, at best, use the Christian vocabulary to cover our own lack of generosity and self-sacrifice, and at worst use the religious profession to cover an immoral lifestyle. Let me cite the wise words of a modern Carmelite, Ruth Burrows.

Let us remind ourselves over and over again that holiness has to do with very ordinary things: truthfulness, courtesy, kindness, gentleness, consideration for others, contentment with our lot, honesty and courage in the face of life, reliability, dutifulness. Intent, as we think, on the higher reaches of spirituality, we can overlook the warp and woof of holiness.[53]

In sum, then, a belief in the holiness of the Church is no substitute for the effort of individuals to strive after holiness themselves. This striving after holiness means following Christ in an effort to imitate Him. We cannot imitate Christ unless we make war on the law of sin in ourselves and strive to obey the moral law. One of the most effective ways of trying to fulfil this Christian imperative is to meditate on the life of Christ and then go on to imitate Him more closely.

Catholicism claims to be true. Truth is not another word for authenticity. Authenticity may demand truth as a condition for its existence, and truth may produce authenticity as its fruit. But truth is concerned with knowing the way things are, and the only way that human beings can know is by an activity that involves language and the use of propositions. Right thinking about faith, a thinking that is based on truth, is the essential basis for our life of prayer. It is through meditation on God's revelation that we begin to assimilate revealed truth in a way that teaches us to live in the newly discovered world of faith, and to do so in such a

53. Burrows, *Interior Castle Explored,* 19.

way that it will gradually make us over into what God wants us to be.[54]

But progress is slow. St. Thomas says that it is "better to limp along the way than stride along off the way."[55] Most Christians have to be content with limping along the way, but that is not to say there is no progress toward the goal, nor that Christ's healing work does not effect at least a partial cure. "For a man who limps along the way, even if he only makes slow progress, comes to the end of the way."[56]

---

54. "Faith would achieve but little," wrote Edith Stein, "if it only instructed the understanding" (*Science of the Cross*, 88).

55. St. Thomas Aquinas, *Exposition on John*, chap. 14, lect. 2, cited in *LH* 3.315–17. The quotation is on p. 316.

56. Ibid., 3.316.

6 ⚘ The Friend

My love then appears as a noble companion

Who succours me and saves me from wretchedness;

He endows me with virtues that lead to salvation.

Can I leave hidden, unsung, the good He has wrought?

6.1 Taking too much for granted

At the beginning of this stage we find the soul more at peace. It has become detached from the will to sin, and begins to treat with God as a companion. Our Lord himself says in the Gospel, "I no longer call you servants . . . but I have called you friends."[1]

The landscape of the spiritual life seems familiar. We have learned to live without an attachment to mortal sin, and to avoid it as well. We have begun, as we say, to get it all together. God is a friend who comforts us, and is there when we need him. We practice the virtues in a quiet and ordered way. Often, it is a period when our work goes well, our friendships are steady, and we have no trouble saying with Browning, "God's in his Heaven, all's right with the world."

St. Teresa describes people in this state in the following way:

They avoid committing even venial sins; they love doing penance; they spend hours in recollection; they use their time well; they practice works

---

1. John 15:15.

of charity towards their neighbours; and they are very careful in their speech and in their dress, and in the government of the household, if they have one.[2]

It should not be supposed that everyone who has arrived at this condition fulfils it quite as well as St. Teresa's description might suggest. But the general lines are clear. This mode reflects the achievements of the person who has won a number of serious battles and now rejoices in a peaceful and successful life in the service of God.

The apparent absence of serious problems is, however, the source of another sort of difficulty. The carefully ordered existence begins to turn even the relationship with God into a routine. The prayers are said, the spiritual exercises are fulfilled, but gradually the zest seems to go out of our relationship with God. St. Teresa says this stage is often a period of great aridity in prayer because the soul refuses to continue to open the door any wider to God. God invites the soul, and the soul refuses to move. As a result, all the freshness and light of the spiritual life is darkened and may even be extinguished.

Part of the reason for this slowing down of the spiritual life is that people who have reached this stage are in danger of losing any sense that their efforts to lead a Christian life are really dependent on God. At the beginning of their conversion, they turned to God and poured out their heart in a simple petition for mercy and for help. Then, through the sacraments, Christ began to heal them of their worst sins. This faithful use of the sacraments was accompanied by meditation and penance, and these practices were an important element in their receiving Christ's healing.

As life begins to settle down, however, they begin to believe it is by their own efforts that they have established themselves as serious and responsible Christians. As a consequence, they are not particularly keen on taking up arms again in the Christian's war-

2. IC III. 1.

fare against self. They have established a self that is useful and moral, and they want no further losing of the self, even to find a better one. They have attained a certain peace and security, and they want to hold onto it. They are unwilling to give up their comfortable, friendly approach to God. They have become too much at ease in Zion, have begun to take God for granted, and their spiritual life is in danger of degenerating into artificiality, mere form, and coldness of heart. St. John of the Cross sums up people in this condition in the following way:

Thus they become bold with God, and lose holy fear, which is the key and custodian of all the virtues; and in some of these souls so many are the falsehoods and deceits which tend to multiply, and so inveterate do they grow, that it is very doubtful if such souls will return to the pure road of virtue and spirituality.[3]

Such a one has reached the limits of what the ascetical self can achieve, and God himself begins to take a more direct part in the lives of those seeking him. He does, that is, if the soul is prepared to open the door once again to his knocking.

This direct action of God is often experienced by us as an apparent failure in our life of prayer and is accompanied by an increasing distaste for our spiritual life as we have known it hitherto. Although we do not realize it at first, the time has now come to let God lead the way in the darkness. God begins to hold us so close to his heart, as Abbot Chapman says, that we can no longer see his face.[4] Our reaction to this new presence of God in our life should be one of gratitude. The gift of God must be met, not with a grudging acceptance, but with a prayer of thanksgiving for all "the good he has wrought me." This prayer of thanksgiving will help us to develop the patience and perseverance necessary to sustain the new presence and action of God. If we are patient and persevere, we will find that a new facility for prayer is gradually

3. *DN* II.2.3.
4. Chapman, *Spiritual Letters*, 60.

developed, and that the virtues of self-knowledge and humility have been taught us through the experience of our own weakness and poverty. The friend has been a noble companion and has begun to share with us the good which he has always possessed.

This third mode (of Jacopone's poem) might be called the mode of the incomplete synthesis. It has been developed through meditation and a certain way of life, both of which were necessary for the relationship with God to be stabilized. On the other hand, the struggle to welcome the Lord's appearing is not over, and we are in danger of deluding ourselves into thinking there is nothing new for us to learn or experience.

6.2 Christ's friendship

In the first letter of St. John, we read: "Beloved let us love one another; for love is of God, and he who loves is born of God and knows God. He who does not love does not know God; for God is love."[5] Our Lord has told us that the first and great commandment is to love God with all our mind and heart and strength, and to love our neighbor as ourself.[6] It is clear that this love, or charity, which we are supposed to have for God and our neighbor is a central Christian concept. It is not so clear, however, how we are to understand this love.

The love we are commanded to give to God and to our neighbor is not something of which we are capable if left to the strengths and capacities of our own nature. The love of God has been poured into our hearts, says St. Paul, and as a result we are able to cry Abba, Father.[7] In a more extended version of the same teaching, we find St. Augustine saying: "In order that we might receive the love whereby we should love, we were ourselves loved, while as yet we had it not. . . . For we would not have the where-

5. 1 John 4:7.   6. See Matthew 22:37–40.
7. See Galatians 4:6.

withal to love Him, unless we received it from Him by His first loving us."[8]

The texts from St. Paul and St. Augustine show us in a forcible way that charity is both the gift of God and a human virtue. That is, it is a human virtue in the sense that it is we who do the loving: "charity is a movement of the soul towards enjoying God for his own sake."[9] Yet the capacity to love God and our neighbor is possible only because our acts of love are the result of endowments God has given to us.

Jacopone here likens the appearing of the Lord to that of a friend. Indeed, friendship plays a central role in St. Thomas's understanding of the virtue of charity. Aristotle had taught that friendship was necessary for a properly human life: "For without friends," he said, "no one would choose to live." The rich and the powerful, the poor and the helpless, the young, those in the prime of life as well as the old, all need friends. But friendship, he goes on to say, is not only necessary, it is also noble: "For we praise those who love their friends, and it is thought to be a fine thing to have many friends; and again we think it is the same people that are good men and are friends."[10]

St. Thomas used Aristotle's discussion of friendship in his analysis of our love for God and our neighbor. He used, that is, a relationship that is familiar to us from our own experience to illustrate the deepest and most mysterious relationship of all. The love of friendship is, for Aristotle and St. Thomas, a settled disposition of wishing the other person well. Such a friendship is recognized by both parties. That is, it must be reciprocal, for unrequited love is not friendship. Furthermore, it is stable and not a matter of the passing moment. The virtue of friendship requires

---

8. St. Augustine, *On the Grace of Christ* XXVI.27, cited in Erich Przywara, *An Augustine Synthesis*, 345–46.

9. This text from *De Doctrina Christiana* III.10, is used by St. Thomas in 2a2ae 23, 2.

10. Aristotle, *NE* VIII.1, 1155a

time and close contact in order to develop. The good will, which
is mutual and stable, is based on the goodness or worth that each
party possesses and that each sees in the other. In other words,
what knits the friends together is the same goodness shared by
each. For this reason, says Aristotle, a friend is called another self.
That is not to say that the other person becomes a kind of appen-
dage or dependent. It means that there is something shared and
admired in both that becomes a common property or quality of
both.

> Perfect friendship is the friendship of men who are good, and alike in
> virtue; for these wish well alike to each other *qua* good, and they are good
> in themselves. Now those who wish well to their friends for their sake
> are most truly friends; for they do this by reason of their own nature and
> not incidentally; therefore their friendship lasts as long as they are good—
> and goodness is an enduring thing.[11]

It is this sort of friendship that St. Thomas takes as the basis
for his discussion of the virtue of charity. Friendship with God is
possible because He shares his beatitude or happiness with us.
This beatitude becomes the shared good that each possesses and
each loves. "Accordingly, it is clear that charity is a kind of friendship that men have toward God."[12]

I do not think what St. Thomas says is particularly clear to us
today. Not that Thomas is wrong, but he puts the truth in a way
we find difficult to grasp, because we are not accustomed to think
of friendship as willing the good of another person. We tend automatically to regard it in the way it affects us, and so we think
of it as pleasant or useful. To look on it as an activity, and as an
activity that requires at least the striving after what is good, seems
foreign to our way of thought. This is not to imply that the love
of friendship exists in isolation from the useful and the pleasant,

---

11. *NE* VIII.3, 1156b7–12.

12. 2a2ae 23, 1: "Unde manifestum est quod caritas amicitia quaedam est
hominis ad Deum."

for these enter into any real friendship, as Aristotle clearly points
out:

And each is good without qualification and to his friend, for the good
are both good without qualification and useful to each other. So too they
are pleasant; for the good are pleasant both without qualification and to
each other, since to each his own activities and others like them are plea-
surable, and the actions of the good *are* the same or like.[13]

We love God with a love that includes elements of all three sorts
of friendship. Ideally, we should move from a love motivated by
the fact that God is useful to us, through one based largely on the
fact that friendship with God is pleasant to us, toward one dominated by the goodness of God, which he shares with us. But that
is not to say that this progress will be a steady one, or that sometimes there are not considerations other than the very highest
which operate in our friendship with our Maker and Redeemer.

The analysis of friendship throws light on the matter of following and imitating Christ. In the Catholic tradition, following
Christ includes an element of trying to imitate Him. Now we
could imitate Him only if He were to share his own goodness with
us. In the love of friendship we do share, and not merely meta-
phorically or figuratively, in that same goodness which He possesses. Thus, imitation of Him becomes a possibility and not a
blasphemy.

Sometimes objections to the idea of imitating Christ are based
on an appreciation of the greatness and holiness of God; but they
are also founded on a view of the Fall that teaches that we are
incapable of doing anything with or to our human nature that will
improve it in the eyes of God. On the Catholic view, as we have
seen, it is possible with grace, and with our cooperation with
grace, gradually to reform our nature. This slow reform is what
the tradition means by the imitation of Christ. We may admit that

13. Aristotle, *NE* VIII.3, 1156b13–18.

the notion is dangerous in the sense that we can easily delude ourselves as to the extent and success of our efforts. It may also be more than dangerous if we imagine that we are successfully imitating Christ by our own unaided efforts. But if we believe that friendship with God is possible, then we have to develop in such a way that God becomes, to recall Aristotle's phrase, "another self" for us. And such a friendship is possible only because we are in fact, and not just in theory, capable of imitating the Lord who took our nature so that we could take His.

6.3 Sloth

It is a fact about our human nature that familiarity breeds contempt. Routine and good habits are essential for the success of any human activity, and we have seen that without the practice of meditation and the effort to lead a good life, there is no growth in the knowledge and the love of Christ. On the other hand, it is just when this growth has begun to take root that we are in danger of taking it for granted. Perhaps we are not so foolish as to think that all our problems are over. Unfortunately, though, we probably do have a secret thought that we can handle by ourselves whatever the future holds.

The inevitable result of this condition, and of this secret self-satisfaction, is a cooling in our life of prayer. The earlier stages in the battle of the spiritual life now seem almost to belong to another person. There may be no explicit avowal that we have achieved our victories by ourselves, but a marked degree of complacency begins to infect our relationship with God. That is, the more sure of ourselves we become, the less we feel we need God. Not unnaturally, if we do not feel we need God, then our spiritual life becomes cold and empty. In addition to this coldness and emptiness, a kind of sadness often seems to sweep over us when we begin to think about anything to do with God or the spiritual life. This feeling can even reinforce our half-admitted thought that we can go it alone. If the spiritual life, that is, is experienced as a source of uneasiness and discomfort, then we are all too liable to conclude that it is something that inhibits getting on with the real job to be done.

This condition was traditionally called *accidie*. It is a much more common sin than we might suppose, and in the sense that it was used in the tradition there is hardly anyone who escapes its pull. Accidie is quite compatible with a great deal of frenetic activity. So while the term includes what we would call laziness, it is not laziness in the sense of never doing anything. Accidie, or sloth, is sadness and unease about God and the things of God. It has several different effects.

Cassian, who, as we have seen, was one of St. Philip's favorite authors, says that we may describe sloth as "weariness or distress of heart."[14] This weariness or distress of heart produces a laziness that is not only physical but spiritual as well. He uses the verse from the psalm that runs "My soul slept from weariness" to illustrate that the root of the trouble is in the soul, not in the body. "In truth," he says, "the soul which is wounded by the shaft of this passion does sleep, as regards all contemplation of the virtues and insight of the spiritual senses."[15] Nonetheless, although sloth is essentially a disease of the spirit, it finds expression in external activity as well. It has three principal observable effects. Sloth produces "dislike of the place and disgust with the cell, and disdain for the brethren who dwell with him. . . . It also makes a man lazy and sluggish about all manner of work."[16] Sloth, then, is characterized externally by three elements: an unwillingness to stay put, dislike of the people with whom we must associate, and laziness.

And so the wretched soul, embarrassed by such contrivances of the enemy, is disturbed, until, worn out by the spirit of accidie, as if by some strong battering ram, it either learns to sink into slumber, or, driven out

14. Cassian, *The Institutes* X.1.   15. Ibid., X.4.
16. Ibid., X.2.

from the confinement of its cell, accustoms itself to seek for consolation under these attacks in visiting some brother, only to be afterwards weakened the more by this remedy which it seeks for the present.[17]

The description should be recognizable. If we change the word cell to room or office or study, it could have been written yesterday. There is a kind of weariness or distress of heart that sweeps over us. This weariness or distress produces three observable symptoms. First, our work seems boring and unprofitable and we find we cannot stand our office or study, and so either we get into bed and go to sleep, or else we leave our room and look for someone to talk to. The people we find, however, seem to us to be covered with the same pall of boredom as is our room. Although they are necessary to us, we do not really like them and we treat them with disdain. Finally, we can observe the evidence of sloth from the obvious fact that we are not working and our work does not get done. Of course, this only makes things worse. Everything gets more stale, and the work seems more boring when we get back to it. The whole thing is made worse by the fact that there is now even more work to do than there was when we first ran away from it.

Accidie, then, is fundamentally a disease of the spirit. St. Thomas quotes St John Damascene's definition that accidie is a "kind of oppressive sorrow"; this sorrow, says Thomas, so depresses a man that he wants to do nothing and "thus acid things are also cold."[18]

> Sloth spreads its bottomless cold
> And the soul, bewildered,
> Cut off from the comforts it knew,
> Is dissolved in terror.[19]

It is important and instructive to see how much attention the classical tradition paid to this sin of sloth. The early writers on the

17. Ibid., X.3.   18. 2a2ae 35, 1.
19. *Laud* 13.

spiritual life saw that laziness attacked not only the practical aspects of existence, but also our spiritual life and our relationship with God. Accidie is not fundamentally a distaste for doing our work in the world. Rather, it is a spirit of weariness or distress, which, if allowed to grow, can kill the joy and peace our faith brings to us. It is quite possible to fulfil in a very adequate way a responsible position even in the Church, but still to have given way to accidie. A grim sense of duty and pleasure in the exercise of managerial skills are quite compatible with an inner emptiness concerning the things of God.

St. Thomas emphasizes this aspect of the matter, and looks on accidie as sorrow concerning spiritual things. That is, boredom, weariness, and indifference over work of any kind spreads to spiritual goods and casts a grey pall over the enjoyment and zest that living in the friendship of Christ is supposed to bring to us. In its most concentrated form, or in its essence, accidie consists in being sad about God's goodness in relation to us personally. "To be sorrowful about the divine good, which charity rejoices in, now that does belong to a special vice. We call it spiritual apathy."[20]

In the final analysis, accidie leads to a spiritual suicide. This suicide consists in rejecting the friendship with God, which is the life of divine charity that God pours into our soul. Sloth, having thus struck at the root and the source of our spiritual life, kills the fruits of the Holy Spirit, which are love, joy, peace, patience, kindness, goodness, faithfulness, gentleness, and self-control.[21]

Given that accidie is both deadly and pervasive, it is clear that it has to be fought, but if we are to fight it, we must first recognize it. We have to be able to distinguish it, on the one hand, from the mere feeling of sadness, and, on the other, from God's action on us in the dark nights of the senses and the spirit.

Some people are temperamentally more light-hearted and easygoing than others. Some are more inclined to a quietness that may

20. 2a2ae 35, 2.   21. See Galatians 5:22–23.

seem to be a kind of sadness. Furthermore, everyone at times has something to be sad about. Cassian and St. Thomas are not talking about this feeling of sadness, or what the Scholastics would have called the passion of sadness. What they are talking about is how we handle the temptation to let this feeling grow into an attitude, or a disposition, or a vice that colors everything we do—or do not do.

The differences between accidie and the symptoms of the dark nights are to be distinguished in a preliminary way, first, by a difference in the behavior of the person concerned. The person really suffering under the hand of God practices the virtues and fights the vices. The person who has capitulated to accidie and claims to be experiencing a dark night is suffering not only from sloth but also from self-deception. The difference, in the abstract anyway, is clear.

It is not only that the behavior in the two cases is different; so is the result. Accidie unchecked leads to spiritual death, but the operation of the dark night leads to "peace, habitual remembrance and thought of God, cleanness and purity of soul and the practice of the virtues."[22]

Accidie, then, is neither the passion of sadness nor the operation of God's loving care over us in the dark night. Accidie is an ever-present danger for the Christian, especially for the Christian who is bound in some formal way to the service of the Church. It kills, and it kills more often than not without ever having been recognized.

6.4 The dark night of the senses

In one of his *Lauds* Jacopone wrote of the apparent disappearance of God.

Love, beloved Love, why have You left me?
Tell me, Love, why have You left me in grief and uncertainty?

22. *DN* I.13.6.

Is it my vileness that repels You? Let me make amends.
If I reshape myself, will You not come back?

Love, why did You give my heart such sweetness,
Only to strip it then of joy?
To give and take back is not chivalrous.
I speak as if out of my mind, but with good reason.

Suddenly bereft of You, I know not where I am;
Confused, I look for You all about,
Look for the sweetness that all unawares,
Little by little was taken from me.[23]

We have seen that one of the elements in our struggle against
the world, the flesh, and the devil consists in a deliberate effort on
our part to deny ourselves so that we may live a more Christ-like
life. In our struggle to live as Christ wants us to live, we engage
in a warfare against all those parts of ourselves that pull us away
from Him. We avoid the occasions of sin; we work at building up
settled dispositions that will lead promptly and efficiently to good
action; we are faithful in our reception of the sacraments and in
our life of prayer; and we mortify ourselves so that we may more
readily fulfil the law of Christ.

At the beginning, with the grace of God, this vigorous discipline bears fruit. Our warfare with the world, the flesh, and the
devil shows every sign of success, and it seems as though victory
is in our grasp. But then we seem to get stuck, and the freshness
and the vitality of our conversion to Christ dries up and withers
away. Although this may be due to sloth, there is another and a
deeper reason for the grey pall that often settles on us at this stage:
We have reached the limits of what we can do by ourselves in our
efforts to put on the "new man, created after the likeness of God
in true righteousness and holiness."[24] Out of the warfare against
our enemies has been developed a self that is no longer the helpless

23. *Laud* 67, "The Soul Laments the Disappearance of God."
24. Ephesians 4:24.

and often consenting victim of the passions and the needs of the moment. Nonetheless, the self we have begun to restore with God's help falls short of what God requires of us; if we imagine that our warfare is over, we are making a fundamental mistake. The sins we have successfully fought in their more obvious forms now return in a way that is harder to recognize and even more difficult to deal with. At this juncture, everything can go terribly wrong, because we are in danger of making a radically false estimate of the value of the self that has been built up through its struggles to live a Christian life. In fact, the self is still very much imprisoned by desire; its condition is dangerous because this is not obvious to it. Unless care is taken, the self at this stage lives in self-deception and hypocrisy, because it imagines itself to be what it is not.

The development of the ascetical life is essential to provide the basis of Christian living. On the other hand, this development is centered in building up the self. Once, that is, we realize that it is *my* pride, *my* anger, *my* lust that I have to overcome, and that this warfare is on home ground, then the home ground becomes a central aspect in the situation. The self, for example, seeks revenge, but the self, perhaps after a difficult and continuing struggle, successfully resolves not to take revenge. Well and good, but one does not need to be a psychologist to see that in one sense the self is still seeking its own way and the gratification of its own desires. It says "no" to sin, and at the same time it says "yes" to its desire to live an ordered and rational moral life. The achievements of the ascetical self are the victories of beginners in the spiritual life. The best that can be achieved, even with grace, is to transfer the satisfactions of the self from a lower to a higher or more spiritual level of self-indulgence. St. John of the Cross says that "however assiduously the beginner practices the mortification in himself of all these actions and passions of his, he can never completely succeed—very far from it."[25]

25. *DN* I.7.5.

The problem seems to be that the self that does the mortifying escapes the mortification. As this self becomes stronger and more successful in living a virtuous life, it falls prey to a spiritualized form of the very sins it has successfully combatted in their obvious and gross form. Pride, avarice, lust, envy, and sloth all come back, and they are all too likely to take possession of the very self that has tried to get rid of them. The fact that the self has conquered the more obvious expression of these sins only makes them harder to recognize and so more difficult to deal with.[26] This built-in dynamic of self-gratification affects even the practice of the virtues. The love of friendship, for example, is more generally talked about than practiced, because it is based on a giving of the good possessed by the lover to the one loved. Yet all human love is based on need. From the earliest times when men began to think about these things, our human love has been viewed as based on need and poverty. Once we begin to understand our own solitude, or to experience it, we cannot bear it. Physical lust is one way of trying to evade the solitude. This escape does not work for very long, but a lot of people discover this only when they find it impossible to do without the physical expression of their need to escape the silence, and somehow to affirm the reality of their own self by imposing it on another.

Not all love is lust, and the Catholic tradition did not need Freud to teach it that the human being is not a ghost in a machine, but an ensouled body. The profession of pure and disinterested love is usually greeted with a certain degree of scepticism, and rightly so. Even the best of human loves is restless and full of hunger, and it is always in danger of devouring and destroying the object of its love, in order to appease its emptiness. Furthermore, it is in constant danger of leading us into self-deception. People

26. St. John of the Cross calls these spiritualized versions of the capital sins "the faults of beginners," and almost half of the text of the *Dark Night of the Senses* in taken up by his discussion of them.

who want something very badly cannot live—so they think—without what they want. The hurt and self-destructiveness brought about by this emotional and confused love is incalculable. It breaks up marriages, it often ruins perfectly useful and happy lives, and it is one of the places in which the effects of original sin are empirically observable.

This desire to possess for ourselves infects even our relationship to God. Religion goes wrong when it becomes the ultimate satisfaction. Von Balthasar puts this in a dramatic way when he writes, "We are capable of encircling in the narrow spell of our ego not only our fellow-men, but also the Creator himself, degrading him to the role of a lever for our egoistic yearning."[27]

In the Gospels there is the description of the unclean spirit who leaves a man "and wanders through the waterless places seeking rest, but he finds none."

Then he says, "I will return to my house from which I came." And when he comes he finds it empty, swept, and put in order. Then he goes and brings with him seven other spirits more evil than himself, and they dwell there; and the last state of that man becomes worse than the first.[28]

A person in this condition finds it hard to pray, and sloth begins to harden the heart. Whether the individual is working at extirpating vice and building up the virtues, or is more directly engaged in trying to practice the love of God, the self not only keeps getting in the way but threatens to take over the whole operation. Both morality and religion are in danger of being sacrificed to the self's possessiveness, and there does not seem much the self can do about the situation.[29] The failure of the individual to recognize

27. Von Balthasar, *Heart of the World,* 40.

28. Matthew 12:43–45; Luke 11:24–26.

29. See Turner, "St. John of the Cross and Depression." See also von Balthasar, *Heart of the World,* 96: "Under the weight of my good conscience and under the ample bosom of my great heart, the voice of Truth has been stifled. It's been silent for a long time now."

this condition, a condition perfectly obvious to those who know him, is the source of the distrust and even hatred with which quite sane and sensible people often view the person who seems to take his morality and his religion too seriously.

The only way we can escape this self-constructed prison is by accepting a love that is given to us in mercy, a love we do not and cannot control.[30] It is God's love for us, and not our love for God, that will "succour us and save us from our wretchedness." This love of God first shows itself to us in our life of prayer, as God in His mercy begins to act in a direct way on the soul.[31] This direct action of God is at first very difficult to perceive. What is perceived are the effects of this new presence, which are both disconcerting and unpleasant; they seem to be a very poor response on God's part to our need for His friendship.

This presence of God brings with it darkness and confusion. Suddenly the awareness of God's presence seems to have been taken away from us. Our spiritual life, which brought such strength and consolation, now appears pointless and without comfort. St. John of the Cross puts it this way:

When they are going about these spiritual exercises with the greatest delight and pleasure, and when they believe the sun of Divine favour is shin-

30. Cf. von Balthasar, *Heart of the World,* 40–41: "For only love redeems. Yet, what love is God only knows, for God is love. There are not two sorts of love. There is not, alongside God's love, another, human love. Rather, when God so determines and he proclaims his Word, love then descends, love then flows out into the void, and God has set up his claim and his emblem over every love."

31. St. John of the Cross uses the soul in the scholastic sense of the first principle of life in living things about us (see St. Thomas, *Summa Theologia* 1a 75, 1). Understood in this broad way, plants and animals have souls, and man has a rational soul. In virtue of his one, rational, soul the human being exercises the vital activities of plants and animals as well as those which are linked with the possession of mind. The dark night of the senses cleanses the sensitive part of the one soul, the dark night of the spirit purges the intellectual aspects of that same soul. See below, 7.2.

ing most brightly upon them, God turns all this light of theirs into darkness, and shuts against them the door and the source of the sweet spiritual water which they were tasting in God whensoever and for as long as they desired.[32]

Now it is obvious that such a state may be the result of back-sliding. Sloth and discouragement may have brought us to this state, and they are certainly not the result of God's action on us. St. John of the Cross, fully alive to this possibility, lists three signs to determine that this condition is not arising from "sins and imperfections, or from weakness and lukewarmness, or from some bad humour or indisposition of the body."[33]

In the first place, the bleakness and lack of pleasure in the things of God has also to be matched by a similar bleakness and lack of interest in the things of this world. If our hearts are really fixed on some temporal satisfaction, then we quickly become fed up with spiritual matters. It should be made clear that St. John is talking not about temptation, but about attachment to a satisfaction we are unwilling to give up. The usual reaction to the sin or imperfection which results from consenting to this attachment is a disgust with self, including our efforts to lead a Christian life. If the sin is not a particularly gross one, then this may manifest itself as an impatience with self at the slowness of our spiritual progress. But in both cases the spiritual tedium we then experience is self-induced. We have fixed our desires on the things of this world, we have become fed up with ourselves, and this over-flows into our relationship with God.

The next sign is the positive side of the first one. The effect on us of the aridity and the darkness should be to induce a deep sense that we are not serving God, and this causes us pain and grief. At such times, St. John says, "the memory is ordinarily centred upon God, with painful care and solicitude, thinking that it is not serving God, but is backsliding, because it finds itself without sweetness in the things of God."[34] When this sign is present, we find that we desire to be quiet and alone, "without being able to think of any particular thing or having the desire to do so." Once again, of course, there may be all sorts of natural explanations for this state, and it may be accompanied by melancholy and a pervasive sense of the drabness of life. If, however, there is at the same time a deep sense that God and the things of God are what really matter, then we can be assured that our condition, at least in part, is the result of God's action on us.

Finally, we find that we cannot meditate. It is not a question of not wanting to, it is a matter of not being able to. God leaves people in this condition "so completely in the dark they know not whither to go with their sensible imagination and meditation; for they cannot advance a step in meditation, as they were wont to do aforetime."[35] Abbot Chapman, it seems to me, has the matter right when he writes that "the essence of the night of the senses is that the senses get into a night, in which they can't be used."[36] The world seems dreary and unattractive, God seems remote, puzzling yet somehow important, and when we come to pray we find we cannot use our imagination. Everything, as St. John says, seems to have gone wrong with us.

This is clearly not what we might have expected from a serious effort to serve God more seriously. Nor, again, does "everything having gone wrong" seem like much of a description of how God saves us from our wretchedness.

We must not imagine that any of this is new with St. John of the Cross. But he was putting a tradition of teaching about Christian prayer into a precise and accessible form. The fourteenth-

34. *DN* I.9.3.   35. *DN* I.8.3.

36. Chapman, *Spiritual Letters,* 281. The passage continues: "St John of the Cross means by 'senses,' all that satisfies the sensual and sensitive part of man; i.e. the imagination (by the help of which the intellect works, in this life), and the emotions and feelings which come from it. So long as these can work, a man *can* meditate, and *ought* to."

century Dominican Johannes Tauler gave a short and eloquent expression of this tradition when he wrote:

From this pursuit of God . . . keen anguish results. When a man is plunged into this anxiety and becomes aware of this pursuit of God in his soul, it is then without doubt that Jesus comes and enters into him. But when one does not feel this pursuit or experience this anguish, Jesus does not come.[37]

St. John and St. Teresa both teach that the scarcity of contemplatives is to be explained by the fact that people are unwilling to face the suffering of the dark night. The apparent withdrawal of the friendship of God is more desolate, lonely, and painful than can be imagined beforehand. The hard beginnings of the direct approach of God seem like the end of the sunny, deep, and tender relationship that has gradually been built up between God and the soul. Jacopone wrote of this change in "The Lament of the Soul for Grace in Hiding."[38]

Who will weep and lament with me?
Let me find someone who will take pity on me,
Someone to whom I can voice my anguish.
O God of righteousness, why have You hardened Your heart?

No longer can I find that compassion
That always led me back to the heavenly court.
I hear the gate as it shuts,
And ingratitude bars me entrance.

Neither tears nor sighs nor prayer nor meditation
Will prepare the way for my return.
O my wretched and forlorn heart,
No words can express your pain!

Tongue cannot say,
Nor can mind conceive;

37. Cited in Garrigou-Lagrange, *The Three Ages of the Spiritual Life*, 2.35. The excerpt is from a sermon by Tauler for the Second Sunday in Lent.
38. *Laud* 66.

They only approach the threshold of pain—
Pain deeper and wider than the sea.

Contemplating my own grief I weep,
The dry tears of a heart in ruins.
That precious, inaccessible sweetness—
Where has it gone?

6.5 Self-knowledge and thanksgiving

God's action on the soul in the dark night of the senses is partly
punitive and partly educative. We need a sharp reminder that we
tend to become careless about the things of God. If our friendship
with God continues on a sunny and equable plain, then we begin
to forget that the friend is also the all-holy Word of God before
whom even the angels tremble. We begin to make God over in
our minds in a way that suits our own self-image and our own
needs. As St. John of the Cross puts it, we begin to measure God
by ourselves, and not ourselves by God.

Even a small dose of the dark night quickly teaches us the foolishness of this attitude. We are punished for our presumption in
trying to treat God as an equal, or even worse, as a convenience.
But the suffering of this night is not so much to punish us as to
teach us how to behave better in the presence of God. The aridities
and trials through which we have passed have altered our reactions
both to God and to ourselves. We begin to have what Newman
would have called a real assent to the truth that God is good and
we are not.

Many books on the spiritual life lay it down that we should
begin with a recognition that we are sinners and that forgiveness
and peace come only from the mercy of the good and all-powerful
God. We may accept this, and we may repeat it as sincerely as we
are able, but our acceptance of the truth does not go very deep. I
may try to force myself to accept the biblical teaching that my
particular heart is "deceitful above all things, and desperately cor-

rupt,"[39] but usually at the beginning I find the thought so distasteful that I put it aside.

The trouble is that we do not know ourselves well enough to recognize our sinfulness. The fundamental change that is wrought by the dark night of the senses is a reassessment, by ourselves, of who we are. "This is the first and principal benefit caused by this arid and dark night of contemplation: the knowledge of oneself and of one's misery."[40] When things were going well for us, as we thought, then we found in God "much pleasure, consolation and support." And, along with this pleasure in our prayer, there also went an assurance and satisfaction that we were serving God and doing his work. Once we have experienced a serious inability to pray in a way that brings consolation, then we also quickly lose the sense that we are helping to spread the kingdom of God in any very effective way. Our prayer seems pointless, and our work appears to have little profit. That is the way things seem to us, and that, St. John says, is the truth of the matter. The soul now considers itself as nothing and experiences no satisfaction in itself, "for it sees that it does nothing of itself, neither can do anything."

And the smallness of this self-satisfaction, together with the soul's affliction at not serving God, is considered and esteemed by God as greater than all the consolations which the soul formerly experienced and the works which it wrought, however great they were, inasmuch as they were the occasion of many imperfections and ignorances.[41]

So out of the painful darkness has grown a real awareness of the truth of the Church's teaching about man. The words of Jeremiah no longer seem like disagreeable and misanthropic ravings from an alien culture, but rather the sober statement of the truth. We now know that the heart of man really is deceitful and desperately corrupt. We know it is true because the kind friend has

39. Jeremiah 17:9.   40. *DN* I.12.2.
41. Ibid.

a severe side and he has forced us to look into the depths of our own being.

Knowledge about ourselves, then, will engender humility. When we are forced to see ourselves as we really are, then pride and an overestimation of our talents and abilities will begin to seem false and will be recognized as very real obstacles in our progress toward union with God.

It may be objected that the arguments of St. John of the Cross complicate a process that is really a very simple one, but also make it unnecessarily painful and dreary. We are often told today to get in touch with ourselves. Once we have done this, it is implied, we will find both that most of our difficult problems will disappear and also that the self we find will be a consolation and support to us. So, it is argued, let us forget all this talk about dark nights, suffering, and self-distaste. Accept yourself as you are and develop your potential.

There is an element of truth in this position. The purpose of self-knowledge is not to cripple its possessor, or to make him hate himself. Both St. John and St. Teresa were quite clear that the purpose of self-knowledge is to free us. To free us, that is, so that we can love God as He deserves to be loved for His own sake. On the other hand, they hold by the truth that self-knowledge is hard to come by and, once come by, is not consoling.

The opposite of self-knowledge is self-deception. It is difficult to develop a satisfactory theory of self-deception, because the person deceived is also the person doing the deceiving. The person, that is, in self-deception knows, as deceiver, what he does not know as victim of deceit. The problem then resolves itself into how the self-deceiver can do something intentionally without at the same time being aware of so doing. However we account for self-deception, its existence is obvious. There is the mother who at one level seems to know all about what an unpleasant little liar her son is, but at another level really seems to believe that he is God's gift to humanity and should be excused every fault of whatever kind. We say she is self-deceived about her son, and so she is. This self-deception is particularly obvious in moral matters. People enunciate a particular moral principle to be binding on everyone, and consciously disobey it themselves. When this is done clearly and lucidly, we have a case of hypocrisy.[42] However, more often than not, there is an element of self-deception involved in this behavior. The self-deceiver seems to blind himself to the fact that the principle applies to him, or else convinces himself that his particular case is not an instance of the moral behavior he condemns. Religious people are all too easy a prey to this sort of self-deception.

One of the lessons of St. John of the Cross is that suffering strips away the various artifices of self-deception that we build up and forces us to look at ourselves as we really are. There is, as Plato said, a lie in the soul. This lie is in the soul of the self-deceiver, who refuses to live in the truth either about himself or anything else. Aridity in prayer and a sense that we have lost our way helps to remove self-deception and the lie in the soul. Self-deception enters into our relationship with God. We strike attitudes before God, we try to leave out all those parts of ourselves which we suspect would not please him (and certainly would not please us if we were to focus our attention on them). We are in constant danger of presenting a self to God that bears little resemblance to what we really are. And, to make matters worse, we more than half believe this false image of ourselves to be the real *I*. We refuse to recognize that the self that sins, that loses its temper, that is unchaste, that is backbiting, that is mean and ungenerous, is as much the real *I* as are any other qualities we might possess. Until the dark night begins to take away our self-satisfaction and strip us of our illusions, we do not have the means or the courage even to begin to live in the truth. It is true, however,

---

42. I have tried to deal with this question at some length in *Duty and Hypocrisy in Hegel's Phenomenology of Mind,* chap. 5. "Conscience and Hypocrisy."

that if we concentrate only on our weaknesses and sins, then we will have escaped self-deception only to end up as cripples of another sort. If we live only with the dry and comfortless taste of self-knowledge, we will fall prey to what St. Teresa calls "cowardice, pusillanimity and fear." In order that our self-knowledge might free us rather than cripple us, she advises us not only to accept the self-knowledge that the dark night brings, but, in addition, to fix our minds on the greatness and the purity of God.

For although, as I say, it is through the abundant mercy of God that the soul studies to know itself yet one can have too much of a good thing, as the saying goes, and believe me, we shall reach much greater heights of virtue by thinking upon the virtue of God than if we stay in our own little plot of ground and tie ourselves down to it completely.[43]

St. John teaches the same message. Out of self-knowledge there flows a deeper knowledge of God. To remain merely with self-knowledge is to miss the point of the difficulties and trials of the spiritual life. It is God we seek and it is God we will find in the obscurity and wretchedness of our own knowledge of ourselves.

So we have now arrived at this, that from this arid night there first of all comes self-knowledge, whence, as from a foundation, rises this other knowledge of God. For which cause Saint Augustine said to God: "Let me know myself, Lord, and I shall know Thee." For, as the philosophers say, one extreme can be well known by another.[44]

The experience of the dark night of the senses that leads to a deeper knowledge not only of ourselves but of God leads Jacopone to write "Can I leave hidden, unsung, the good He has wrought?" and this practice of thanksgiving is one aspect, or movement, of prayer. St. Paul in the Letter to the Colossians says: "As therefore you received Christ Jesus the Lord, so live in him, rooted and built up in him and established in the faith, just as you were taught, abound-

43. *IC* I.2.   44. *DN* I.12.5.

ing in thanksgiving."[45] Again he says, in the same letter: "Continue steadfastly in prayer, being watchful in it with thanksgiving."[46]

When someone gives us something, the natural unspoiled human response is to be grateful: gratitude is the proper response for favors received. Furthermore, one of the means by which we hold onto the reality of God's particular providence in our lives is by practicing the prayer of thanksgiving. If we believe in the God of Christianity, we acknowledge that all we have comes from God: "Do not be deceived, my beloved brethren. Every good and perfect gift is from above, coming down from the Father of lights with whom there is no variation or shadow due to change."[47] Each one of us has many things to be grateful for, and it is a good exercise from time to time to try to enumerate them. All too often it is only when we lose something, or somebody, that we realize how blessed we in fact were. One of the best ways of keeping our spiritual life fresh and vital is to thank the Lord for what we have in fact received. We thus make ourselves more deeply aware of the reality of God who cares for each one of us as an individual. In the same way that a temptation, if we resist it, can become the occasion of drawing nearer to our Creator, so the grateful recognition of the gifts of God leads us at the same time from the gift to the Giver. Francisco de Osuna, whose writings had such a great influence on St. Teresa, expresses this point in the following way:

Faithfully remember the gifts bestowed by nature as well as those you enjoy by chance and grace and by the promised glory that, unless you happen to lose it through your own fault, is as certain as the rest. Think intently about the special and general graces from the Lord and admit truthfully that you received them from his hand. Preserve them assiduously in greatest possible purity and love them dearly, but even more, love him who so blessed you.[48]

---

45. Colossians 2:6.   46. Colossians 4:2.
47. James 1:17.
48. De Osuna, *The Third Spiritual Alphabet* II.3. The *CCC* teaches the same:

Giving thanks takes three forms, the first of which is by our deeds, the second by our hearts, and the third by our words.

The first way of thanking God for what he has done is by trying to use his gifts in our lives: "We can . . . say that thanksgiving through deed is to serve God with the talents with which he endowed us, and an excellent way of proving gratitude, therefore, is to make good use of the grace the Lord gives us."[49]

The second way of giving thanks to God pertains to the heart, and it is the "frequent and loving attention to favours already enjoyed, those promised, and even the ones lost through sin, for you are to be no less grateful for them than for those you safeguarded."[50] We protect the gifts God has given us by keeping them in our heart, by quietly going out to the Giver of all good gifts through the careful, tender, and prayerful movements of a grateful heart.

The third way we show gratitude toward God is through the words in which we recount the favors God has done for us.

I will bless the Lord at all times;
   his praise shall ever be in my mouth.
My soul makes its boast to the Lord;
   let the afflicted hear and be glad.
O magnify the Lord with me,
   and let us exalt his name together![51]

There is a natural movement of gratitude for gifts that we perceive as good. We can recognize a natural link between what we see as good and gratitude for these good things. It is much more difficult to see any link between gratitude and things we perceive as hurtful or evil that may happen to us.

We should thank the Lord in adversity as in success, like the nightingale that sings day and night. There are many who sing in the day of happy

---

As in the prayer of petition, every event and need can become an offering of thanksgiving (2638).

49. Ibid.   50. Ibid.
51. Psalm 34.

fortune, thanking God for success and joy, and David says of them: They will praise your holy name when you do them good. But in the night of adversity few sing and thank God, and so the nightingale is more fitting in his praise than men.[52]

The first reason we should rejoice in adversity is because we have been told to take up our cross and to follow Christ. "We should not thank God begrudgingly for adversities, especially if we consider that he does us no small favour by allowing us to assist Simon of Cyrene to carry the cross and remember that we could suffer no evil unless God permitted it for our welfare."[53]

This position concerning the need to thank God for what appears hurtful demands both faith and trust. We must believe in the Providence of God, and we have to trust (or hope) that this Providence is leading us to be with Him forever. To help Simon of Cyrene to bear our Lord's Cross, and to give thanks for this privilege, require faith and hope, but such thanksgiving is possible, and it is required of us.

St. John of the Cross gives us another reason for giving thanks in the midst of pain. He writes:

Better is it to be heavy-laden and near one that is strong than relieved of one's load and near one that is weak. When thou art heavy-laden thou art near to God, Who is thy strength and is with them that are in trouble. When thou art relieved, thou art near but to thyself, who art thine own weakness. For the virtue and strength of the soul grows and is confirmed by trials of patience.[54]

St. John is telling us we are always close to our Lord when we are suffering, and He is close to us. Sometimes generous people who have tried to accept the trials of life, and even to rejoice in them, when they find the trial removed have also a sense that they

---

52. De Osuna, *Third Spiritual Alphabet* II.3.

53. Ibid.

54. *Spiritual Sentences and Maxims,* no. 4, in Peers, *Complete Works of Saint John of the Cross,* 3.219.

are less close to our Lord than they were. The world, although more pleasant from many points of view, because the difficulty has been removed, now seems to lack the weight and depth it had before. Once the trial is over, we look back and recognize that through our suffering we were in the presence of the Redeemer on His way to the Cross.

Still, there is no doubt that this can be taken the wrong way. There is nothing in our faith that tells us that suffering is not suffering. Pain is pain, loss is loss, and grief is grief. There is no escape, and no promise of escape, from these realities for a Christian. Our faith teaches us that both *in* the pain, and *because* of the pain, God draws nearer to us and we can draw nearer to God. It is this presence of God, hidden in the darkness of our own grief, that is the source of our prayer of thanksgiving.

It all sounds more complicated than it is. It is not so hard to understand, but it is not always easy to do. We have to build up gradually an almost automatic reflex of referring everything that happens to us to God. We believe in a general way that God loves us, and this is the cause of our rejoicing and hope in this life. We make this general belief particular especially by applying it to ourselves in the hard times as well as the easy. We thereby realize that it is often in the hardest times that we are closest to God. We should develop the habit of saying: "Blessed be the Lord in His gifts."

The practice of the prayer of thanksgiving is the refusal to accept the incomplete synthesis of Jacopone's third mode.[55] In a direct way, thanksgiving is a cure for sloth, because it helps to dispel the sadness over spiritual things that is the hallmark of sloth. It also teaches us the reality of God's action in our own lives. As we begin to recognize the dangers and limits of the ascetical life, the prayer of thanksgiving forces us to realize that without God's help we cannot break out of the achievements of the ascetical self.

55. See above, 6.1.

7 ❦ The Father

In the fourth mode He appears as a tender father

With gifts of great largesse;

Once the soul tastes of that goodness, that love,

It exults in its inheritance.

7.1 The harsh side of paternity

The recognition of fatherhood involves the experience of dependency. A father is someone who is in charge whether we like it or not. Jacopone characterizes this stage of the spiritual life as being one of fatherly love. To the note of friendship in our relationship with Christ, there is now added a healthy measure of respect and awe for the holiness and the greatness of God. Difficulties in prayer, the experience of aridity and discouragement, the recognition that our good will has its limits, all this begins to teach us in a painful way that God is greater than we are. Gradually there is developed in us a living sense of the fatherhood of God and of our dependence on him. It is this awareness of God's paternity that is now the dominant theme in our lives.

The love of a father for his children, as we know from Scripture, from history, and probably from our own experience, is neither a simple nor an unclouded love. Paternity, as we find it in Saul's relationship to Jonathan, or Abraham's to Isaac, is not an

easy and sunny relationship for either father or son. In fact, the
contrary is the case. Yet the relationship does in fact exist and our
Lord taught us to pray to our heavenly Father.

In relation to contemporary concerns about the paternity of
God, only two things have to be said here. In the first place, in
the Christian religion the term "Father" is applied to the first person of the Trinity in relation to the Son, and to God in relation
to his creatures, but not to the being of God as such.[1] Fatherhood,
in other words, is a relational concept used to refer to the truth of
God's own life and of our relationship to him.[2] Secondly, this relationship of paternity is a revealed truth of our faith. God is Father in relation to the divine Son, and he is our Father in an
analogous way. The truth that God is our Father is not the expression of a sociologically conditioned attitude, but is an essential
aspect of our revealed faith. It is also an aspect of this same faith
that our Father loves and cares for us.

But the paternity of God, as we experience it, has also a dark
and terrible side, and the fatherhood of God does not always manifest itself in a way that can be seen as benevolent. God loves his
people, yet the reality of suffering is visible everywhere. Suffering,
as we have already seen, can be related to both justice and reform
or education. The discipline from a father we know loves us may
be painful, but it can be borne.

1. 1a 33.

2. St. Augustine, *Ennarationes in Psalmos* 68.1.5: "He is not called father with
reference to himself but only in relation to the Son; seen by himself he is simply
God"; quoted in Ratzinger, *Introduction to Christianity*, 131. Ratzinger goes on to
say: "'Father' (in God) is purely a concept of relationship. . . . Relationship is not
something extra added to the person, as it is with us; it only exists at all as relat-
edness.

"Expressed in the imagery of Christian tradition, this means that the First
Person does not beget the Son in the sense of the act of begetting coming on top
of the finished Person; it *is* the act of begetting, of giving oneself, of streaming
forth. It is identical with the act of giving" (131–32).

For the Lord disciplines him whom he loves, and chastises every son whom he receives. It is for discipline that you have to endure. God is treating you as sons; for what son is there whom his father does not discipline?[3]

The Book of Job, however, and many of the psalms remind us that our God is a consuming fire, whose treatment of us often seems so cruel and unfair that we cannot understand how it could be productive of any sort of good.

He has torn me in his wrath, and hated me;
he has gnashed his teeth at me;
my adversary sharpens his eyes against me.[4]

And, to make matters worse, any sense of God's presence often disappears just when we need it most:

Behold, I go forward, but he is not there;
and backward, but I cannot perceive him;
on the left hand I seek him, but I cannot behold him;
I turn to the right hand but I cannot see him.[5]

When we reflect on this sort of experience, or when we go through it ourselves, we should not be surprised that people have said that either God is not all powerful or, if he really is the omnipotent God of Scripture, then he cannot be good. On the one hand, he must be weak and no true God or, on the other, he must be either mad or bad.

The foundations of morality are said to be laid in the reason and not in the will of God, yet in the light of history and experience, this contention often seems to be an idle mockery. The horror of God's command to Abraham[6] that he should sacrifice

3. Hebrews 12:6–7.   4. Job 16:19.
5. Job 23:8–9.
6. Genesis 22:2: "And he (God) said: 'Take your son, your only son Isaac, whom you love, and go to the land of Moriah, and offer him there as a burnt offering upon one of the mountains of which I shall tell you.'"

his only son is not really blotted out by the fact it was rescinded at the last moment. Professor Zaehner has argued with passion that people are afraid to look into the face of what he called "our savage God." In our heart of hearts, we want to turn religion into a gutless formula for a peaceful state of mind based on ignoring the reality of suffering and of evil in the world.

They want the timeless blessedness allegedly supplied by Marcion's oh! so kind and gentle God, because they dare not face that frenzied God who storms and rages throughout the Old Testament, is tamed and muted in the Apocrypha and the New, only to reappear with a literal vengeance in the Revelation of St John the Divine which brings this terrible book to an end.[7]

Within the context of the Fatherhood of God, some of the Christian's most bitter trials and difficulties are encountered. It is not merely that he may be faced with agonizing conceptual difficulties about the relationship of the omnipotence and the goodness of God. These are real enough, but often they are coupled with a complete breakdown of the moral certainties that heretofore have enabled him to keep going. In addition, there may be ill health and exterior difficulties that seem insurmountable.

St. John of the Cross teaches that this terrible suffering of the dark night of the soul is used by God to purify and strengthen faith, hope, and love. Left to ourselves, even with the grace of God, we only partially succeed in detaching ourselves from the world, the flesh, and the Devil. God's action in the darkness of suffering and confusion has a twofold effect. First, it removes our attachment to the things that hinder our progress. Secondly, it strengthens our capacity to receive the gift of union with God himself, and "no eye has seen, nor ear heard nor the heart of man conceived, what God has prepared for those who love him."[8]

St. John is a Catholic thinker, and for such a thinker suffering

7. Zaehner, *Our Savage God*, 233–34.
8. Cf. 1 Corinthians 2:9.

is never an end in itself. The trials and difficulties of the contemplative life are brought about in order to purify the soul and to prepare it for a deeper and more intimate union with God himself. For, as St. John says in a lovely passage: "He never mortifies save to give life, nor humbles save to exalt, which comes to pass shortly afterwards."[9]

The suffering described by St. John of the Cross can be viewed as the establishment of the Fatherhood of God over the individual soul. The purpose of the realization of God's Fatherhood is not so that we may be dominated or humiliated, but so that we can begin here and now to live the life of God himself. The relationship through which the Son is eternally engendered by the Father is meant to be reproduced in each individual.

The soul now loves God, not through itself, but through Himself; which is a wondrous brightness, since it loves through the Holy Spirit, even as the Father and the Son love One Another, as the Son Himself says, in St. John: "May the love wherewith Thou hast loved Me be in them and I in them."[10]

St. John of the Cross is not providing us with a theodicy after the manner of Leibniz. He is not, that is, trying to justify the ways of God to man by providing a philosophical explanation for the existence of suffering and of evil. St. John takes suffering and evil as given and shows how they are used, within the context of faith, to establish a living sense of the fatherhood of God in the individual soul.

7.2 The dark night of the spirit

Contemplation, as the loving and peaceful infusion of God into the soul, had as its first effect the dark night of the senses. This influx of God into the soul resulted in a reversal of our life of

9. *DN* II.23.10.   10. *LFL* (2d redaction) III.82.

prayer. We were no longer able to meditate, while at the same time, the silent approach of God to us was all but imperceptible to sense. This meant we had to learn to be silent and to wait for God. The well-organized spiritual life, centered on meditation and mortification, appeared to collapse, and our prayer stopped being consoling in any obvious way.

At the same time, however, there remained a deep sense that it is important to pray and, if we persevered, we gradually accommodated ourselves to the new situation. This led to the beginnings of a contemplative form of prayer that is peaceful and loving and that is capable of "enkindling the soul with the spirit of love."

It would seem as though all would be plain sailing from now on. The soul has been taught self-knowledge and humility and has learned to pray without the props of sense and meditation. In its newfound freedom it may be tempted to say *non movebor in aeternam*—I shall never be shaken. But this is not the way things develop. The darkness that has taught the soul to pray in this new and more profound way begins to assume a menacing aspect. Like thunder heard in the distance on a fine day, a sense of uneasiness returns to the soul, and then, suddenly, the storm breaks and there is no escaping it. The self, which underwent the refashioning of its sensible nature is unable to put up any defense against "this inflowing of God into the soul,"[11] and "the understanding is deprived of light, the will of its affections and the memory of meditation and knowledge."[12]

The first darkness resulted in "a correction and restraint" of the senses and taught them at least to be quiet when the higher aspects of the self were engaged with God. However, the roots of our sins have remained firmly implanted and entwined around the self that is seeking God. There is nothing for it but to pull up the roots by violence. This God proceeds to do, but in the process the self in which the sins were lodged is reduced to nothingness. In

11. *DN* II.5.1.   12. *DN* II.8.2.

this second darkness, God appears as the terrible Father of the Old Testament, who demanded the sacrifice of Isaac and who punished Saul for sparing the Amalekites. There seems to be neither justice nor love in the way he treats his chosen ones. St. Teresa's complaint that God has so few friends because he treats them so badly was meant in all earnestness.

Carl Jung, in his *Answer to Job,* writes of the many testimonies, before Job, which had given a contradictory picture of Yahweh:

. . . the picture of a God who knew no moderation in his emotions and suffered precisely from this lack of moderation. He himself admitted that he was eaten up with rage and jealousy and that this knowledge was painful to him. Insight existed along with obtuseness, loving-kindness along with cruelty, creative power along with destructiveness. Everything was there, and none of these qualities was an obstruction to the other. [13]

From Marcion in the second century to Simone Weil[14] in our own there have been people who have been so repelled by the picture of God in the Old Testament that they have tried to separate the God of love they see in the New Testament from the angry, jealous, revengeful Lord of Armies they find portrayed in the Old.[15] The Church holds that it is the same God in both the Old and the New Testaments. Probably Marcion and Simone Weil did

13. Quoted in Zaehner, *Our Savage God,* 219.

14. Weil, *Letter to a Priest,* 13: "Zeus, in the *Iliad,* orders no cruelty whatever. The Greeks believed that 'suppliant Zeus' inhabits every creature that implores pity. Jehovah is the 'God of Hosts.' The history of the Hebrews shows that this refers not only to the stars, but also to the warriors of Israel. Now Herodotus enumerates a great number of Hellenistic and Asiatic peoples amongst whom there was *only one* that had a 'Zeus of Hosts.' This blasphemy was unknown to all the others."

15. Pétrement, *Simone Weil,* 347: "Simone was not surprised to find accounts of massacres in the Bible. . . . What filled her with indignation was the fact that the order for extermination is presented in the Bible as God's order and that neither the person who wrote the story nor the majority of those who read it, including Christians, had found it repugnant to admit that God could give such an order."

not reflect enough on the fact that the God portrayed in the New Testament is not a comfortable figure. The God of Jesus Christ demanded the sacrifice of his own innocent Son, and this is as terrible and frightening as anything found in the Old Testament.

There is no doubt that the fatherhood of God as portrayed in Scripture has a dark, forbidding, and cruel aspect. However we come to grips with this aspect of our religion at a reflective theological level, it can at least be said that this portrayal is adequate to the mystery of suffering and cruelty. That is, when we think about man's history, we are confronted with a darkness we cannot explain. Christianity recognized this terrible surd in man's experience, and it is not foreign to its sacred writings.

The suffering of Abraham represents the incomprehensible demands God sometimes makes on those he has chosen. Kierkegaard said that one cannot weep over Abraham: "One approaches him with a *horror religiosus*"[16] as we view him, alone in the darkness, called on to sacrifice the child of his promise, and trudging up the mountain to fulfil in anguish and desolation the incomprehensible exactions of his terrible God.

. . . But Abraham said to himself, "I will not conceal from Isaac whither this course leads him." He stood still, he laid his hand upon the head of Isaac in benediction, and Isaac bowed to receive the blessing. And Abraham's face was fatherliness, his look was mild, his speech encouraging. But Isaac was unable to understand him, his soul could not be exalted; he embraced Abraham's knees, he fell at his feet imploringly, he begged for his young life, for the fair hope of his future, he called to mind the joy in Abraham's house, he called to mind the sorrow and loneliness. Then Abraham lifted up the boy, he walked with him by his side, and his talk was full of comfort and exhortation. But Isaac could not understand him. He climbed Mount Moriah, but Isaac understood him not. Then for an instant he turned away from him, and when Isaac saw Abraham's face it was changed, his glance was wild, his form was horror.[17]

16. Kierkegaard, *Fear and Trembling*, 71 ("Problem 1").

17. Ibid., 27 ("Prelude 1").

In the *Dark Night of the Spirit* St. John of the Cross discusses the experience of the individual in the face of a God who is no longer the kind friend, or even the strict but fair-minded Father. Now we are in the presence of the God "who did not spare his own Son"[18] and will spare no one else.

St. John compares this dark night to a sea that overflows into the soul and both purges and instructs it at the same time. In our former trials we sometimes may have been in darkness and confusion. Now, however, the darkness invades the innermost parts of our nature and we seem to lose our way. All the familiar landmarks disappear, and doubt, anxiety, and confusion become our staple fare. The Divine Wisdom, which transcends the capacities of the soul, appears to it as a darkness against which it has no defense and which throws it into confusion. In addition, however, the darkness itself causes us to suffer and is the source of nameless sorrow and bitter grief. This he puts down to our impurity, our weakness, and the incommensurability of the soul and God.

But what the sorrowful soul feels most in this condition is its clear perception, as it thinks, that God has abandoned it, and, in his abhorrence of it, has flung it into darkness; it is a grave and piteous grief for it to believe that God has forsaken it . . . when this purgative contemplation is most severe, the soul feels very keenly the shadow of death and the lamentations of death and the pains of hell, which consist in its feeling itself to be without God, and chastised and cast out, and unworthy of him, and it feels that he is wroth with it. All this is felt by the soul in this condition—yea and more, for it believes that it is so with it for ever.[19]

In addition to the sense that we have been deprived of all goods, whether temporal, natural, or spiritual, there is also a terrible sense of isolation. This makes it impossible for anyone else to help the person who is really suffering in this way. He does not believe anyone else has ever suffered quite the way he is suffering and so he doubts the ability of anyone else to help or understand him.

18. Romans 8:32.   19. *DN* II.6.2.

Not unnaturally, this condition results in an apparent destruction of the spiritual life. The soul ". . . is unable to raise its affection or its mind to God, neither can it pray to him, thinking, as Jeremiah thought concerning himself, that God has set a cloud before it through which its prayer cannot pass."[20] God is "passively working in the soul," and the soul can do nothing but submit to the hand of its creator.

Hence it can neither pray nor pay attention when it is present at the divine offices, much less can it attend to other things and affairs which are temporal. Not only so, but it has likewise such distractions and times of such profound forgetfulness of the memory that frequent periods pass by without its knowing what it has been doing or thinking, or what it is that it is doing or is going to do, neither can it pay attention, although it desire to do so, to anything that occupies it.[21]

It is clear that a great many of the symptoms of the dark nights are similar to unhealthy and destructive psychological states. Many of the characteristics of the dark night of the senses are similar to a depression, while some of those encountered in the dark night of the soul seem indistinguishable from a more serious breakdown. St. John of the Cross is perfectly aware of this, and his three signs that enable us to detect the presence of God's activity in the soul are also to be understood as three ways of separating the results of God's activity from those caused by psychological factors.

The three signs, it will be remembered,[22] are the following. In the first place, the soul finds no pleasure or consolation in the things of God, and it also fails to find it in anything created. Secondly, the "memory is ordinarily centred upon God, with painful care and solicitude, thinking that it is not serving God, but is backsliding, because it finds itself without sweetness in the things of

20. *DN* II.8.1.   21. *DN* II.8.1.
22. See above, 6.4, and *Ascent* II.13.

God." The third sign is the inability to use the imagination and the senses for a prayer of meditation.

The cause of the dark nights of the soul is the action of God on the soul. St. John uses traditional language to describe what he is talking about. He speaks of the soul receiving the gift of wisdom, or of the blinding brightness of the presence of God, or of the inflowing of the dark sea. These descriptions point to a cause that cannot be experienced. All that is experienced are the effects. If all three signs are present in an individual, then it is safe to assume the presence of God's activity in the soul.

The causes of depression and of more serious psychological disturbances are also not experienced. The effects are recognized but, for example, in the case of depression, it is a part of the sickness that it is experienced as uncaused. Thus it is often difficult to separate conditions of the soul that are psychologically produced from those which are the result of God's direct action. The result of both a depression and the action of God may be a condition which is likely to induce worry, tension, and depression, and all this may lead to a destructive reaction if the individual gives way to the fears and uncertainties that beset it at these times.

The presence of the three signs is in principle the means to discern the direct action of God on the soul. The fruits of a genuine night of the spirit are not depression and psychological disorder. God breaks down and even destroys only so that his love for us may become the principle of all of our activity. The love of God has been poured into our hearts. Gradually, as a result of the darkness this has caused, we begin to love God with that love he has given to us. God is indeed a tender Father to the person at this time of his spiritual life. The soul has believed and trusted, and he has begun to see the secrets of the King.

7.3 Contemplation

Jesus said to the Samaritan woman that if she knew the gift of God, and who was talking to her, then she would have been given the gift of living water.[23] The gift that God wants to share with us is Himself. Yet we do not recognize the signs of His drawing nearer to us and so we do not know how to respond to His approach. Like the Samaritan woman, we are not aware that God is touching our lives in a new way and so we often miss the opportunity to enter into a new and deeper relationship with our Creator.

The traditional map of progress in prayer is something like this. As we go on practicing petition, meditation, and thanksgiving, our prayer becomes less and less a matter of words, acts of the imagination, and motions of the will. It becomes more and more a loving attention to God that is still largely the result of our own activities. St. Francis de Sales says, "At the beginning we consider the goodness of God to excite our will to love him, but love being formed in our hearts, we consider the same goodness to content our love."[24] Sometimes this simple, loving attentiveness to God is called "acquired contemplation." That is, by our own efforts we have gradually trained ourselves to remain quiet and content in the presence of God, and so we can be said to be contemplating God rather than meditating about him.

[The soul] no longer needs to meditate in order to learn to know and love God. The way has been left far behind, the soul is resting at its goal. As soon as it begins to pray it is with God and remains in his presence in loving surrender. Its silence is dearer to him than many words. This is what today is called "acquired contemplation." It is the fruit of man's own activity.[25]

23. John 4:4.
24. *TLG* VI.3.
25. Stein, *The Science of the Cross,* 86.

There is nothing wrong with this usage in itself, but it is not what St. John of the Cross means by contemplation.[26] "Contemplation," he says, "is nothing but a secret, peaceful and loving infusion from God which, if it be permitted, enkindles the soul with the spirit of love."[27] The saint's definition may not seem to accord with what we usually mean by contemplation. In the first place, we usually think of contemplation as a kind of seeing, either seeing in a literal sense or seeing as understanding. For example, we say I contemplated the beauty of the landscape, or I contemplated the possibility of this or that course of action. Secondly, we sometimes use "contemplation" for any kind of prayer including meditation. Thus we say, I contemplated the third of the glorious mysteries of the rosary. Or again, we may use contemplation for a largely wordless, serene, and attentive prayer of the presence of God. The love of God having been formed in our hearts through our life of prayer, we then quietly "consider this same goodness to content our love."

None of these usages is really adequate to convey how contemplation has been understood in the tradition. In the first place, contemplation is not a question of seeing anything—either literally, as in visions or revelations, or in the extended sense of understanding new truths or the connections of truth.[28] The writer of *The Cloud of Unknowing,* after writing of Mary Magdalene, who "was so heartily set to love him, that nothing beneath him might comfort her, nor yet hold her heart from him," goes on to say:

This is she, that same Mary, who, when she sought him at the sepulchre with weeping, would not be comforted by angels . . . because she thought that whoso sought verily the King of angels, he would not cease for angels.[29]

26. Abbot Chapman is particularly good on this question. See for example Chapman, *Spiritual Letters,* 68.

27. *DN* I.10.6.

28. St. John of the Cross discusses this at great length, and in a magisterial way, in Book Two of the *Ascent.*

29. *Cloud,* chap. 22.

The contemplative must neither seek, nor rest in, anything other than God, for God is beyond anything we can understand, much less see, in this life. Now if God is beyond what can be imagined or understood, then it is clear that any direct dealings God may have with us will not be accurately described in language that uses visual terms. So contemplation is not a visualizing of anything in any way.

Secondly, the use of contemplation to include any kind of prayer, including meditation, obscures the essential point that contemplation is marked by an approach of God to us in a radically new way. His grace has been with us from the beginning of our life of prayer, but now the control of our prayer is taken out of our hands, and God begins to operate on our soul in a new way. Once again, the author of *The Cloud,* in expressing the tradition, anticipates St. John of the Cross.

But one thing I tell thee: he is a jealous lover and suffereth no fellowship, and he liketh not to work in thy will unless he be only with thee by himself. He asketh no help but only thyself. He will thou do but look upon him and let him alone.[30]

Thirdly, what has been called "acquired contemplation" obscures the fact that contemplation is something given to us by God. Contemplation is infused into the soul by God, and is not the result of anything we have done or not done. The dominant theme in the movement of our prayer becomes the approach of God to the soul, rather than of our efforts to draw nearer to Him by petition and meditation. It should, however, be emphasized that the prayer of the contemplative is not passive in the sense that he does nothing. The writer of *The Cloud* insists that contemplation is a work, "a travail," and he writes both of God's work and the work of the soul. God's work he describes as "that devout stirring of love that is continually wrought in his will, not by himself, but by the hand of Almighty God, who is evermore ready to

30. Ibid., chap. 2.

work this work in every soul that is disposed thereto."[31] The work of the contemplative, he says, consists largely in removing the obstacles to this work of God:

But wherein then is this travail, I pray thee? Surely, this travail is all in treading down of the thought of all the creatures that ever God made, and in holding of them under the *cloud of forgetting*. . . . In this is all the travail; for this is man's travail, with the help of grace. And the other above—that is to say, the stirring of love—that is the work of only God.[32]

This movement is the reverse of what our prayer has been like until the present. That is, heretofore our prayer has focused on the effort to make the truths of our faith so real to ourselves that they will affect our conduct. With the beginning of contemplation all this is taken out of our hands and we have to learn to pray in the darkness of faith.

This contemplation is no mere acceptance of the message of faith that comes by hearing, no mere turning to God who is known only from hearsay; it is an interior touch and an experience of God capable of detaching the soul from all created things, of elevating it and at the same time immersing it in a love that does not know its object.[33]

The writer of the *Cloud of Unknowing*, St. John of the Cross, and the Blessed Edith Stein all teach that the purpose of this darkness is to strengthen faith, hope, and charity. The beginnings of the contemplative life are hard, and our prayer becomes more difficult, more arid, or, to use St. John's favorite word, more dark. The intellect now has less and less to do to, and prayer becomes a question of loving attentiveness to the will of God. The Father now appears to us in the form of darkness that clouds our minds, empties our memories of hope, and paralyzes our will.[34]

31. Ibid., chap. 26.
32. Ibid.
33. Stein, *Science of the Cross*, 89.
34. Von Balthasar, *The Glory of the Lord*, 3.133: "The critique of forms and

And therefore shape thee to bide in this darkness as long as thou mayest, evermore crying after him whom thou lovest. For if ever thou shalt see him or feel him, as it may be here, it must always be in the cloud and in this darkness. And if thou wilt busily travail as I bid thee, I trust in his mercy that thou shalt come thereto.[35]

At first sight, none of this seems readily intelligible, much less very credible. It is the opposite to what we would expect. When we study a subject, we begin to understand it better. Our knowledge may develop to the point where we may be said to have mastered the subject. An expert in a particular branch of knowledge is someone who has a good conceptual grasp of the material as well as the ability to handle it properly. We say of such a person that he has the subject at his fingertips.

It is a natural enough mistake to think that progress in prayer will follow this pattern. Surely, it might be said, growth in prayer will be accompanied by an increasingly clear awareness of the being and of the nature of God, and the person who knows a great deal of mystical theology is someone who knows more about God than the person who never studies or reads about God. Now, in one obvious sense this is true. The student, as a student, will have a much greater facility in using the concepts of theology, and in explaining their connection, than will the person who does not study.

Yet what of the man who prays and can in no way be a called a student? We have already seen that it is quite possible that such a person may love God in a deeper and more profound way than

---

states in its full context is connected with the positive element of transcendence; it is for this that John makes his critique, and it is this that John, in one of his great architectonic simplifications, identifies with the theological virtues. For him these are fundamentally a single reality (only differentiated by the powers of the soul), the reality of participation in God." This is correct, but it leaves out the role of the gifts of the Holy Spirit, which, unlike the theological virtues, operate *modo divino*. See 1a2ae 68.

35. *Cloud*, chap. 3.

does the scholar. St. Thomas and St. Francis de Sales both insist that, although knowledge is required to give birth to love, none-theless, once we have some knowledge of God, then the will goes out to God as He is in Himself by means of our love. And so St. Francis de Sales says that knowledge "gives birth, but not measure to love. The passions do not follow the knowledge which moves them, but very often, leaving this quite in the rear, they make towards their object without any measure or limit."[36]

The simple, prayerful man, then, may "bear away heaven," while the learned may be swallowed up in hell. This analysis, between the success of the unlearned and the shipwreck of the scholar, identifies the difference as basically a moral one. That is, the one succeeds in virtue of his humility and the other fails be-cause he is proud. It is certain that this analysis remains true in-sofar as it points to the truth that pride is the great enemy in the spiritual life, and that progress in prayer demands an ever-deep-ening humility based on a real assent to our own unworthiness and incapacity to follow the good. On the other hand, there are intelligent people who are humble enough to pray seriously, and what are we to say about them? Surely, we are tempted to say, their intelligence and their learning will be a great help in their spiritual life.

It is clear why people want to say that intelligence and prayer have a direct relationship to each other. In the first place, there is the Christian imperative, which comes from the Gospel itself, that we are to use and develop what God has given us.[37] If intelligence and the opportunity to learn are gifts entrusted to us, it seems hard to see how the definition of progress in our relationship with God can actually consist in not developing them. Furthermore, it is not at all clear how ignorance is related to "bearing away heaven." Ignorance can be a very unlovely thing, often closely

---

36. *TLG* VI.4.

37. See the parable of the talents, Matthew 25:14–30.

connected with pig-headedness and a positive unwillingness to consider anything beyond the horizon of the individual's immediate needs.

These questions and these hesitations develop because we have not paid close enough attention to the truth that the Christian life, as a Christian life, is based on faith, is nourished in hope, and is completed by charity. It follows that the success or otherwise of a Christian life is to be determined in relation to how one's gifts are used. Furthermore, the proper use of these gifts will have to be determined in the light of the nature of the gifts and the sort of demands they make on the baptized Christian. Learning and morality do not determine the proper exercise of faith, hope, and charity. Rather, faith, hope, and charity provide the dynamic for the understanding of learning and morality.

It is God who gives us the means to live a Christian life, and the most important of these means are the theological virtues. Furthermore, since without faith there can be neither hope nor charity, a Christian life is in the first instance a life of faith. Faith, St. Thomas says, by its very nature, precedes all other virtues.[38] It is one of the many great merits of St. John of the Cross that the whole of his teaching is based on this primacy of faith, and it is the nature of faith that, for him, determines the nature of the spiritual life.

When, therefore, we wonder about the importance of intelligence or about the role of morality in the spiritual life, we have

---

38. 2a2ae 4, 7: "Faith by its very nature precedes all other virtues. For since the end is the principle in matters of action, . . . the theological virtues, the object of which is the last end, must needs precede all the others. Again, the last end must of necessity be present to the intellect before it is present to the will, since the will has no inclination for anything except in so far as it is apprehended by the intellect. Hence, as the last end is present in the will by hope and charity, and in the intellect by faith, the first of all the virtues must, of necessity, be faith, because natural knowledge cannot reach God as the object of heavenly bliss, which is the aspect under which hope and charity tend toward Him."

to ask these questions within the framework of the nature of faith and its demands. St. Thomas's discussion of faith begins, not with the believer, but with what he believes. This object of faith is God Himself and what He has revealed. God as He is in Himself, the first truth, is beyond anything we can imagine or know. Furthermore, most of what has been revealed to us is beyond our capacity to understand. And so, St. John, building on St. Thomas, compares the light of faith to a darkness that "oppresses and disables that of the understanding."[39]

It is essential to put these strong expressions about faith in their proper context. We have to remember, first, that St. John is talking about a type of prayer that is experienced as an inability to meditate, together with a desire to be alone with God and an unwillingness to fix our minds on worldly things. If this experience is to be Christian, it must have grown out of meditation and be continually referred to it. However, the experience, as an experience, is a darkness to the senses, the imagination, and the intellect.

We have seen that this darkness is God's response to a serious effort on our part to deepen our grasp on the truths of the Christian faith, as well as to bring our lives into harmony with what we believe. This approach of God appears as darkness for different reasons. First of all, although we have made some progress in the love of God, we are still a long way from Christian perfection. We are still not fitted even morally to be able to bear the light of the divine presence and so we are like bats flying around blind in the daylight.[40]

There is, however, more to the question than this. God's approach to us is a darkness to the intellect because He is drawing

39. *Ascent* II.3.1.

40. Cf. Walter Hilton, *The Ladder of Perfection* II.24: "He who loves God dwells entirely in light. Then whatever man perceives and sees the love of this world as false and failing, and therefore chooses to forsake it and seek the love of God, he must abide a while in the night. He cannot go suddenly from one light to the other, that is, from the love of the world to the perfect love of God."

near to us in the truth of His own being. Our understanding works in a discursive way, that is, by analyzing and synthesizing, but not by a direct, intuitive intellectual grasp of the truth. At best, we can obtain an analogical knowledge of God, which is derived from a consideration of the material object of faith. Discursive knowledge is essential, and prayer based on this kind of knowledge is essential. On the other hand, if we accept that contemplation results from God's direct approach to us as He is in Himself, then it is clear that our understanding is not equipped to deal with this new advent of God, who is beyond anything we can conceive or imagine.

He who would attain to being joined in a union with God must not walk by understanding, neither lean upon experience or feeling or imagination, but he must believe in His Being, which is not perceptible to the understanding, neither to the desire nor to the imagination nor to any other sense, neither can it be known in this life at all.[41]

Von Balthasar is surely correct in saying that St. John's explanations limp rather prosaically in the wake of his poetry.[42] In the *Spiritual Canticle* there is a verse of outstanding loveliness that brings together many of the themes we have been discussing. In the verse he compares faith to a clear spring:

O spring like crystal!
If only, on your silvered-over face,
You would suddenly form
The eyes I have desired,
Which I sketched deep within my heart![43]

The silvered-over face constitutes the propositions and articles of faith that faith sets before us. They reveal to us the truth about

41. *Ascent* II.4.4.

42. After discussing St. John's analysis, Von Balthasar writes: "All this is beautiful and true but how hopelessly it limps behind the vision!" (*Glory of the Lord*, 3.125).

43. *Spiritual Canticle* (2d redaction), stanza 12.

God, but in a propositional way that the mind grasps according to its own nature. Faith gives us God, "but covered with the silver of faith."[44] They are silver to us now and here, and only in heaven will they reveal the gold that lies beneath them. "When faith comes to an end, when it terminates through the clear vision of God, the substance of faith, in having been stripped of the veil of silver, will have the colour of gold."

The propositions of faith are accompanied by "divine truths and rays," which are "formless and hidden" and which at the same time reveal "the greatness and the presence of the beloved." These truths are called eyes "because of the remarkable presence of the beloved she experiences." The formal object of faith is God as the first truth. The experience of the dark nights is at the same time God's drawing near to us as this first truth and a refashioning of the person who prays so that he is progressively more capable of sustaining this approach.

For St. John of the Cross contemplation is, in the final analysis, a development or exercise of the infused virtues of faith, hope, and charity. "For him these are fundamentally a single reality (only differentiated by the three powers of the soul), the reality of participation in God."[45] The remorseless destruction of images, of forms, and of states which characterize his discussion of both the positive and active aspects of the dark nights is directed to one end. This end is that we will come closer to worshipping God as He is in Himself, and we are able to do this because He has given Himself to us.[46]

That is the outline of the contemplative life as St. John of the Cross understands it. It is not something an individual takes up

44. Ibid. The following quotations are also from stanza 12.

45. Von Balthasar, *Glory of the Lord*, 3.133. This is true, so long as we remember that the "use" of the gifts is not in our control. Cf. note 34 to this chapter.

46. Ibid., 3.134: "This triune attitude of faith that loves and hopes and of love that believes and hopes is . . . defined by John as both the *experience* of God (beyond all psychological experience) and as the state of *contemplation*."

when he feels like it, but rather it is something that comes to possess the contemplative. Furthermore, this possession by God of the soul is always, at first, the cause of darkness and difficulty and of great spiritual anguish. If God is beyond anything we can think or imagine, it is not surprising that His approach should be anything but easy for us.

7.4 The sacrament of the present moment

Suffering is a mysterious reality that characterizes the human situation in a fundamental way. That is, surely, the lesson of human experience and, as such, it is not based on faith. Christianity, however, adds another dimension to the matter. St. Paul said: "In my flesh I complete what is lacking in Christ's afflictions for the sake of his body, that is, the Church,"[47] and this shows that suffering is irremediably entwined with how we, as Christians, experience life. Our faith teaches us that in suffering we come into contact with the redeeming power of Christ, who conquered sin and death through His suffering on the Cross and His rising from the dead.

In his letter *The Christian Meaning of Human Suffering,* Pope John Paul II emphasizes that the only way to approach suffering is through the mystery of God's creative and redeeming love. On the one hand, Christ's suffering and death "created the good of the world's redemption," and no one can add anything to it.

But at the same time, in the mystery of the Church as His Body, Christ has in a sense opened His own redemptive suffering to all human suffering. In so far as man becomes a sharer in Christ's suffering—in any part of the world and at any time in history—to that extent *he in his own way completes* the suffering through which Christ accomplished the Redemption of the world.[48]

The pope is not engaged here in an attempt to justify or vindicate the divine attributes of holiness and justice. He is reformulating

47. Colossians 1:24.   48. *SvD*, sect. 24.

an old tradition concerning the use of suffering in Christian experience. Yet, while this tradition has to do with the use of suffering, and while it makes sense only within the context of faith, nonetheless it does teach us a lesson that should become the staple fare of the Christian life. The lesson applies to everything that happens to us in life, and this includes what occurs in our life of prayer.

In the dark nights, God's action takes away our initiative in prayer and, along with this initiative, the incomplete synthesis of the ascetical self. Yet the response on our part to God's action must never be one of pure passivity. In the dark night of the spirit we are left with either saying yes to the will of God as it shows itself in our life, or else rebelling against what we cannot change. Neither alternative is easy to practice. To accept the will of God as it shows itself to me at the present moment may mean assenting to exterior and interior suffering, which can achieve such a level of intensity that I am aware only of the darkness, confusion, and pain. Yet refusing to accept the will of God only adds to weariness and discontent with the situation.

We believe in a God who acts and whose loving care is leading us back to himself. But this providence of God often shows itself in ways that are beyond our understanding, that outrage our sense of justice, and do violence to everything we thought we believed. Faith is a darkness to the understanding, we have been told, and we thought we accepted this. Now we are taught that the darkness of faith is intended for us as well.

Our prayer at these times needs to be an effort to will what God wants for me in the here and now in my present situation. This prayer has been called the "sacrament of the present moment"; it consists in fidelity to God's plan. This fidelity has both an active and a passive side:

The active practice of fidelity consists in accomplishing the duties imposed on us by the general laws of God and the Church, and by the particular state of life which we have embraced. Passive fidelity consists in the loving acceptance of all that God sends us at every moment.[49]

It is not necessary to speculate if this is an adequate theory for the whole of life; what we are concerned with here is how to pray when we are laboring under the hand of God in a way we cannot understand. Yet one of the effects of this state is, as we have seen, an apparent inability to pray at all, or to believe in anything. At such times, rather than running away, we should ask the Father that this cup may be taken away; nevertheless not as we will, but as He wills.[50] Through the active acceptance of what we cannot change or understand, our faith is purified and strengthened, and God's life begins to grow in us. *Solus Deus deificet:* only God is capable of making us over into Himself, says St. Thomas.[51] Only God can turn us into the image of His beloved Son.

We must learn to listen to God from moment to moment in order to be learned in the theology of virtue which is wholly practical and experimental. Set aside what is said to others, listen to what is said to you for your own use: you will find enough to exercise your faith, for this interior language of God by its very obscurity exercises, purifies and increases faith.[52]

This practical knowledge, based on faith, of God's loving care is entirely compatible with intense suffering. Indeed, in the Christian view of things, it is those who have suffered most who most truly understand their faith.

Do not be afraid to live constantly in this great emptiness which you discover within yourself. Remain in it, without any thoughts, unperceiving, and insensible to all things. Delight in this state since, in your

49. De Caussade, *Self-Abandonment to Divine Providence* I.1.3. De Caussade uses the expression "the sacrament of the present moment."

50. Cf. Luke 22:42.

51. 1a2ae 112, ad 1. Cited by Denys Turner in "St. John of the Cross and Depression," 162.

52. De Caussade, *Self-Abandonment,* I.1.2.8.

case, it is God's gift and the source of all good. I have never met with a favoured soul whom God has not forced to pass through these barren wastes before it reaches that promised land which is perfection's earthly paradise.[53]

In our own terrible century, the Blessed Edith Stein lived and died this doctrine of the sacrament of the present moment. In her case, the acceptance of the will of God, day by day, hour by hour, and minute by minute, led to martyrdom. It was a martyrdom that, like St. Thomas More, she did her best to avoid. But once it was clearly inevitable, she went forward serenely and courageously to meet her death. The account of her last week in the deportation camp at Westerbork, in Holland, before she was shipped off to the East to be gassed, is a compelling lesson in the triumph of the Cross in a human life. Whatever her life of prayer may have been before she was taken away to die, we know that it had done God's work in her. She died a martyr for Christ, but not, so far as one can see, actually in the dark night of the spirit.[54] Her concern as she went to her death was, literally, for the little ones for whom Christ died.

It was Edith Stein's complete calm and self-possession that marked her out from the rest of the prisoners. There was a spirit of indescribable misery in the camp; the new prisoners, especially, suffered from extreme anxiety. Edith Stein went among the women like an angel, comforting, helping and consoling them. Many of the mothers were on the brink of insanity and had sat moaning for days without giving any thought to their children. Edith Stein immediately set about taking care of these little ones. She washed them, combed their hair, and tried to make sure they were fed and cared for.[55]

Edith Stein faced the wickedness and insanity of our century head on. She did it, not with her intelligence and her scholarship,

---

53. Ibid., VII.1.5.
54. The prioress of the Carmel in Cologne is of the same opinion.
55. Cited in Waltraud Herbstrith, *Edith Stein*, 105.

but in the power of the Cross. She had seen her end in her beginning, and she was not disappointed in her hope.

We cannot acquire a *scientia crucis*—a knowledge of the Cross—unless we receive a deep awareness of the Cross. I have been convinced of that from the beginning and, with all my heart, I said: Ave, Crux, Spes unica![56]

It is our unique and irreplaceable relationship of faith to our Creator and our Redeemer that gives sense to our existence. If we have forgotten this, or if we have never learned it, then God the Father will have to teach it to us. That is what St. John of the Cross and Edith Stein are trying to explain.

56. Stein, *In Der Kraft des Kreuzes* (my translation).

8 ❧ The Lover

In the fifth mode Love leads me to the conjugal bed
And I lie in the embrace of the Son of God. O my soul,
Led by grace, you are the queen of the angels,
In wondrous fusion transformed into Christ.

8.1 Union with Christ

We seek God, and God desires to give Himself to us. The way of our seeking must be through Jesus Christ, who has always been with us seeking our love. St. Teresa writes in her description of the Sixth Mansion, a state which is closely united to the very highest degree of the spiritual life, that we must never try to abandon the humanity of Christ:

. . . the last thing we should do is to withdraw of set purpose from our greatest help and blessing, which is the most sacred humanity of our Lord Jesus Christ. I cannot believe that people can really do this; it must be that they do not understand themselves and thus do harm to themselves and to others . . . if they lose their Guide, the good Jesus, they will be unable to find their way.[1]

This is the first principle. The second is that, in our search for God and in his loving search for us, the will outstrips the under-

1. IC VI.7.

standing, and our love of God is greater than our knowledge. This love runs on ahead of our intellect to God Himself, and God, in the darkness, takes possession of the soul in a real and lasting way. It is the teaching of St. Thomas and of the great mystics that even in this life we can be taken up into the life of the Blessed Trinity and united in love with our Creator, our Redeemer, and our Sanctifier. This is what the tradition of the Church has meant by the final stage of Christian perfection.[2]

What do you suppose his will is, daughters? That we should be altogether perfect, and be one with him and with the Father, as in his majesty's prayer.[3]

Perfection is not a question of visions or ecstasies, or of a secret knowledge.[4] Christian perfection is the love of God and of neighbor brought to such a height that its possessor can say with St. Paul: "I have been crucified with Christ; it is no longer I who live, but Christ who lives in me."[5]

It remains true, however, that we cannot see or understand God in this life. This means that union will always be based on the obscurity or darkness of faith, and from this it follows that union is something about which we can say very little. We do know, though, that union is the Lord living in us and we in him. It is for this reason that all the mystics, including Jacopone, talk about union as being like a marriage. The importance of the marriage imagery is that it is marital, not merely sexual. Marriage, on the

2. For a modern discussion of the notion of Christian perfection, see Aumann, *Spiritual Theology,* chapter 5.

3. *IC* V.3.

4. Hans Urs von Balthasar writes: "What is secret here is precisely what is proclaimed and taken for granted in all public places and (especially) in the Church. And yet no one can make it his own. Of its very nature it can be recognised only as a mystery, and an eternal mystery it remains and becomes so more and more for one who encounters it once and eternally" (*Glory of the Lord,* 3.114).

5. Galatians 2:20.

Catholic view, is union for a lifetime, and ideally the sexual union of the partners expresses this unity and helps to develop and maintain it.

We should not think that when Jacopone writes of the soul's union with God as a wondrous fusion that he is writing about anything less complete than the experience of married love. The sexual imagery is used because the love of desire and its expression in marriage is the most immediate and the most nearly total experience (outside of the mystical union itself) known to most people.

Married love is not merely a taking; it also requires a mutual giving.[6] Union with God in this life demands a complete giving of the self to the God who seeks to possess it. But marriage is ordered to fruitfulness, and Christ's union with the soul is brought about not so that we may be satisfied, but that we may imitate Christ more faithfully.[7]

When the mystical union is described as Christ marrying the soul, we have to remember these elements of stability, intimacy, and fruitfulness. The soul that is to be taken by Christ has to be prepared by a long process of trials and purifications as well as by a growth in the exercise of the virtues, especially charity. It must have been taught to be steadfast, to hold nothing back and to be defenseless before its Lord. Finally, the reality of the union is shown in the growth of the love of God and of our neighbor. The note of this final stage in the development of our spiritual life is peace and quietness. "So tranquilly and noiselessly, does the Lord

6. The teaching of the pope in *FC* (1980) on the Christian family is to the point here.

7. Cf. St. Teresa *IC* VII.4: ". . . none of you shall think that he (grants so many favours) simply to give these souls pleasure. That would be to make a great error. For his majesty can do nothing greater for us than grant us a life which is an imitation of that lived by his beloved Son. I feel certain therefore that these favours are given us to strengthen our weakness . . . so that we may be able to imitate him in his great sufferings."

teach the soul in this state and do it good [says St. Teresa] that . . . he and the soul alone have fruition of each other in the deepest silence."[8]

In this final stage of Jacopone's account, the Lord's appearing is close at hand, and the world is no longer experienced as a temptation to draw us away from God, nor as a hostile and threatening force that develops with no concern for our own good. The dark night has given way to the beginning of a new day, and our own existence and the whole of the created universe is shot through with the experience of the glory of God.

The prayer that is most appropriate to this condition of tranquillity and peace is the prayer of the heart. It is also true that the prayer of the heart is a prayer particularly suited to our own time. The elegant certainties of the British and French Enlightenment mean very little to anyone but the writers of newspaper editorials and television commentators. The storm and stress of nineteenth-century ideologies are all a bit too much for most of us. It appears to be our lot to live in a world that offers few certainties of either a negative or a positive kind. The post-Enlightenment and the post-Ideological man or woman approaches life with neither a penchant for chaos nor a nostalgia for system.[9] What is needed is a prayer of quietness and security, which is content to live and work within an unbounded confidence of the love of God.

In this final stage of the life of prayer, the self has been lost in God. God is now able to do with it what He wants, for the self no longer puts obstacles in His way. In the classification of St. Thomas, the union of the soul in God is called the *studium* of the

8. *IC* VII.3.

9. Kolb, *The Critique of Pure Modernity*, 270: "Our life can be lived without the possibility of final or formal grounding, but also without the spectre of the lack of such grounding. We can understand our multiple context, our rootedness and our rootlessness, and get on with what and where we are. Modernity has been much in the thrall of the fear of scepticism, moral or epistemological. Perhaps we might live without either scepticism or security."

perfect, and marks the attainment of a condition in which the self loves God for who He is and not for His gifts. The unknown author of the *Cloud of Unknowing* puts it this way:

So though it may be said, when we speak of ordinary perfection, that the great goodness and the great kindness that God has shown us in this life are noble and worthy reasons for loving God, yet the perfect lover of God, who directs his gaze to the bull's-eye in the target of perfection (and it is toward this that I intend to direct you by writing in these terms), for fear of missing his perfection—that is to say, its supreme point—now seek no other reasons for loving God except God himself. This is what I mean when I say that pure love is to love God for himself and not for his gifts.[10]

This perfect love of God flows over into love of neighbor.[11] This love of neighbor, however, is a consequence of and a participation in the loving union of the soul and God. What has to be guarded against here is a political or communitarian understanding of this love of God and neighbor. Only if we love our neighbor do we know that we love God; it does not follow, however, that the love of neighbor *is* the love of God. The being of God has to be maintained against the effort to reduce Him to the community—even a religious community. It may be true, as Charles Taylor puts it, that "the vast majority of us in this civilization" are committed "to the goodness of being and benevolence,"[12] but the goodness of being is not the object of Christian worship, nor is benevolence identical with Christian love. It is the glory of God that is the final goal of the spiritual life, and this must not be reduced to

10. *The Pursuit of Wisdom*, "Letter on Prayer," 170.

11. See St. Thomas's discussion in 2a2ae 25, 1.

12. Taylor, *Sources of the Self*, 85: "Practical charity is enjoined on us. The Enlightenment took this up in intensified form, and it has become one of the central beliefs of modern Western culture: we all should work to improve the human condition, relieve suffering, overcome poverty, increase prosperity, augment human welfare. We should strive to leave the world a more prosperous place than we found it."

anything that can be understood and interpreted in purely human categories.

8.2 *The prayer of the heart*

Prayer in the end is the recognition in a deep and abiding way of what has been true for us from the beginning. It has always been true that God has been with us in our prayer, and the prayer of the person united to God is the overwhelming yet quiet sense of the indwelling of the Blessed Trinity in his soul. From the first moment God's grace touched our heart and we turned and were turned, He has inspired us and has taught us to pray. Petition, meditation, thanksgiving, and the prayer of darkness have all been responses to the presence of God.

For those whose will has become united with the will of God, the prayer of the presence of God is nothing more than a continual act of recognition and of loving surrender to the God within. For most people, however, becoming aware of the presence of God requires a specific sort of prayer. Abbot Chapman says he is surprised how much space is expended in books on prayer on this question of the presence of God. [13] This remark is often made by people whose existence is ordered or directed toward praying. A monk who lives in an observant house and spends several hours of the day in choir, singing the psalms and canticles and listening to the readings from Scripture which comprise the Divine Office, should not need a great deal of time to put himself consciously into the presence of God. His whole existence is geared toward meditation

13. Chapman, *Spiritual Letters,* 38: "I have never been able to understand why some authors lay so much stress upon preparation, meaning some formal preparation.

"It seems to me that common sense teaches us that, when a man is distracted, a certain amount of preparation is needed before he is in the right frame of mind to pray. But, on the contrary, when his life is one of quiet and recollection, he more often comes to his prayer as to a relief, as though a spring were released."

upon and contemplation of the mysteries of God. But few people live in monasteries. Most people, even priests and nuns, live in the world. Their lives are not geared to the practice of meditation and contemplation, and they need to pull themselves away from the world, at least for a time, so that they can concentrate on God. It was the recognition of this need that led saints like St. Francis de Sales and St. Ignatius of Loyola to formulate ways of recalling to the mind and heart the truth of the presence of God.

St. Francis de Sales, in his *Introduction to the Devout Life,* gives four different ways for putting ourselves into the presence of God.[14]

First of all, we should consider the truth that God is in all things and in every place.[15] We are like blind men who do not see the prince who is present among us but behave with respect when we are told of his presence. Although our faith assures us of His presence, we have to reflect on it if we are not to act as though he were far away.[16] In Psalm 138 (139) there is a moving description of this presence of God in the whole of the visible creation:

> Whither shall I go from thy Spirit?
> Or whither shall I flee from thy presence?
> If I ascend to heaven, thou art there!
> If I make my bed in Sheol, thou art there!
> If I take the wings of the morning
> > and dwell in the uttermost parts of the sea,
> > even there thy hand shall lead me,
> > and thy right hand shall hold me.

14. See *IDL* II.2.

15. These four ways of St. Francis should be compared to Question 8 of the Prima Pars of the *Summa Theologiae* of St. Thomas. The question is "The Existence of God in Things," and it provides the theological basis for St. Francis's teaching.

16. *IDL* II.2: "Although we well know that he is present in all things, because we do not reflect upon it we act as if we did not know it. That is why before prayer we must always excite in our souls a lively thought and apprehension of the presence of God."

Secondly, God is also present in a special way in the depth of our being. David calls Him the God of my heart, and our Lord says, "I will love him and take up my abode with him." We have to balance the recognition of God's presence in the visible creation with His presence within us. He is nearer to us than our distractions, our thoughts, our desires, and our imaginings.

Then, says St. Francis, we ought to try to think specifically of our Lord in His humanity watching us from heaven as we try to pray. It is as though He is looking at us through a chink in the wall, or looking over our shoulder. He is a watcher of whose presence we are aware, but whom we cannot precisely identify.

Finally, we should imagine our Lord in His humanity, present with us, perhaps sitting beside us, and helping us to pray. If we are before the Blessed Sacrament, we ought to make a formal act of faith in His presence in the tabernacle.

All this may seem somewhat too detailed. But gradually the four ways can be shortened until they become hardly more than shorthand statements of the truths they contain. We can, after a time, reduce them into a formal kind of rehearsal of the fact that God is everywhere, that God is within me, that Christ is watching me from heaven, and that our Lord is sitting here with me in His humanity, helping me, consoling me, and strengthening me.

This simple prayer of the presence of God may be all that is required to bring us back to an awareness of the presence of God. Obviously, this prayer will vary enormously with the experience and the state of the person doing the praying. For the beginner, engaged in the warfare of the first *studium,* the prayer itself will often be a struggle. For the person in the way of proficients, it may be a bleak effort to remind himself of a truth he can no longer sense or experience in any sort of way. For the people whose habitual state is "to depart and to be with Christ,"[17] the prayer will hardly be adverted to, and will be as natural as breathing itself.

17. Philippians 1:23.

It is a very natural mistake to spoil this prayer of the presence of God by thinking that more depends upon ourselves than in fact it does. Our part in this prayer is to become aware of the reality of God's presence with us. The prayer itself does not create the reality. People seem to suspect, although they may not voice the suspicion even to themselves, that if they relax, or "let go," even for a moment, then somehow God's presence will disappear. Probably they do not actually think that their efforts somehow or other *create* the God they are praying to, but they certainly seem to act as though this is exactly what they do believe. The stress and strain they impose upon themselves would lead one to believe they conceive of God as a genie in the bottle, a genie who is produced with the right words and sufficiently vigorous efforts. All this indicates that they have very little faith either in the reality of God or in his presence.

The prayer of the presence of God often develops into a prayer of the heart. Here there is no strain, and the person rests content with a loving awareness of the presence of God. One of the most effective statements of this prayer is by De Caussade, who presents his doctrine in the form of questions and answers.[18] Four of his points will help us to understand the prayer of the heart. In the first place, what is the prayer of the heart? Secondly, how is it practiced? Thirdly, what is its result? And finally, what is its value?

Prayer is never a merely intellectual exercise. In the most general way we could say that De Caussade's work is an effort to describe the other aspects of our nature that play a role in prayer. These other aspects he calls the heart, and he says quite simply that all prayer, no matter what sort it must be, must come from the heart if it is to be worth anything. It would seem that his use of the term covers much of the same territory as does the word *will* in Scholastic thought, and he seeks to put his usage firmly within the Catholic tradition by mentioning some of the authors who have

18. See De Caussade, *Traité sur l'oraison du coeur* and *Instructions spirituelles.*

spoken about this prayer, even if they have used other terminology to describe it.[19]

Prayer that is purely from the heart is made by acts that are not enunciated even interiorly; the person praying does not even recognize their existence. They are, however, really practiced in the depths of the heart by what Bossuet called "a real and effective tendency of the heart towards God and the things loved for the sake of God."[20]

An example of this unremarked going out of our being to what we seek is a mother's love for her baby. She may look at the child, and she may think about him, but at the same time there is a long, drawn out and unarticulated movement of love on her part toward her child. We may characterize this movement as a series of loving turnings toward the object of her love, or describe it as the same act which is maintained all during the time she is looking at him or thinking of him.

This experience of setting our affections on an object without deliberately focusing the attention on our affections is a very common one. It is clear in the case of a sinful attraction to another person. One may spend hours on end, even while doing other things, with the heart engaged by the memory, as well as the anticipation, of being with another person. The acceptance of the temptation is like the ground bass of a piece of music; that is, like a note that endures, unheeded some of the time perhaps, but nonetheless qualifying all our experience. Furthermore, we know perfectly well that we are accepting and encouraging the temptation even while we are not explicitly adverting to it. The pull is there and we breathe out our yes in a way that can be described as a series of acceptances that reinforce our first failure, or as one sustained reception into ourselves of the object of our desire.[21]

19. He includes St. Teresa and St. Francis de Sales.
20. De Caussade, *Traité* I.1.
21. Ibid.

The practice of this prayer is simple once we understand what it is. Often, while we are reading, or meditating, we find our heart touched in a holy way by a movement of piety, or of the fear of the Lord, or of regret for the past, or of a desire to do better in the future. The prayer of the heart consists in giving ourselves over to these movements, and allowing them to take possession of us without disturbing them by further activity. If we find they disappear and we begin to be distracted, then we should continue with our reading or meditation. When the heart is touched again we should once more accept what is happening and do our best to maintain "the simple but saving impressions."[22]

When we pray in this way we allow room for those movements of grace which all too often we smother either by too much inner disturbance or even by the ordinary workings of our mind. God is always calling us toward a closer union with Himself, and this calling is like an attraction to which we give consent even when it is not the direct object of our understanding. The gateway to the prayer of the heart is the practice of attentive pauses in which we learn to fix our heart on God in silence. We do this as a response to the often unnoticed pull or attraction that God has constantly on us.

We are a long way here from the prayer of meditation with its resolutions and efforts to develop particular virtues and get rid of specific vices. But the difference is one of method, not of purpose. De Caussade sees this prayer within the context of the Christian life and insists that the prayer he is describing demands both purity of conscience and purity of heart. By purity of conscience he means having no attachment to anything sinful, and by purity of heart he means being detached even from objects that are apparently innocent. The heart was made for God, and even so-called innocent attachments are very often an obstacle to this love.

Purity of conscience is necessary for the prayer of the heart, and

22. Ibid., I.5.

for the practice of the attentive pauses that are its gateway. Even when we are talking about ordinary recollection, which is achieved by our own efforts and ordinary grace, it is clear that the purer our conscience is, the easier it will be for grace to operate and for the faculties to concentrate on the hidden things of God. Distractions are very often the result of an imperfect break with a habit of sinning in a particular way. I do not mean that we fully intend the sin, but we have not broken the cord that binds us to it.

If we are talking about the prayer of the heart that is infused, supernatural, and the result of the direct action of God, then we cannot hope God will grant it to us if we refuse to detach ourselves from what leads us to sin. Purity of conscience will best be attained by paying attention to how we react in the real situations in which we find ourselves, and how we are tempted to break the law of God. This practice will lead to a recognition of our own weakness, and such self-awareness will be painful. The self-knowledge should not lead to a quasi-despair, or to a paralysis of our will. On the contrary, it should lead us to a heightened sense of the mercy of God, to deep repentance and firm purpose of amendment.

Purity of heart is a development of purity of conscience. It involves the effort to see where our nature pulls us away from God and so interferes with the fundamental pull that God exercises on us. The things toward which we incline may not in themselves be sinful, but they can as effectively interfere with what God wants to give us. St. John of the Cross says it does not matter if you tie a bird to a branch with a string or with a thick piece of cord, if the bird cannot fly. So a small attachment will prevent our flight to God just as effectively as a serious fault.[23] If we are to love God and His creation with the same love with which God loves us, then we must be free, and we are not free so long as we are attached to anything that interferes in our relationship with God.

23. *Ascent* I.11.4.

De Caussade makes it clear that he accepts the view of St. John of the Cross and of St. Francis de Sales that one cannot build anything solid in the spiritual life except on the basis or foundation of peace. Peace, as St. John of the Cross says over and over again, is one of the fruits of prayer; but peace is also one of the requirements for a prayer that is more than a preoccupation with self. It is God we are seeking, and if we are in such a constant turmoil emotionally, mentally, or even physically that we cannot be still, then we will never be aware of the God who is within us.[24] The spirit of God dwells and operates only where there is peace. The absence of this peace is for the soul what the absence of good health is to the body. Sickness weakens the body and makes it incapable of attending to its own needs. In a similar way, the absence of peace of soul makes it sick in every way and almost incapable of any spiritual function. This is why St. Francis de Sales repeats so often that, with the exception of sin itself, nothing is so deadly as agitation, vexation, disquiet, and sadness.

It should be clear by now that this peace is not the result of passively accepting ourselves as we find ourselves. Nor is it the result of a misguided effort to try to keep our faculties quiet when we should be meditating, reading the Bible, or studying the Fathers. We are not supposed to be turning ourselves into vegetables, which accept a rotting nature as it is. The peace required for the prayer of the heart, as well as the peace this prayer brings, involves an effort to remove those aspects of our nature which militate against living in that peace our Lord wants to give us. The prayer of the heart demands detachment, and it teaches detachment. God, finding the soul patient and open to His suggestions, operates in that soul as He sees fit. He acts upon the soul in ways that are best for that person and not as that person would like. "Thy will be done" is the key to this active offering of our soul to the silent work of God. Here we are taught to live peacefully in the will of

24. *DN* I.9.6; *Ascent* III.3.6.

God and to live peacefully in the will of God even in that which
concerns our prayer.[25]

8.3 The glory of God

With the beginning of contemplative prayer, the structured,
discursive type of meditation becomes an impossibility for us and
this is usually a confusing and painful period in our lives. The
suffering experienced at this time is the result of our putting up a
resistance to the "loving, peaceful infusion" of God into the soul.
This resistance has several different sources. First of all, we may
fail to recognize that God is with us in a new way and so try to
continue with our structured meditations with their compositions
of place, their considerations, and their resolutions. The result, as
St. John of the Cross insists, is that we miss what God wants to
give us and, at the same time, our meditation becomes unprofitable and increasingly difficult to do.

There are, however other reasons for our resistance. There is
the fact that our sinful and weakened nature experiences the near-
ness of God as something painful. The sun of God's love impresses
itself on us as a darkness, which not only blinds but also seems to
cripple. We leave off praying because it is painful as well as apparently pointless. We do not, as we say, seem to be getting anything out of it, and the dry desert is more satisfying to read about
than to experience first hand. But the contemplative life is not only
the apparently hostile and fearful blackness of a midnight in which
we do not know which way to turn. It is often also a darkness that
is friendly and peaceful and that is almost the dawn of another and
more radiant day.

The Blessed Edith Stein, in an analysis of our experience of the
night, has reminded us that what she calls "the cosmic night" (to

---

25. De Caussade is very impressive on the need for peace even amid the greatest trials and aridities. See his *Lettres spirituelles,* chap. 2, letter 1.

distinguish it from night used as a metaphor) has a double aspect. "The contrast of the dark and uncanny night is the gentle, magic night, flooded by the soft light of the moon."[26] Again, the darkness just before the coming of the dawn already seems to have about it the promise of the light of a new day. Even the darkness of midnight has a value of its own. "It ends the bustle of the day; it brings quiet and peace."[27]

The mystical night of St. John of the Cross is not a night in the literal sense, as something physical and exterior to us. It arises from the interior of our being and affects only the person whom God is approaching. Yet its effects are similar to those of the cosmic night. The aridity and the sense of helplessness that seize the soul—and the certainty that it has lost its way—all this removes our interest and awareness of everyday existence. "It effaces the outside world, even though this may be flooded with daylight,"[28] is how Edith Stein puts it. Yet the dark night is a sure path because we are walking in faith. Faith is the hidden light, which is always about to break through so that it illumines the darkness and opens up to us the reality of God's hidden love and the mystery of His dwelling with us.

Our discovery of the reality of God's indwelling in the soul brings with it a new attitude toward the rest of creation. The overwhelming sense of God's presence, which the various trials of the mystic night bring with them, also causes us to participate in some small way in God's own love for His creation. The night of faith, once it has broken our misuse and false love of the world, gives us back the world. It gives us back the world not as something to

26. Stein, *The Science of the Cross*, 26. The passage continues: "This night does not swallow up things, but lights up their nocturnal aspect. All that is hard, sharp and crude is now softened and smoothed; features which in the clear daylight never appear are now revealed; voices, too, are heard which the noise of the day tends to drown."

27. Ibid.

28. Ibid., 27.

be coveted or dominated but as seen by faith[29] and as revealing the glory of God. Jacopone, in one of the last of the *Lauds,* describes the man who has allowed himself to be led by faith and hope and so has been reduced to an emptiness that only God can satisfy:

Faith and hope have estranged me from myself,
Struck at my heart, annihilated me.

Within and without I am shattered,
reduced to nothingness:
This is the fruit of centring my life on love.
I am no longer able to flee or to pursue;
Caught in the swell of the sea
I drown, and my words drown with me![30]

The darkness has done its work, and the result is not merely the obscure awareness of his presence in the light of faith; it is also the gift of recognizing Him in His creation.

My speech is silence and shout.
I know where He is hidden, for though I see Him not
I recognize the signs of his presence
In every creature that is one with Him.
Being and nonbeing I have fused together,
And out of love banished my will with its "yes" and "no."[31]

The journey toward God in a union of love has been made possible by the destruction of the grasping, selfish, and disordered aspects of our nature: "And out of love banished my will with its 'yes' and 'no.'" The purpose of the journey, however, is to become more the sort of person God had always intended we should be. The end of the darkness is not the destruction but the remaking of our own individuality and particularity. Again, in a similar way,

29. Ibid.: "Yet here, too, there is a nocturnal light opening up a new world in the interior and illuminating, as it were the outside world from within, so that it is given back to us completely changed."

30. *Laud* 92.   31. Ibid.

although we have to say no to all created things in order to find God, nonetheless it is a kind of madness to say they do not really exist.[32] The result of a closer communion with God is to become more closely united with His creation.

We are presented then with a twofold movement. There is, first of all, the movement away from the things of this world to God. But there is also the movement of God to His creation. The first movement is described in the famous passage in St. Paul's Letter to the Romans: "Ever since the creation of the world his invisible nature, namely his eternal power and deity, have been clearly perceived in the things that have been made."[33]

This passage has been used by the Church to insist that we can know of the existence of God by thinking about His creation, and that it is possible to know of the existence of God through a rational process. The reality of the world around us, the fact of existence, is the ground, or can be the ground, for our certainty that God exists. St. Augustine describes the testimony of creation to the reality of God:

The very order, disposition, beauty, change and motion of the world and of all visible things silently proclaim that it could only have been made by God, the ineffably and invisibly great and the ineffably and invisibly beautiful.[34]

The beauty of the visible creation can strike us in such a way that we hunger for the beauty that created it. The experience is much more common than it might sound, and it is certainly not confined to Christians. The high mountains, a quiet lake, the silence of the woods in wintertime, the raging of a storm—these

---

32. This is the burden of the second volume of Georges Morel's *Le Sens de l'Existence selon S. Jean de la Croix*. "Whatever else may be the case, the discovery of a real dimension that is truly mystical will entail the destruction only of the unreal aspect of the phenomenal, but not of the phenomenal itself" (2.348) (my translation).

33. Romans 1:20.   34. *The City of God* XI.4.2.

experiences can strike a person with a sense that there is something more, or something behind, the immediate experience. This sense of there being something more, often leads to a process of an almost automatic referring of the glory of creation to the reality of the hidden God.

On the other hand, if we are not careful, it is possible to undervalue or even to ignore the creation that is the starting point for our knowledge of God. Sometimes religious people are so bent on finding the creator that, at least in practice, they develop a very impoverished view of the world in which we live. It is of course true that we have to say no to everything that stands in the way of our journey toward union with God. Until we can become detached from everything else save God, then anything—even holy thoughts and meditations (not to speak of visions or private revelations)—can become a comfortable resting place, and so an obstacle to becoming what God wants us to become.

If we look again at the passage from Romans, we can see another sense in it, a sense that in no way contradicts the way the First Vatican Council used the text,[35] but another sense all the same. If we were to read the words "his invisible nature . . . has been clearly perceived in the things that have been made" without any preconceptions, we might summarize them by saying that God is seen in His creation, and that His invisible nature is perceived in the things that have been made.

Von Balthasar's great work *The Glory of the Lord* is based on this interpretation of the text. He maintains that, in Greek thought, the cosmos is experienced as "the presentation and manifestation of the hidden and transcendent beauty of God,"[36] and that Christian thought, at its best, took over this aesthetic and metaphysical scheme. This perspective—that creation is not merely a stepping stone to God but itself is a revelation and participation in the

35. Denzinger, 1795, 1801.
36. Von Balthasar, *Glory of the Lord*, 2.154.

beauty of the creator—has always been influential in Christian thought.[37] The world is not a veil, or an unreality that hides God from us. The world is real, and it really manifests the beauty of God.

This movement of God to his creation is the fundamental one. It is God who created all things and it is God who sustains them in being. Our seeking after God through the works of His creation is dependent on this primary activity of God in sustaining, creating, and redeeming the universe. With the grace of a union with God, we awaken to awareness of the primary and fundamental movement of God's love for His creation, and we begin to see the loveliness of God in all His works. St. John of the Cross wrote of "the great delight of this awakening; to know creatures through God and not God through the creatures; to know the effects through their cause and not the cause through the effects; for the latter knowledge is secondary and this other is essential."[38]

Gerard Manley Hopkins beautifully expressed the view that the creation is itself a manifestation of the beauty of God:

> The World is charged with the grandeur of God.
>   It will flame out, like shining from shook foil;
>   It gathers to a greatness . . .
>
> . . . .
>
>   . . . nature is never spent;
>   There lives the dearest freshness deep down things;
> And though the last lights off the black West went
>   Oh, morning, at the brown brink eastward, springs—
> Because the Holy Ghost over the bent
>   World broods with warm breast and with ah! bright wings.[39]

37. Von Balthasar gives a long list of the earliest Christian writers who were influenced by this perspective. None of them, however, he says, "approaches in power and will to achieve expression the theological composition of Denys the Areopagite" (ibid., 2.154).

38. *LFL* IV.5.

39. Hopkins, "God's Grandeur," in *Poems and Prose,* number 6.

Or again, in the poem "Pied Beauty" he thanks God for the lovely things in creation and ends with the line: "He fathers-forth whose beauty is past change: / Praise him."[40]

Yet, seeing creatures in God goes far beyond physical beauty. In the Bible the notion of the glory of God[41] means God's self-manifestation and self-communication without His ceasing to be a transcendent being. This self-giving by God is to be found not only in what is physically lovely and uplifting, but also in human lives and in history, which, often enough, are not beautiful in any ordinary sense of the term. The glory of God is to be found in the most unlikely settings, for it is found among all those whose will is one with His.

In the first instance God's self-manifestation and self-communication are found in the history of His dealings with His chosen people, and in His particular care He has for this people. It is seen in the Exodus, in the events connected with the Ark of the Covenant, and in the dedication of the Temple. It is also seen in the Suffering Servant of Isaiah who had labored in vain but to whom God said: "You are my servant, Israel, in whom I will be glorified."[42]

In the New Testament the glory of God is most fully revealed in Jesus Christ. The glory of the New Israel, which is the Church, is a participation in the glory of God made visible in our Lord. In 2 Corinthians 4, St. Paul speaks of "the light of the Gospel of the glory of Christ who is the likeness of God" and he continues:

For it is the God who said "Let light shine out of darkness" who has shone in our hearts to give the light of the knowledge of the glory of God in the face of Christ.[43]

The glory of God in Christ will be fully revealed only at the end of all things,[44] yet this same glory also shone in Christ's life

---

40. "Pied Beauty," in *Poems and Prose,* number 14.
41. See Andrès and Deseille, "Gloire de Dieu," in *DS* 6.421–87.
42. Isaiah 49:3.   43. 2 Corinthians 4:6.
44. Mark 13:26.

on earth. In St. John this is found in two related themes. In the first place, all that Jesus does is a manifesting of the life of God himself. It is a manifesting of the life of God himself because all that Jesus does is done in union with the Father through the Holy Spirit. Christ's actions are, to put it simply, the actions of God Himself, and so reveal the glory of God. Secondly, in a mysterious way, St. John links the Passion and death of Christ with His glory.

Jesus, in the teaching of St. John, is the Word of God made into our flesh. "And the Word was made flesh, and dwelt amongst us, full of grace and truth; we have beheld his glory, glory as of the only Son from the Father."[45] The first miracle of Christ "manifested his glory,"[46] and this same glory is shown in the raising of Lazarus: "Jesus said to her, did I not tell you that if you would believe you would see the glory of God?"[47]

But the glory of God shows itself in its most striking way in the Cross of Christ. It is in the pain and desolation of the Suffering Servant prophesied by Isaiah that the glory of the Lord shines out most brightly. Jesus "consecrates"[48] Himself to His Passion, so that we may be consecrated in the truth. He does this knowing exactly what He is doing,[49] and out of obedience to the Father and for the glory of His name.[50] Finally, He explicitly identifies His Passion and death with His glory:

The hour has come for the Son of Man to be glorified. Truly, truly, I say to you, unless a grain of wheat falls into the earth and dies, it remains alone; but if it dies, it bears much fruit.[51]

45. John 1:14.   46. John 2:11.
47. John 11:40.   48. John 17:19.
49. ". . . Jesus knew that his hour had come to depart out of this world" (13:1); "Then Jesus, knowing all that was to befall him, came forward and said . . ." (18:4); "After this Jesus, knowing that all was now finished, said (to fulfil the scripture), I thirst" (19:28).
50. John 12:28.
51. John 12:23.

We see then that the text from Romans may be used to describe a twofold movement. In the first place it teaches us that the wonders of the visible creation point us toward the existence of the God we do not see. Yet, at the same time, the greatness of God Himself is revealed in all His works. To see creatures in God, as St. John of the Cross puts it, is to see them as resplendent with the glory of God. To see the world in this way means, in the first place, that we have to take the aesthetic dimension of existence much more seriously than we often do. The beauty of nature and the world of artistic creation are not mere "extras" thrown in to help us relax before we return to the hard business of reality. They are, in themselves, the way we are given the reality of the dependence of all things on God for their being. Secondly, the greatness of God is to be found in mankind made in the likeness and image of God. Thirdly, it is found in a preeminent way in the life of Jesus Christ who is the image of his Father's glory.

The culmination of the spiritual life is not the achievement of a static condition but a living of this twofold movement. It is the passage away from everything to find the love Who is infinitely greater and more wonderful than all His creation. Yet, having found Him in Himself, we then begin to love Him in all things. "The soul seems to be more God than soul," says St. John of the Cross, "and is truly God by participation."[52] God loves His creation, and in that love His saints have loved the world. They have had the courage to deliver themselves in the here and now to the power of love, and love has taught them to love the world.

It is not in some vague tomorrow, reserved to other generations, that men can live the life of God Himself. It is today, it is in the here and now, that we must give ourselves to God and do His will. What Father Morel calls "the sovereign presence" has not waited on "our efforts to offer himself unceasingly in the shadows and

52. *Ascent* II.5.7.

perplexities of our existence."[53] God's love for us demands a response. St. John of the Cross, St. Teresa, and Jacopone have taught us how to say no to all things so that we can deliver ourselves over to that love. Then, having said no to everything but God, we find Him in everything He loves.

Love, I flee from you, afraid to give you my heart:
I see that You make me one with You,
I cease to be me and can no longer find myself.

I see evil in a man or defect or temptation,
You fuse me with him, and make me suffer;
O love without limits, who is it You love?

It is You, O Crucified Christ,
Who take possession of me,
Drawing me out of the sea to the shore;

There I suffer to see Your wounded heart.
Why did you endure the pain?
So that I might be healed.[54]

8.4 Sedes Sapientiae

It is a commonplace to say that, with the tremendous growth in knowledge of all sorts, no one can possibly master more than a small segment of what there is to know. Specialization and fragmentation are realities, even if they have become buzzwords, and the need for syntheses and for overall views is constantly being expressed.

When we come to consider the tradition of the spiritual life in

53. Morel, *Le Sens de l'Existence*, 3.157. Fr. Morel is not an entirely satisfactory guide to St. John of the Cross, but he does have the capacity to put aspects of the saint's thought in a striking manner. See Henri Bouillard, S.J., "Sagesse Mystique chez S. Jean de la Croix," *Recherches de Science Religieuse*, t. 50 (1962) 481–529; and "Mystique, Métaphysique et Foi Chrétienne," ibid., t. 51 (1963) 30–82.

54. *Laud* 82. ("How the Soul through the Senses Finds God in All Creatures").

the Church today, we are tempted to say with Yeats that "The centre cannot hold." How are we to find and live a spiritual life that is nourished and deepened by the tradition of the Church, yet which leaves room for the Lord who makes all things new?[55] Where is the center that will at once contain and reflect the timeless truth and yet be open and suffering before all the realities of our existence? Where is the center that will not depend on our efforts but will maintain itself and, in so doing, maintain us as well?

If the answer to these questions is to be anything more than just another theory about tradition and spiritual life, then it must already be a living, and lived, reality in the Church. Where are we to find the wisdom to respond to the Lord's appearing in our prayer and in the life He wants us to lead? Where is the seat of wisdom? We all know the answer when the question is asked in this way. The place where wisdom has deigned to dwell is in the womb of the Blessed Virgin Mary, and the instinctive response of the Catholic is: *Sedes Sapientiae, ora pro nobis;* Seat of Wisdom, pray for us. Our answer may rest on something that seems hardly a memory, and our instinctive response on something we only faintly understand. Nonetheless, the answer is the right one, and our response is the gateway to the living tradition of the Church.

In the last of his University Sermons, Newman took St. Luke's words that Mary "kept all these things, and pondered them in her heart"[56] as the model for the believing Church, and in doing this he united the two aspects of tradition in a way that is still as pointed and as necessary as ever it was. The blessed Virgin received and guarded the Word of God, but she also pondered it, and it developed within her.

55. Revelation 21:5: "And he who sat on the throne said, 'Behold I make all things new.'"
56. Luke 2:19.

St. Mary is our pattern of faith, both in the reception and in the study of divine truth. She does not think it enough to accept, she dwells upon it; not enough to possess, she uses it; not enough to assent, she develops it; not enough to submit the reason, she reasons upon it; not indeed reasoning first, and believing afterwards, with Zacharias, yet first believing without reasoning, next from love and reverence, reasoning after believing.[57]

Mary was a human being who was the mother of Jesus of Nazareth. It was in Bethlehem of Judea in the reign of Caesar Augustus that she gave birth to her child. The conceiving of the child was miraculous, and so was the birth itself. But the coming of Christ was not an example of the dialectic of redemption; it was the event in history with which our redemption began. If we are Christians we must be prepared to accept what Kierkegaard called the scandal of particularity, and what Hegel called positivity. This may be a "stumbling block to Jews and folly to Gentiles," but, to those of us who are called, Christ is "the power of God and the wisdom of God."[58]

So, in the first place, Mary is the human being in whom Jesus Christ, "the power of God and the wisdom of God," was pleased to dwell.[59] In a miraculous yet human way, she became *Sedes Sapientiae,* the place where wisdom took up its abode. When we turn our mind and heart to Mary we are reminded of the historical reality of our religion, that we are dealing not with theories or

57. *US,* serm. 15 ("The Theory of Development in Religious Doctrine"). This sermon itself developed into *An Essay on the Development of Christian Doctrine.*

The passage in the text continues: "And thus she symbolizes to us, not only the faith of the unlearned, but of the doctors of the Church also, who have to investigate, and weigh, and define, as well as to profess the Gospel; to draw the line between truth and heresy; to anticipate or remedy the various aberrations of wrong reason; to combat pride and recklessness with their own arms; and thus to triumph over the sophist and the innovator."

58. 1 Corinthians 1:23–24.

59. I owe many of the ideas in this section to vol. 3 of Philippe, *L'Étoile du Matin.*

archetypal images, but with the Incarnation of the Word of God in time and in a particular place.

Yet the blessed Virgin is not merely the mother of the humanity of Christ; she is the mother of the Word made flesh, true God and true man. Because of this she is the model of the contemplative life in a new and awesome way. In her human nature she received the eternal Word of God who is "the image of the invisible God, the first-born of all creation."[60] St. John of the Cross defined contemplation as a "secret, peaceful and loving infusion from God," and this was fulfilled in the blessed Virgin in a unique way when she assented to the will of God and gave herself to the Holy Spirit: Sedes Sapientiae, the mother of the Word of God and of "the unsearchable riches of Christ."[61]

Eve said, "I have gotten a man with the help of the Lord."[62] Those words of the first mother remind us that motherhood is not merely a biological process, but giving existence to a new human being. Life is the gift of God, and all motherhood is a cooperation with this gift of God. Our Lady was the mother of the Word, but the Word is life,[63] and so she is the mother of the Word of life. For this reason she represents to us the tradition of the Church. Tradition brings to us the Word "which is living and active,"[64] and her continual receptivity to the living Word nourishes and strengthens the living tradition of the Church.

It is a tradition that is rooted in history and accepts only the "faith which was once for all delivered to the saints."[65] It is a tradition that brings us the Word of God in Jesus Christ. It is a tradition that is living and active and helps us to distinguish the wheat and the tares in the philosophy of the modern world. It is a tradition that will guide us into the truth of Christ, so that we may

60. Colossians 1:15.   61. Ephesians 3:8.
62. Genesis 4:1.
63. John 1:4: "In him was life, and the life was the light of men."
64. Hebrews 4:12.
65. Jude 1:3.

joyfully live in his love until we awake and our eyes shall see him and be satisfied.[66]

> Holy Father, Eternal God,
> Who in your mercy didst set up the royal throne
> Of your wisdom in the Blessed Virgin Mary,
> Illumine your Church, we beseech you,
> By the light of the Word of Life,
> That joyfully going forward in the splendour of the truth,
> It may achieve the full awareness of your love.[67]

66. Cf. Psalm 17:15: As for me, I shall behold thy face / in righteousness, / when I awake, I shall be satisfied / with beholding thy form.

67. Prayer from the Mass of Our Lady Seat of Wisdom.

❀ Bibliography

Classic Works

Aristotle. *Nicomachean Ethics*. Trans. W. D. Ross. In *The Basic Works of Aristotle*, ed. Richard McKeon, 935–1112. New York: Random House, 1941.

Augustine, St. *Basic Writings of St. Augustine*. Ed. Whitney J. Oates. 2 vols. New York: Random House, 1948.

Bacci, Pietro Giacomo. *The Life of St Philip Neri, Apostle of Rome and Founder of the Congregation of the Oratory*. New and rev. ed. 2 vols. London: Kegan Paul, Trench, Trübner & Co., 1902.

Bernard of Clairvaux, St. "On Conversion." In *Bernard of Clairvaux: Selected Works*, trans. G. R. Evans, 65–97. New York: Paulist Press, 1987.

Bonaventure, St. *The Soul's Journey into God*. In *Bonaventure*, trans. Ewert Cousins, 53–116. New York: Paulist Press, 1978.

Cassian, John. *The Conferences*. Trans. Edgar Gibson. In Nicene and Post-Nicene Fathers of the Christian Church, ed. Philip Schaff and Henry Wace, 2d ser., 11:295–545. New York: Christian Literature Co., 1894.

———. *The Institutes*. Trans. Edgar Gibson. In Nicene and Post-Nicene Fathers of the Christian Church, ed. Philip Schaff and Henry Wace, 2d ser., 11:201–90. New York: Christian Literature Co., 1894.

The Cloud of Unknowing and Other Treatises [including *Epistle of Privy Counsel*]. Ed. Justin McCann. 6th ed. London: Burns & Oates, 1952.

De Caussade, Jean-Pierre, S.J. *Lettres spirituelles*. Ed. M. Olphe-Galliard. Paris: Desclée de Brouwer, 1963.

———. *Self-Abandonment to Divine Providence*. Trans. Algar Thorold. Ed. John Joyce. London: Burns & Oates, 1959.

———. *Traité sur l'oraison du coeur et Instructions spirituelles*. Ed. Michel Olphe-Galliard. Paris: Desclée de Brouwer, 1979.

Devotio Moderna: Basic Writings. Trans. John van Engen. New York: Paulist Press, 1988.

Francis de Sales, St. *Introduction to the Devout Life.* Ed. and trans. John K. Ryan. Garden City, N.Y.: Image Books, 1955.

———. *Treatise on the Love of God.* Trans. Henry Benedict Mackey. Westminster, Md.: Newman Press, 1953.

Francisco de Osuna. *The Third Spiritual Alphabet.* Trans. Mary E. Giles. New York: Paulist Press, 1981.

Guigo II. *The Ladder of Monks and Twelve Meditations.* Trans. Edmund Colledge and James Walsh. New York: Image Books, 1978.

Hilton, Walter. *The Ladder of Perfection.* Ed. M. L. del Mastro. Garden City, N.Y.: Image Books, 1979.

Hopkins, Gerard Manley. *Poems and Prose.* Ed. W. H. Gardner. London: Penguin Books, 1968.

Ignatius of Loyola, St. *The Spiritual Exercises of Saint Ignatius.* Trans. Henry Keane, S.J. 5th ed. London: Burns, Oates & Washbourne, 1952.

Irenaeus. *Against Heresies.* In The Ante-Nicene Fathers, ed. Alexander Roberts and James Donaldson, 1:315–567. Repr., Grand Rapids: Eerdmans, 1950.

Jacopone da Todi. *The Lauds.* Trans. Serge Hughes and Elizabeth Hughes. New York: Paulist Press, 1982.

John of the Cross, Saint. *The Complete Works of St John of the Cross: Doctor of the Church.* Ed. and trans. E. Allison Peers. 3 vols. London: Burns, Oates, & Washbourne; Westminster, Md.: Newman Press, 1953.

A Letter of Private Direction and Other Treatises. Ed. and trans. John Griffiths. New York: Crossroad, 1981.

Newman, John Henry, Cardinal. *Apologia Pro Vita Sua.* New York: Image Books, 1956.

———. *An Essay in Aid of a Grammar of Assent.* Notre Dame, Ind.: University of Notre Dame Press, 1979.

———. *An Essay on the Development of Christian Doctrine.* Garden City, N.Y.: Image Books, 1960.

———. *Essays Critical and Historical.* 2 vols. London: B. M. Pickering, 1871.

———. *Fifteen Sermons Preached before the University of Oxford.* New ed. London: Longmans, Green, 1892.

———. *Historical Sketches.* 3 vols. London: Longmans, Green, 1914.

———. *The Idea of a University.* New York: Image Books, 1959.

———. *Lectures on the Doctrine of Justification.* 6th ed. London: Longmans, Green, 1892.

———. *The Letters and Diaries of John Henry Newman,* Volume XXIX. Ed. Charles Stephen Dessain and Thomas Gornall, S.J. Oxford: Clarendon Press, 1976.

———. *Meditations and Devotions.* 3d ed. London: Longmans, Green, 1894.

———. *Parochial and Plain Sermons.* 8 vols. London: Longmans, Green, 1896.

————. *Sermons Bearing on Subjects of the Day.* London: Longmans, Green, 1909.

————. *Sermons Preached on Various Occasions.* London: Longmans, Green, 1904.

————. *The Via Media of the Anglican Church.* 3d ed. 2 vols. London: B. M. Pickering, 1877.

Origen. *Letter to Gregory Thaumaturgos.* In The Ante-Nicene Fathers, ed. Alexander Roberts and James Davidson, 4:393–94. Repr., Grand Rapids, Mich.: Eerdmans, 1956.

Plato. *Phaedrus and Letters VII and VIII.* Trans. Walter Hamilton. Harmondsworth, England: Penguin Books, 1973.

————. *Symposium.* Trans. B. Jowett. In *The Dialogues of Plato,* 1:301–48. New York: Random House, 1892.

Pursuit of Wisdom and Other Works, by the Author of the Cloud of Unknowing. Ed. and trans. James A. Walsh, S.J. New York: Paulist Press, 1988.

Rule of St. Benedict. Ed. and trans. Justin McCann, O.S.B. London: Sheed & Ward, 1972.

Scupoli, Lorenzo. *The Spiritual Combat.* London: Burns, Oates & Washbourne, 1935.

Teresa of Avila, St. *The Complete Works of Saint Teresa of Jesus.* Ed. and trans. E. Allison Peers. 3 vols. New York: Sheed and Ward, 1946–50.

Thomas Aquinas, Saint. *Summa Theologiae.* Blackfriars ed. 61 vols. London: Eyre & Spottiswoode; New York: McGraw-Hill, 1964- 80.

————. *Summa Theologiae.* Trans. Fathers of the English Dominican Province. 3 vols. Repr., New York Benziger, 1947.

Thomas à Kempis. *The Imitation of Christ.* Ed. Harold C. Gardiner, S.J. Garden City, N.Y.: Image Books, 1955.

Valier, Cardinal. *Philippus sive de Christiana Laetitia Dialogo.* Ed. Antonio Cistellini. Brescia: Editrice la Scuola, 1975.

Modern Works

Adnès, Pierre, and Placide Deseille. "Gloire de Dieu." In *Dictionnaire de Spiritualité,* 6.421–87. Paris: Beauchesne, 1967.

Anscombe, G. E. M. *Intention.* 2d ed. Oxford: Basil Blackwell, 1963.

Aumann, Jordan. *Spiritual Theology.* London: Sheed and Ward, 1980.

Blommestijn, Hein. "Progrès-Progressants." In *Dictionnaire de Spiritualité,* 12–2.2383–2405. Paris: Beauchesne, 1986.

Bouillard, Henri, S.J. "Sagesse Mystique chez S. Jean de la Croix," *Recherches de Science Religieuse,* t. 50 (1962) 481–529.

————. "Mystique, Métaphysique et Foi Chrétienne," ibid., t. 51 (1963) 30–82.

Bouyer, Louis. *The Church of God: Body of Christ and Temple of the Spirit.* Trans. Charles Underhill Quinn. Chicago: Franciscan Herald Press, 1982.

————. *The Spirituality of the New Testament and the Fathers.* Vol. 1 of *A History of Christian Spirituality.* Trans. Mary P. Ryan. London: Burns & Oates; New York: Seabury Press, 1963.

————. *Orthodox Spirituality and Protestant and Anglican Spirituality.* Vol. 3 of *A History of Christian Spirituality.* Trans. Barbara Wall. London: Burns & Oates; New York: Desclée, 1969.

————. *Introduction to Spirituality.* Trans. Mary P. Ryan. Collegeville, Minn.: Liturgical Press, 1961.

Bradley, F. H. *Essays on Truth and Reality.* Oxford: Clarendon Press, 1914.

————. *Principles of Logic.* 2d ed. 2 vols. London: Oxford University Press, 1922.

Burnyeat, M. F. "Reading Silently." *Times Literary Supplement,* April 19, 1991.

Burrows, Ruth. *Interior Castle Explored.* London: Sheed and Ward, 1981.

Capecelatro, Alfonso, Cardinal. *The Life of St Philip Neri, Apostle of Rome.* Trans. T. A. Pope. London: Burns, Oates & Washbourne, 1926.

Cassirer, Ernst. *The Philosophy of the Enlightenment.* Trans. Fritz Koelln and James P. Pettegrove. Boston: Beacon Press, 1955.

Chapman, John, Abbot. *Spiritual Letters.* 2d ed. London: Sheed and Ward, 1946.

Cistellini, Antonio. *San Filippo Neri e la congregazione Oratoriana.* 3 vols. Brescia: Morcelliana, 1989.

Congar, Yves M.-J. *Tradition and Traditions: An Historical and a Theological Essay.* Trans. Michael Naseby and Thomas Rainborough. New York: Macmillan, 1967.

Coulson, John. *Newman and the Common Tradition: A Study in the Language of Church and State.* Oxford: Clarendon Press, 1970.

Da Genova, Umile, O.F.M. Cap. "Catherine de Gênes." In *Dictionnaire de Spiritualité,* 2.290–321. Paris: Beauchesne, 1953.

De Guibert, Joseph, S.J. *The Theology of the Spiritual Life.* Trans. Paul Barrett, O.F.M. Cap. New York: Sheed and Ward, 1953.

de Lubac, Henri. *Exégèse Médiévale: Les quatre sens de l'Écriture.* 4 vols. Paris: Aubier, 1959.

Dessain, Charles Stephen. *John Henry Newman.* 3d ed. Oxford: Oxford University Press, 1980.

Eliot, T. S. *Selected Essays.* 3d ed. London: Faber and Faber, 1951.

Evennett, H. Outram. *The Spirit of the Counter-Reformation.* Ed. John Bossy. Notre Dame: University of Notre Dame Press, 1970.

Faber, Frederick William. *Spiritual Conferences.* 32d American ed. Baltimore: John Murphy, n.d.

Garrigou-Lagrange, R., O.P. *Christian Perfection and Contemplation.* Trans. M. T. Doyle. St Louis: B. Herder, 1937.

————. *The Three Ages of the Spiritual Life.* Trans. M. T. Doyle. 2 vols. St. Louis: B. Herder, 1954–59.

Geiselmann, Josef Rupert. *The Meaning of Tradition.* Quaestiones disputatae 15. New York: Herder and Herder, 1966.

Groeschel, Benedict J. *The Courage to Be Chaste.* New York: Paulist Press, 1958.

——. *Spiritual Passages.* New York: Crossroads, 1988.

Herbstrith, Waltraud. *Edith Stein: A Biography.* Trans. Bernard Bonowitz. San Francisco: Harper & Row, 1985.

John Paul II, Pope. *Meditations and Devotions.* Ed. Peter Canisius van Lierde, O.S.A. Trans. Firman O'Sullivan. New York: Viking Penguin, 1994.

Journet, Charles. *The Meaning of Grace.* Trans. A. V. Littledale. London: Geoffrey Chapman, 1962.

Kerr, Fergus. *Theology after Wittgenstein.* Oxford: Basil Blackwell, 1986.

Kierkegaard, Soren. *Fear and Trembling and The Sickness unto Death.* Trans. Walter Lowrie. Garden City, N.Y.: Doubleday Anchor Books, 1954.

Kolb, David. *The Critique of Pure Modernity.* Chicago: University of Chicago Press, 1986.

Lash, Nicholas. "Production and Prospect: Reflections on Christian Hope and Original Sin." In *Evolution and Creation,* ed. Ernan McMullin, 273–89. Notre Dame: University of Notre Dame Press, 1985.

LeClercq, Jean. *The Love of Learning and the Desire for God: A Study of Monastic Culture.* Trans. Catherine Misrahi. New York: Mentor Books, 1961.

MacIntyre, Alasdair C. *After Virtue: A Study of Moral Theory.* 2d ed. London: Duckworth, 1985.

——. *A Short History of Ethics.* New York: MacMillan, 1966.

——. *Three Rival Versions of Moral Enquiry: Encyclopedia, Genealogy and Tradition.* Notre Dame: University of Notre Dame Press, 1990.

Matthews, V. J. *St Philip Neri: Apostle of Rome and Founder of the Congregation of the Oratory.* London: Oates and Washbourne, 1934.

Morel, Charles. "Mortification." In *Dictionnaire de Spiritualité,* 10.1791–99. Paris: Beauchesne, 1980.

Morel, Georges. *Le Sens de l'Existence selon S. Jean de la Croix.* 3 vols. Paris: Aubier, 1960–61.

Nichols, Aidan, O.P. *From Newman to Congar: The Idea of Doctrinal Development from the Victorians to the Second Vatican Council.* Edinburgh: T & T Clark, 1990.

Murdoch, Iris. *The Fire and the Sun: Why Plato Banished the Artists.* Oxford University Press Paperback, 1978.

Nietzsche, Friedrich. *The Anti-Christ.* Trans. Walter Kaufmann. London: Penguin Books, repr. 1977.

Passmore, John Arthur. *The Perfectibility of Man.* London: Duckworth, 1970.

Pastor, Ludwig. *The History of the Popes.* 40 vols. London: Routledge & Kegan Paul, 1898–53.

Peck, George T. *The Fool of God: Jacopone da Todi.* Alabama: University of Alabama Press, 1980.

Pelikan, Jaroslav. *The Christian Tradition: A History of the Development of Doctrine*. 5 vols. Chicago: University of Chicago Press, 1971–89.

————. *The Vindication of Tradition*. New Haven: Yale University Press, 1984.

Pétrement, Simone. *Simone Weil: A Life*. Trans. Raymond Rosenthal. New York: Pantheon Books, 1976.

Philippe, Marie-Dominique, O.P. *L'Étoile du Matin: Entretiens sur la Vierge Marie*. Le Sarment: Fayard, 1989.

Ponnelle, Louis, and Louis Bordet. *St Philip Neri and the Roman Society of his Times (1515–1595)*. Trans. R. F. Kerr of the Oratory. London: Sheed and Ward, 1932.

Pourrat, Pierre, P.P.S. "Commençants." In *Dictionnaire de Spiritualité*, 2.1143–56. Paris: Beauchesne, 1953.

Przywara, Erich, ed. *An Augustine Synthesis*. New York: Sheed and Ward, 1936.

Rahner, Karl, S.J. *Theological Investigations*. 23 vols. Trans. Cornelius Ernst. New York: Crossroads, 1974–92.

Ratzinger, Joseph. "Dogmatic Constitution on Revelation: Origin and Background." In *Commentary on the Documents of Vatican II*, ed. Herbert Vorgrimler, 3:155–66. Freiburg: Herder and Herder; Montréal: Palm, 1968.

————. *Introduction to Christianity*. Trans. J. R. Foster. New York: Seabury Press, 1979.

Rist, John M. *Augustine: Ancient Thought Baptized*. Cambridge: Cambridge University Press, 1994.

Robinson, Jonathan. *Duty and Hypocrisy in Hegel's Phenomenology of Mind: An essay in the real and ideal*. Toronto and Buffalo: Toronto University Press, 1977.

Sieben, Hermann Josef. "*Lectio Divina* et lecture spirituelle, II: De la *Lectio Divina* à la lecture spirituelle." In *Dictionnaire de Spiritualité*, 9.487–96. Paris: Beauchesne, 1976.

Stein, Edith. *In der Kraft des Kreuzes*. Ed. W. Herbstrith. Breisgau: Herder, 1987.

————. *The Science of the Cross*. Ed. L. Gelber and Romaeus Leuven. Trans. Hilda Graef. Chicago: Regnery, 1960.

Taylor, Charles. *Human Agency and Language*. Vol. 1 of *Philosophical Papers*. Cambridge: Cambridge University Press, 1985.

————. *Sources of the Self: The Making of the Modern Identity*. Cambridge: Harvard University Press, 1989.

Trevor, Meriol. *Apostle of Rome, a Life of St Philip Neri, 1515- 1595*. London: Macmillan, 1966.

Türks, Paul. *Philip Neri: The Fire of Joy*. Trans. Daniel Utrecht of the Oratory. Edinburgh: T & T Clark; Staten Island: Alba House, 1995.

Turner, Denys. "St John of the Cross and Depression." *Downside Review* 106 (1988): 157–70.

von Balthasar, Hans Urs. *The Glory of the Lord: A Theological Aesthetics.* Ed. Joseph Fessio and John Riches. Trans. Erasmo Leiva-Merikakis. 7 vols. Edinburgh: T & T Clark, 1982–91.

————. *Heart of the World.* Trans. Erasmo S. Leiva. San Francisco: Ignatius Press, 1979.

————. *Prayer.* Trans. A. V. Littledale. London: Sheed and Ward, 1961.

————. *Presence and Thought.* Trans. Mark Sebanc. San Francisco: Ignatius Press, 1995.

von Goethe, J. W. *Italian Journey 1786–1788.* Trans. W. H. Auden and Elizabeth Mayer. San Francisco: North Point Press, 1982.

von Hügel, Friedrich. *The Mystical Element of Religion.* 2 vols. London: J. M. Dent, 1908–9.

Weil, Simone. *Letter to a Priest.* Trans. A. F. Wills. London: Routledge & Kegan Paul, 1953.

Wulf, Friedrich. "The Call of the Whole Church to Holiness." Trans. Richard Strachan. In *Commentary on the Documents of Vatican II,* ed. Herbert Vorgrimler, 1:261–72. Freiburg: Herder and Herder; Montréal: Palm, 1968.

Zaehner, R. C. *Our Savage God.* London: Collins, 1974.

Church Documents

Catechism of the Catholic Church. Ottawa: Canadian Conference of Catholic Bishops, 1994.

Christian Meditation. Congregation for the Doctrine of the Faith. Boston: St. Paul Books and Media, 1989.

Canons and Decrees of the Council of Trent. Trans. H. J. Schroeder, O.P. Rockford: Tan Books, 1978.

Dei Verbum (Dogmatic Constitution on Divine Revelation). In *The Documents of Vatican II,* ed. Walter M. Abbott, S.J., and Joseph Gallagher, 111–28. New York: Guild Press, 1966.

Denzinger, H. *Enchiridion Symbolorum,* Editio 29. Fribourg: Herder, 1953.

Pope John Paul II. *Familiaris Consortio.* Ottawa: Canadian Conference of Catholic Bishops, 1980.

The Liturgy of the Hours. 4 vols. New York: Catholic Book Publishing, 1975.

Pope John Paul II. *Reconciliation and Penance.* Boston: St. Paul Books and Media, 1984.

Sacrosanctum Concilium (Constitution on the Sacred Liturgy). In *The Documents of Vatican II,* ed. Walter M. Abbott, S.J., and Joseph Gallagher, 137–78. New York: Guild Press, 1966.

Pope John Paul II. *Salvifici Doloris.* Boston: St. Paul Books and Media, 1984.

✿ Index of Names

A Kempis, Thomas, 44
Abraham, 166, 173
Alvarez de Paz, J., 53n
Anonymous author of the *Cloud of Unknowing, etc.*, 37, 64, 81n, 85n, 129, 178–80, 181n, 196
Anscombe, Elizabeth, 65n
Aquinas, St. Thomas, 30, 38, 67, 78, 79, 82n, 83, 91, 92, 96n, 102, 103, 104, 106, 107n, 108, 109n, 112, 14n, 136, 141, 142, 147, 181n, 182, 183, 184, 189, 193, 195, 196n, 198n
Aristotle, 81, 104n, 127, 141–44
Athanasius, St., 17, 23
Augustine, St., 10, 29, 30, 38, 47, 74, 75, 88, 89n, 95, 104, 110, 111, 140, 141, 161, 167n, 208
Aumann, Jordan, 77n, 193n

Bacci, Pietro Giacomo, 38n, 102n, 121n
Balthasar, Hans Urs von, 21, 22, 30n, 43n, 57, 61, 152, 153n, 180n, 185, 193n, 209, 210n
Benedict, St., 50
Benedict XI, Pope, 57
Bernard of Clairvaux, St. 30, 31, 38, 66, 67
Blommestijn, Hein, 80n
Blondel, Maurice, 17
Bonaventure, St., 37
Boniface VIII, Pope, 57

Bossuet, Jacques Bénigne, 201
Bouillard, Henri, 214n
Bouyer, Louis, 11, 25n, 52n, 77n, 78n, 118n, 124
Bradley, F. H., 19n
Burnyeat, M. F., 51n
Burrows, Ruth, 135

Caesar Augustus, 216
Capecelatro, Alfonso Cardinal, 39n
Carafa, Pietro (Pope Paul IV), 41
Cassian, John, 39, 113, 145, 148
Cassiodorus, 103
Cassirer, Ernst, 87n
Catherine of Genoa, St. 41, 55, 59
Chapman, Abbot John, 125n, 139, 155, 178n, 197
Charlesworth, M. J., 90n
Cistellini, Antonio, 49n, 55n–56n
Clement VIII, Pope, 58n
Congar, Yves, 14, 15n, 16, 19n, 24n, 27, 28n
Coulson, John, 20n, 36n, 42n

Damascene, St. John, 104, 107, 146
David, 199
De Bérulle, Pierre Cardinal, 126n
De Caussade, J. P., 5, 188, 189n, 200, 201n, 202, 204, 205n
De Guibert, 56n
De Lubac, Henri Cardinal, 13, 14n, 27
De Osuna, Francisco 162, 164n

❧ Index of Subjects